SEP 2010

Photograph of Thomas Merton by John Lyons. Used with permission of the Merton Legacy Trust and the Thomas Merton Center at Bellarmine University.

BOOKS BY THOMAS MERTON
(PARTIAL LIST)

A Vow of Conversation

Conjectures of a Guilty Bystander

Contemplation in a World of Action

Echoing Silence

*Honorable Reader: Reflections
  of My Work*

Love and Living

New Seeds of Contemplation

No Man Is an Island

The Seven Storey Mountain

The Sign of Jonas

The Wisdom of the Desert

Thoughts on the East

*The Collected Poems of
  Thomas Merton*

*The Literary Essays of
  Thomas Merton*

The Inner Experience

The Monastic Journey

The Asian Journal

*The Journals of Thomas Merton
  (seven volumes)*

Zen and the Birds of Appetite

BOOKS BY MARK SHAW

Melvin Belli, King of the Courtroom

*Miscarriage of Justice: The Jonathan
  Pollard Story*

Dandelions in the Moonlight

Down for the Count

Forever Flying
  (with R. A. "Bob" Hoover)

Testament to Courage

The Perfect Yankee (with Don
  Larsen)

Bury Me in a Pot Bunker
  (with Pete Dye)

*Clydesdales: The World's Most
  Magical Horse*

*Jack Nicklaus, Golf's
  Greatest Champion*

*How to Become a Published Author:
  Idea to Inspiration*

Diamonds in the Rough

Let the Good Times Roll
  (with Larry Goshen)

From Birdies to Bunkers
  (with Alice Dye)

Larry Legend

BENEATH *the* MASK *of* HOLINESS

THOMAS MERTON AND THE FORBIDDEN LOVE AFFAIR THAT SET HIM FREE

MARK SHAW

palgrave
macmillan

Dedicated to my wife, Wen-ying Lu

The light of my life

BENEATH THE MASK OF HOLINESS
Copyright © Mark Shaw, 2009.
All rights reserved.

First published in 2009 by PALGRAVE MACMILLAN® in the US–a division of
St. Martin's Press LLC, 175 Fifth Avenue, New York, NY 10010.

Where this book is distributed in the UK, Europe and the rest of the world, this is
by Palgrave Macmillan, a division of Macmillan Publishers Limited, registered in
England, company number 785998, of Houndmills, Basingstoke, Hampshire
RG21 6XS.

Palgrave Macmillan is the global academic imprint of the above companies and
has companies and representatives throughout the world.

Palgrave® and Macmillan® are registered trademarks in the United States, the
United Kingdom, Europe and other countries.

ISBN: 978-0-230-61653-0

Shaw, Mark, 1945–
    Beneath the mask of holiness : Thomas Merton and the forbidden love affair
that set him free / Mark Shaw.
        p.   cm.
    Includes bibliographical references (p.) and index.
    ISBN 0-230-61653-4
    1. Merton, Thomas, 1915–1968.   2. Trappists—United States—Biography.
3. Merton, Thomas, 1915–1968—Relations with women.   4. Smith, Margie.
I. Title.
BX4705.M542S53   2009
271'.12502—dc22
[B]
                                                                    2009021749

A catalogue record of the book is available from the British Library.

Design by Letra Libre

First edition: November 2009
10 9 8 7 6 5 4 3 2 1
Printed in the United States of America.

CONTENTS

PROLOGUE

During the 1950s and 1960s, he was the most famous Catholic monk in the world. During his lifetime he wrote more than 70 books read by millions of readers. One, *The Seven Storey Mountain (SSM),* an autobiography published when he was only 33 years old, sold more copies during its initial printing than another classic, *For Whom the Bell Tolls,* by Ernest Hemingway, had a few years earlier. Later, some critics mentioned *SSM* as one of the 100 greatest books ever written.

During the height of his fame, he was promoted by the Catholic Church and its superiors at the Vatican in Rome as the poster boy for the contemplative life detached from the material world. Together, they portrayed him as peaceful, happy, and content to be at the Abbey of Gethsemani, the oldest Trappist monastery in the United States. After his death in 1968, acclaimed Dutch priest and spiritualist Henri Nouwen called him "the most important spiritual writer of the twentieth century." Others labeled him a "genius," and he became an inspiration to everyone from renowned authors Ann Lamott and Sue Monk Kidd to famed singer and songwriter Joan Baez to His Holiness, the Dalai Lama. Calling him a brother whose impact would remain until his last breath, His Holiness applauded his understanding of Eastern religions, his inclusionary beliefs regarding spirituality, and his nonviolent stance as a political activist who was among the first to denounce the Vietnam War.

Without question, he was the most widely read monastic writer since Saint Bernard of Clairvaux, the twelfth-century French abbot. His books have been translated into nearly 30 languages and are read because of their appeal to those dedicated to a life of serious prayer, peace, love, and contemplation. His poetry is revered for its inspirational tone, and his gifts as a wordsmith cause comparisons with the land of the giants, contemporaries such as Hemingway, F. Scott Fitzgerald, Jack Kerouac, and Henry Miller. As of 2008, no fewer than *ten* full-bore biographies had been written about him, along with thousands of dissertations, essays, and articles chronicling his inspiring life story at every turn. At both Nazareth College in Rochester, New York, and the Graduate Theological Union in Berkeley, among others, entire courses are focused on his life and extensive body of work.

One of his books, *The Wisdom of the Desert,* was listed by Oprah Winfrey as "one of the five books everyone should read at least once."[1] In December 2008, the main display of famous Catholic writers in London's Westminster Cathedral bookshop featured only him, Pope Benedict, and Pope John Paul II.[2] In what may be seen as a tribute to his writing prowess, the archbishop of Canterbury, during a 2008 Christmas address, quoted his description of himself as being like a "feather on the breath of God."[3] As 2009 dawned, he remained a spiritual guru and beacon of light for a multitude of followers around the world. There are more than thirty chapters of his international society in North America, and many more around the world in countries from Australia and New Zealand to Brazil, Canada, France, Great Britain, Italy, and Spain.

All this and more is true, but there is another side of the story, one never before told in its entirety. It relates to a man who, while admitting character flaws, hid important details of a sinful pre-monastic past that shadowed him from his days as a teenager to the moment he walked through the gates of the Abbey of Gethsemani in December 1941. Unbeknownst to friends, fellow monks, and his legion of followers, he was, despite periods of happiness during a ten-year period, a tormented and suffering monk imprisoned by the abbot of the monastery he sought to leave. Despite writing several books about how *others* should lead a contemplative life and be one with God, he lived in a secret world haunted by ghosts of past conduct related to irreverent behavior with women, as well as the knowledge that he had never learned how to love, and be loved.

In addition, he felt guilt and remorse about not being the contented man he was proclaimed to be by enablers, including the powers-that-be in the Catholic Church who controlled his image. Deliberately hidden from view, his torment was known only to God. Such emotions denied him any chance to totally discover the solitude and freedom he coveted most of his life.

When all seemed lost, and this celebrity monk truly believed he would never escape inner demons and completely cleanse his lost soul, the sky opened in late March 1966 and he was presented with a chance at salvation. The instrument of hope was a beautiful, sensual student nurse half his age named Margie Smith, with whom he fell deeply in love at first sight. Given the blessing of love from a true-to-life angel and the prospect of a forbidden affair, could he discover his true self and come closer to being with "God alone," or would he decide that the woman of his dreams could replace his love for, and dedication to, the God who had saved his life?

This man in turmoil, in crisis, was the famous Catholic monk Thomas Merton, and here, finally, is the true story of his life, warts and all, providing inspiration for anyone who has ever suffered during a search for the meaning of love. Through struggle, anguish, and a belief in God that wavered but stood strong, Merton's saga reflects a confusion in all of us, and shows why his writings, especially about love and freedom, are as relevant to today's perplexing world as they were a half-century ago.

By experiencing the "Margie affair" and its positive effect on his troubled soul, Merton learned a valuable lesson in life. As he pondered the lasting effects of knowing true love, he would realize that people who attempt to be something they are not suffer torment and unhappiness; while those who live as their true selves will be enlightened, discover love and freedom, and find, if they so desire, the kingdom of heaven.

BOOK I

BLOSSOMING LOVE

"The man who loves for the sake of love only—he is completely free."

—*Thomas Merton, May 4, 1963*

CHAPTER ONE

"PERFECT FREEDOM EQUALS PERFECT LOVE"

A light rain shower on April 20, 1963, cleared the skies over the Abbey of Gethsemani, lodged in a wandering, holy valley 60-plus miles southeast of Louisville, Kentucky, near Bardstown. The abbey's common room had a humid, sticky feel to it as the short, balding monk sat before the young, wide-eyed students studying to become Trappist monks who had gathered to hear him speak.[1]

There was little that was notable about the 47-year-old priest's appearance. He had a round face, bushy eyebrows, small hands and feet, and delicate ears fitting the mix; at times, he wore black horn-rimmed glasses. Perhaps his probing blue eyes had a bit of sparkle to them, but they were not revealing eyes. Instead, they appeared to be reflective, darting here and there as his distinctive voice spouted inspiring words often peppered with humor to curious minds thirsting for insight into his wisdom. When this gifted storyteller relaxed, a soft, gentle appearance filled his face as he smiled, or laughed, his best characteristic. To see Thomas Merton laugh was to know the image he wished to project, that of the congenial, learned, happy, and humble Catholic monk whose celebrity was widespread.

Fourteen years had passed since his autobiography, *The Seven Storey Mountain,* became an international best-seller, catapulting him to instant fame.

Since then, he had written numerous books, including *New Seeds of Contemplation, The Wisdom of the Desert,* and *No Man Is an Island.*

On this unseasonably cool morning, as the novices' hungry minds anticipated in silence Merton's inspiring message, he shuffled a pile of papers while monastery bells clanged in the background.[2] An avid reader, he was currently completing early twentieth-century French Thomistic philosopher Etienne Gilson's *The Unity of Philosophical Experience,* a book he found compelling. Teaching was something Merton loved, and these lectures were important to him since they focused on two of his favorite topics: love and freedom. Today he would speak for more than an hour, but in the end, there would be three or four phrases that were more memorable than others.

Merton certainly had no idea that God would tempt him with forbidden love in future years, and he thus spoke with no knowledge that he would be put to the test regarding the subject he was about to discuss. His heartfelt message, focused around a letter of charity and love written by Saint Bernard and a letter Merton had received from a depressed Catholic layperson seeking his guidance, rang through the crowded room as the students leaned forward to hear every word.

Merton, his voice crisp and lively, first called the depressed man who had written the letter a baby, someone who was quite immature due to being self-centered. After noting the man's need for love, Merton told the students that love was the only way to change a person's heart and, using the gender-exclusive language of the day, that any man who loved based solely on desire was then dominated by desire—but "the man who loves for the sake of love only—he is completely free."[3]

Continuing, Merton, sitting erect in a wooden chair and gesturing gently as he spoke, explained that Saint Bernard wrote of three forces in a person: fear, desire, and, most important, pure love. When he resumed the two-part lecture on May 4, Merton told the students that any man's life could be measured by how he loved. The problem with the man who wrote the letter, Merton explained, is that he loved himself.

Checking his notes, Merton explained that when love occurred, people had to take a risk, because if they simply took and never gave, they were "buffaloed [stymied]." Saint Bernard, Merton believed, sought a complete conversion of the soul. But any fear or desire impeded this goal, while charity and real love overcame all barriers.

Addressing what such a conversion meant, Merton, after covering his mouth to cough, told the eager students this required a "change of one's whole self . . . one's whole life, you see." He noted that Saint Bernard called this "a revolution." Fear and desire may change one's direction, Merton added, but when partial love exists, so does partial hate, triggering the need for total love.

Merton, his voice bursting with enthusiasm, next suggested that any true conversion demanded significant changes in the depth of the soul. He agreed with Saint Bernard that one could never be totally free without true conversion, which was only possible through love. Total, perfect freedom, he decided, meant one desired nothing contrary to the will of God.

Interrupting Merton's thought pattern, a novice in the rear of the room raised his hand with the question: "Does this mean perfect freedom equals perfect love?" Without hesitation, the gifted wordsmith and teacher agreed. He then released the students to their manual labor for the day, none of them realizing he had spoken about his own personal struggles with love, something that would not be clear until his words were considered in the context of other events in his life.

As Merton picked up his papers, ready to return to monastic duties, little did he know that God would give him the chance to see if perfect freedom could indeed be discovered through perfect love. A surprise—a gift, really—was waiting for the famous monk, and in the unlikeliest of places.

CHAPTER TWO

MARGIE

I t began with a sponge bath—a spiritual baptism of sorts.

Fifty-one-year-old Thomas Merton sat uncomfortably on the side of a narrow bed at St. Joseph's Hospital in Louisville, Kentucky. He had just endured a painful back operation in late March 1966, when the raging war in Vietnam was an eyesore for the world at large. He had first spoken out in protest as early as late 1963, when he called the assassination of President Ngo Dinh Diem a "sickening affair," since he was the symbol of corrupt Catholic rulers "operating through a combination of Church power and American weaponry."[1] This was an extension of his disgruntlement with church hierarchy, one boiling over the years through personal experiences of disillusionment and anger. Disgust with the escalation of the war was on Merton's mind as he gazed at the blank hospital ceiling, still groggy from the medication. His thoughts were of the writings of German theologian Meister Eckhart and focused on words he might use in a sermon about the theologian, philosopher, and mystic renowned during the Middle Ages.[2]

A few days later, on the final day of the month, a student nurse, dark-haired Margie Smith, entered the small room to check Merton's status. She was in her mid-twenties, pretty, and sweet. Later, he would describe her as "small, shy, almost defiant, with her long black hair, her grey eyes, her white trench coat . . ."[3] After the celebrity priest and the aspiring nurse chatted and shared jokes about the Snoopy cartoon character, the first order of business was a sponge bath and back rub to soothe Merton's aching body. With gentle touches, Margie electrified his senses as her fingers massaged a warm sponge into his nakedness.[4] As he relaxed to enjoy the comfort, Merton could not take his eyes off of the young nurse's lovely face. She returned his stares, giggling as they shared more thoughts about Snoopy.

A few days later, Merton, resting in the infirmary at Gethsemani,[5] believed the operation was a success. He had enjoyed his time with Margie, and her devotion to taking care of him. She had made the experience, he decided, livelier. Appreciative of her bedside manner, he was nonetheless concerned that perhaps they had been too friendly before she left on her Easter vacation. But her caring ways, raw and deliberate, had helped to make him feel better. Ruminating about the experience, he decided he felt "a deep emotional need for feminine companionship and love." But monastic rules forbade this, and he concluded that he must live without such things. This conclusion, he decided, "ended up tearing me up more than the operation itself."[6]

Earlier, during the snowy month of January, when the thermometer neared zero, Merton, walking up "Heart Attack Hill" from the main abbey to the white rectangular stone-block hermitage where he lived, projected the happy, contented person others believed him to be. The famed bishop Fulton J. Sheen visited Merton at Gethsemani, as had several others, including his close friend Robert Lax, literary agent Naomi Burton Stone, and *SSM* publisher Robert Giroux. Ever the naturalist, Merton, wearing his robe underneath a jacket, loved the beauty he spied while walking through the dense woods where bushy-tailed red squirrels flocked. He enjoyed "tiny flashes of ice . . . falling, a kind of mist of ice . . . only a thin coat over the hard frozen snow of the other day." The white powder had been falling for several hours, and deer footprints were visible on the trails.[7]

Despite the brave front, all was not well. For some time, Merton's health had been deteriorating, with back pain a daily killer. Dermatitis had affected his hands. On his 51st birthday, the final day of January, Merton lamented that he was growing old.[8]

Experiencing a sense of loneliness in his solitude even though the day exhibited unexpected signs of spring on the horizon, Merton vented his frustrations in the direction of Gethsemani's abbot, Dom James, a constant target during times of unhappiness. He had taken over the reins at the abbey after Dom Frederic Dunne died, and was much more authoritarian than the previous abbot. Dom James worked hard to control Merton's image as the famous contemplative monk and poster boy for the Catholic Church. But Merton had no confidence in the man, believing he was neurotic. Worse, Merton felt as if he were a prisoner and helpless to change his status. He resented the "sadomasochism" Dom James introduced into everything Merton said and did, calling it "life-defeating, depressing, hopeless—no wonder so many [brother monks] leave."[9]

Forced to endure tumbling temperatures in the hermitage, which was heated only by a fireplace, full of anger at Dom James, besieged by ill health and facing mortality for the first time, and exhibiting all of the earmarks of a mid-life crisis, Merton was bored while reading the recently edited manuscript of his new book, *Conjectures of a Guilty Bystander*. It was only when he returned to nature and relaxed while watching deer through field glasses that he found peace. Five deer stood by the brush pile in silence trying to understand his presence, spreading their ears out at him. He gazed into their big, brown eyes and admired their black noses. He was mesmerized by the perfection of these beautiful creatures. Silence, his favorite sound, permeated the air.[10]

Unfortunately, such moments of tranquility did not ease the pain Merton felt when he walked through the woods near his hermitage. He was confused about a life he did not fully understand, despite all of the glory and fame thrown his way from writing book after book after book. As the soggy, cold month of March appeared, Merton was distracted and obsessed with his plight, deciding that he was spending too much time thinking about the past and that he needed to return to what was occurring in the present. Despite this promise, he felt alone with failures leading to "confusions, weakness, hesitation, fear—and the way through to anguish and nightmares." As he cut firewood and carried it back to the hermitage, he decided that he had become too hostile, too mean, too desperate, and totally unjust.[11]

As a lonely dog howled in the distance, Merton set a glass of water from the rain barrel by the hearth to warm it so he could brush his teeth and stirred the fire to bring it to life with new wood. With the fragrance of the smoke to keep him company, he sat at his rectangular work table by the front window and addressed his pressing concern: pending back surgery on March 25. Despite enjoying the surroundings, there was little sign of the joyful Merton, the laughing Merton whose full-mouthed smile caused crows' feet to appear around his eyes and wrinkles to ease across his neck. In essence, he exemplified a schizophrenic persona, passive on the outside while pangs of anguish and fear patrolled within.

During a day when the thermometer dropped to 20 degrees, Merton, warming himself by rubbing his hands together as a tiny bird pecked away at breadcrumbs left on the windowsill, continued to flagellate himself for past indiscretions, both real and imagined. He believed even having the surgery was a defeat in itself, an admission that he had not lived a proper life, that he had been the prisoner of a very unreasonable culture. His believed it was too late to escape his predicament. Catching a glimmer of light during a period of darkness, perhaps a premonition of things to come, Merton wondered if he could salvage something positive from his life. When the operation was over, he hoped he could start fresh and get his life in order.[12]

On the day before the operation, he took a hot bath at the abbey infirmary and then changed into secular clothes for the hour-plus trip to Louisville. Enjoyment of the eggs he had boiled for dinner the night before, and the coffee drunk to wash them down, was fresh in his mind.[13]

After Merton had returned from surgery in Louisville, he rested in the infirmary but he could not get Margie Smith off his mind. Meeting her had changed everything. Like a schoolboy with a first crush on a girl with pigtails, Merton was smitten, his monastic world turned upside down. An outside force, a sensual, caring woman, had infiltrated his contemplative mind, which coveted solitude. Now the violins began to play as Merton turned his attention to a long-lost feeling, the capacity to love a woman. "One thing has suddenly hit me," he admitted, "that nothing counts except love and that a solitude that is not simply the wide-openness of love and freedom is nothing." Propped up on his infirmary bed, Merton decided love and solitude were the "one ground of true maturity and freedom."[14] Additional details regarding the interaction between Merton and Margie during their first meeting, including the sponge bath she gave him, would emerge later, but there was no question that Margie had touched his heart and soul with feelings unknown for many years.

The hermitage, with his brick chimney poking up outside the flat roof that covered white cinderblock walls, was Merton's hideaway from any sense of both the real world and even the monastic realm. This was his private place on Earth. Permitted to occupy the cement-floored structure with only the bare essentials of simple living, he enjoyed rising at 2:30 A.M. to recite psalm-centered offices of monastic prayer. This was followed by an hour of meditation and reading the Bible before he enjoyed a simple breakfast. At 9:00 A.M., Merton read psalms again before settling in at his desk, where his typewriter was positioned to the right of his chair, away from piles of paper, his pen, and a writing pad. Here he wrote letters to his many correspondents, some famous, some not. Then it was off to the monastery for Mass before he returned to the hermitage to read before saying psalms again. Meditation and another reading of psalms consumed the early to middle part of the afternoon before he enjoyed a light supper, perhaps some tea or soup with a sandwich. More mediation preceded his lying down to sleep around 7:30 P.M. on a cot positioned toward the back of the hermitage in the small bedroom around the corner from the main living quarters. Across the way was a tiny room he had turned into a chapel, where he prayed daily.[15]

When Merton had time, he sat on the front porch in one of the old wooden rockers or ventured into the woods where the deer slept in the hollow behind the hermitage with their safety secured through the cover of brush and fallen trees.[16] Upon return to the hermitage, he could rest easy on his cot, sit and read new books in the rocker by the hour, or sip coffee with a bit of honey to sweeten the taste. Even cleaning the cabin, sweeping the fireplace with a small broom, or washing dishes in the rain barrel provided peace and quiet away from a world infested with killing in Southeast Asia.

Before being permitted to return to the hermitage, Merton had rested his sore back in the abbey infirmary. His hands quivered as he opened an unauthorized letter from Margie delivered to his bed. As he scratched two-day old chin whiskers and whiffed the smell of linseed oil, he noted the tender nature of her words and admitted the obvious—he loved this woman even though he had just met her. Without hesitation, he decided to "risk loving with Christ's love when there is so obvious a need for it. And not fear!"[17] Suddenly reflective, Merton, alive with spring as the dogwood blossoms began to appear outside the abbey, assessed his past conduct and conceded that concerning any questions of love, of loving a woman, he had to honestly admit that he had avoided them. That evening he decided he would face love as a man who could not only be dedicated to God but one who could care for a woman with "selfless, detached, free, completely open love."[18]

Merton's thoughts two days later reflected a tug-of-war emotional state for a man obviously desiring affection. Addressing his obsession with seeing Margie, he attempted to convince himself he wanted simply to help her, even though he recognized doing so would be fraught with complications that would try to interrupt the love affair. Regardless of the risk, and the gray mood of an overcast sky, he began to strategize how they might be together, all while juggling conflicting feelings that he must not become too enamored with her but instead concentrate on being free and sure of his love for Christ.[19]

A day later, Merton relished the feeling of love in the air, connecting his journal entries about the natural surroundings to the fresh romance. He first rejoiced over the mating of two bumblebees before lamenting the death of a cardinal killed by a hawk and being saddened that a pair of birds had been separated by death.[20]

Merton admitted that his heart was still struggling with new emotions about Margie. After an hour of meditation, he placed an illegal telephone call to her from the abbey cellarer's office while the other monks were dining. The lovesick monk was excited to hear Margie's voice and her cry of joy when she realized he was calling. It was a lengthy talk, one causing "another link in an uncomfortable kind of karmic chain." Slipping soundlessly back into bed, he chastised himself for not simply enjoying the exchange of letters and leaving it at that.[21]

Merton was tempted to see Margie, but he realized the futility of any relationship. He considered the complicated nature of the new love but was fearful that of things were proceeding too fast and could not be stopped, only perhaps slowed down.[22]

On the Feast of Saint Mark in late April 1966, Merton appeared certain the risk was worth it, that he could take the risk of loving and handle any anxiety it aroused in him until fear was cast out through perfect love. As for Margie, he was certain of her love less than a month into the relationship. He truly believed she loved him and needed from him a supporting type of love. He decided he would help her become free from "some destructive patterns and attachments that are likely to wreck her," a possible reference to Margie's engagement to a man she did not love.[23]

Totally immersed in the romance, Merton considered flinging himself into her arms despite being jealous of her sleeping with her fiancé,[24] a thought that tormented him so much he lay awake most of the night. Bolstered by a shot of aged bourbon shared with Brother Camillus, Merton slept intermittently before arising with the belief that his love for Margie was meant to be. He convinced himself that he had been truthful, that love had taken hold of him despite his fear. He promised to love her for who she was and share his deep faith with her.[25]

In spite of these good intentions, Merton worried about sex, about breaking his vow of chastity in view of the "deep, clear, strong, indubitable resonance between us."[26] He knew their hearts were in tune and their communication strong, but he swore he would not touch her too intimately and would make his intention clear. He knew, based on their conversations and despite having only seen each other at the Louisville hospital, that she must recognize his temptations as well.[27]

On April 26, Merton, his back tender but mending daily, decided to take the big step, and for the first time since the hospital visit, met Margie alone at the sparsely decorated office of Louisville psychiatrist James Wygal. Merton had seen Dr. Wygal sparingly, but the professional relationship had turned into a close friendship.

Merton and Margie enjoyed a wonderful lunch and responded to each other on every level. He knew she was as scared as he was since "there is a sense of awful, awesome rather, sexual affinity."[28] Careful to be chaste, Merton, recognizing he was "in deep," repeated the promise to his vows and the need to be faithful to them, believing he could be while also admitting moments of being scared.[29]

Regardless, the romantic obsession based on whatever words of love Margie whispered to him increased in intensity, with Merton deciding they were deeply in love but it was the "kind of love that could virtually tear you apart." Noting her passion was overwhelming, causing him to feel her trembling even over the telephone, and that the potential existed for them to cause each other distress, he nonetheless hoped his affection for her would not "turn into an ugly, bloody conflagration." Dr. Wygal had spoken to Merton with "prophecies of doom and gloomy insinuations,"[30] warnings Merton ignored.

Each day, during times when he would have otherwise meandered through the woods toward his favorite streams and kicked at fresh grass cuttings, Merton questioned his motives and those of his lover. He decided she was "terribly inflammable, and beautiful," and certainly not a nun, but instead full of passion with no inhibitions about displaying her emotions. Merton worried that he had been too honest, too forthright and that the couple had admitted too much, too soon, of their deep love for each other. Confessing to himself his confused state of mind as he walked near the hermitage, he decided he was not as smart or as stable as he had imagined.[31]

Despite the threat of punishment for his irreverent deeds, Merton pressed ahead two days after their visit by calling Margie from Gethsemani even though it was imprudent and risky. But the risk was worth it, he noted, recalling that "she was perfectly happy and at peace, with a blissful, childlike kind of happiness. . . ." He believed all the fear was gone, that the love affair could continue if it remained "pure." He enjoyed the uniqueness of her voice, and the sound of her laughter. He was filled with joy while just wanting to be with her forever. Pinpointing why he loved Margie, Merton described her as "a wonderful sweet little-girl" who was simple and caring—characteristics, he believed, of her true self.[32]

After Margie told him during the half-hour telephone call, "I will love you *always*,"[33] his eyes were moist as he sat alone in a rocking chair near his bed thinking of her. Normally he would have eased into his hermitage sleeping room, undressed, lain down on the cot, and, perhaps being unable to sleep, returned to the porch for another glimpse at the nightly stars as fireflies danced about. But this night he simply undressed and gingerly lay down. He was soon fast asleep with Margie on his mind and a smile on his face.

Buoyed by her affection, Merton decided he loved her so deeply he could think of little else. Separating Margie from previous pre-monastic relationships, he concluded her love was special, with no one having ever given themselves to him in such a complete, open, and frank manner. As he sat writing and daydreaming, he realized he had never responded like this to a woman. Recognizing the danger of exposure, he knew the affair conflicted with accepted social mores, causing him to realize that "*everyone,* the pious and the feisty, will use it for one thing only—to crush and discredit us."[34]

Envisioning the challenges, Merton appeared pessimistic that anything long-term might come from the affair. Citing the self-righteousness of those in power and their cruel tone, he nevertheless believed that by supporting each other, the two could endure. Admitting what Margie meant to him, he knew how much he needed her warmth and understanding, something he had never responded to so completely. After he enjoyed the silence of a morning meditation, he felt lonely being without her before scolding himself by exclaiming, "Some talk for a hermit! But it is true and I may as well admit it."[35]

Still, doubts existed based on so many factors, but Merton was concerned with going "back to the old routine of drawing into my shell and putting up the defenses."[36] This would be a betrayal, he decided. Instead, he looked forward to a relationship in which he wanted to share his heart and soul so that he and Margie might be transformed in each other. This would lead, he prayed, to a closeness in which they would always love each other, no matter the consequences. He hoped it might be possible, even though when he thought clearly about the relationship, he knew it bordered on the ridiculous.[37] As Merton noted on April 28, this had not kept him from kissing her and "in the chastity and tenderness of it (as I knew it would be), felt this deep, total, vibrant resonance." The response, he recalled as he lay on the cot with his eyes wide open despite the early hour of the day, was of "a whole warm little being, totally surrendered."[38]

To keep the affair secret, the conspirators decided to wait until Abbot Dom James was away so that letters between them could pass more easily. Regardless, Merton, as determined as the heavy rain outside was to coat the spring flowers, decided any risk of exposure by the abbot was worth it, since all he could think of was to pray as hard as he could for her and leave all the rest to the God he loved.[39]

That Margie had infiltrated Merton's very soul within the short time they had known each other was evidenced by his inability to now write in his journal about anything else *but* her. Consumed day and night with her presence, whether physical or spiritual, he continued pulling at his emotions two days into May. He was not lonely without Margie, but in a strange fashion lonely when he was "with her." He knew Margie was now a part of that loneliness and the life he had dedicated to God.[40]

Ignoring risk again, the famous monk was enchanted with the thought of an upcoming picnic on the Gethsemani grounds with Margie in early May. Debating within, Merton felt lost due to loving so much and being loved despite being in violation of monastic regulations, which forbade such relationships. It was clear, he knew, that the affair was wrong, absurd, and quite insane. Buoyed by the blessing God had provided, Merton was nonetheless excited by the beauty of Margie's heart and how she gave herself totally to him.[41]

Merton's mission, he knew, was to answer Margie's need for a deep commitment of love with love. He wanted to make her happy, give her joy, and permit her true happiness. This allowed him to feel quite peaceful, because his actions exposed her feelings of love and goodness.[42]

Unable to wait until the day of the picnic, Merton, accompanied by publisher James Laughlin and Chilean poet Nicanor Parra, roamed the countryside near Gethsemani in Laughlin's automobile. Merton decided to call Margie from Bernheim Forest to see if she could meet him, despite his wearing of Trappist overalls and having a bit of a beard. After greeting her outside Louisville's Lourdes Hall, where she looked more lovely than ever in her brown dress, the couple headed for the Louisville airport's Luau Room, where monied people had gathered for the Kentucky Derby. Despite the presence of others, he enjoyed a wonderful time with Margie, feeling as he did like a "convict" but satisfied to simply gaze at her with loving eyes as the aroma of tasty dishes danced in the air.[43]

Desiring more privacy, the couple left after dinner and sat by themselves on the chilly grass by some trailers parked in a nearby field and "loved each other to ecstasy." As he wrote about the interlude in his journal next to the Coleman lamp on his work table, Merton recalled it as "beautiful, awesomely so, to love so much and to be loved." He was most impressed that the two could talk without fear and "without observation (not that we sexually consummated it)."[44]

Reveling in the glee of his love's warmth and tenderness, Merton arose early on the morning of May 13 and, after toast and coffee and an hour of meditation, began to write Margie a 55-line poem. He told her he felt like a "newborn" celebrating a "first creation" of love through their "wet eyes and cool lips," hands worshipping as one, all bent toward a "voiceless beginning of a splendid fire" arising from their respective hearts.[45]

On the day of the picnic, May 20, after tasting a fine bottle of St. Emilion, Merton and Margie wandered into the woods as lovers do, in full view of brother monks who happened upon them. As puffs of clouds hovered overhead and the sound of machinery nearby seem to stop just for them, they sat by a little creek where they chatted and shared secrets deep within their hearts. Back at the hermitage later, he sat on the porch in the moonlight thinking that their time that day, while not as ecstatic as moments at the airport, was nonetheless unforgettable.[46]

This caused him to realize "the deepest capacities for human love in me have never even been tapped, that I too can love with an awful completeness."[47]

BOOK II

the SEVEN
STOREY MOUNTAIN

"Thomas Merton was the most important spiritual writer
of the twentieth century."

—Dutch priest and spiritualist Henri Nouwen

CHAPTER THREE

the ORPHAN

Thomas Merton had discovered the woman of his dreams in Margie Smith. He now had what he wanted, what he may have very well prayed for—the chance to share the covenant of love with a woman who loved him back.

Was this the panacea he sought? Could he now be truly happy? Apparently conflicted despite the bliss, Merton knew there was an itch to scratch, the question of whether he could love Margie and love God at the same time. Could he do both, pledge allegiance to a woman who made him feel ten feet high, who caused his heart to pound whenever he thought of her, who excited every bone in his body when she pressed her body against his, and still be obedient to his God, this God who had saved his life and become ingrained in the deepest part of his soul? Could he climb yet another mountain in his life, one as steep and slippery as ever encountered, and if he was to climb this mountain, what courage might he need to make a most important, if not *the* most important, decision of his life?

To understand the measure of the man, the Merton entrenched in this intense romantic relationship, and whether he would choose her, choose God, or attempt to please both, background information about him is essential. That Merton was a gifted, loving, caring, inspiring, determined man with immense ability as a writer is a given. Through his celebrity-monk status, he never failed to stand up for what he believed in when ugly social issues such as war and racism reared their heads. He was a vehement opponent of the Vietnam War and all wars, with one colleague calling him the "pastor of the peace movement" and a man who highly influenced peace activists such as Daniel Berrigan and Dorothy Day.[1]

Posthumous accolades regarding Merton abound. Scholar Robert E. Daggy described him as "Poet and essayist, biographer and critic, translator and diarist, novelist, autobiographer, sometime satirist . . . a letter writer of extraordinary ability."[2] Legendary folk singer Joan Baez said "he was a caring and brave, creative human being . . . [he] left behind a lot of people who loved him."[3] *Traveling Mercies* author Anne Lamott recalled, "A [great deal] of my spiritual seeking began with Merton. He [was] an incredible source of light and comfort and humor."[4] *The Globe and Mail* reporter Elizabeth Renzetti called Merton "the first celebrity monk of the modern age, long before Gregorian-chanting brothers of Santo Domingo de Silos hit the world-music charts. He was Christianity made, briefly, cool."[5] Sister Joan Chittister said Merton was "a fascinating, engaging, offbeat, charming, and provocative personality . . . what he directed the world to see was far more than the mystique, the mystery of the cloistered life."[6]

His Holiness the Dalai Lama said of Merton, "I felt that I had lost personally one of my best friends, and one who was a contributor for harmony between different religions and for mental peace."[7] Revered Vietnamese Zen Buddhist monk Thich Nhat Hanh observed, "He was filled with human warmth . . . he was open to everything, constantly asking questions and listening deeply."[8]

A special tribute to Merton had been emblazoned on a citation he received along with the University Medal of Excellence from Columbia University in 1961. It read, "Gifted master of language, in poem and prose, light-hearted as you are grave, you have reached out with winged words to the world you left . . . you are much less lost to the world than many who insist they are still in it."[9]

Merton's wise words about compassion, love, fear, true self, inclusion, contemplation, freedom, and living with "God alone" (as it is written on a wall in Gethsemani) reverberate today as new readers discover his illuminating books. His life story, especially detailing early years from birth to sinner to Gethsemani monk/priest, should be easy to recall, since the *SSM* autobiographical sketch he provided was supposedly all-encompassing. The writing was superb, solidifying Merton's lofty perch as one of the finest wordsmiths in the history of literature. The inspiring book was an overwhelming success. Through the years, it has never been out of print, continuing to be a classic read by millions of people around the world, whether they are Christian, nonbelievers, or attuned to Eastern religions.

Unfortunately, Merton's story, as portrayed in the book, was not the whole truth, but instead a watered-down version of what really occurred during his pre-Gethsemani years. And the misrepresentation was intentional, the result of a concerted effort to disguise a tormented sinner as some sort of a plastic saint rehabilitated through monastic practices.

Why is *SSM* not a "whole truth" account of Merton's early years? The answer lies in a quiet conspiracy, a cover-up if you will, by not only Merton, but also the Catholic Church hierarchy, stretching from the United States to the Vatican, Abbot Frederic Dunne, Merton's literary agent, and his publisher, none of whom did anything other than promote the book as factual even though critical parts did not disclose the whole truth. Strict censorship, in effect, issued a restraining order on Merton's true story, omitting critical information about him, and readers were hoodwinked and misled into believing that while Merton may have been a sinner prior to entering Gethsemani, *he was not "that bad" a sinner.*

Through this false impression, an act of omission just as severe as one of commission, readers were, and are today, left with a portrayal of Merton as a poor, lost soul who was converted to Catholicism and entered the monastery seeking salvation. In fact, he was a sinner of the first degree who was never held responsible for more serious conduct that would have tarnished the Merton "image" being promoted. Based on this motive, a cover-up was necessary so the Catholic Church and Gethsemani would not be embarrassed over Merton's pre-monastic conduct, which was, as the complete truth indicates, reprehensible at best, and downright despicable at worst.

Protecting the image of the church thus continues, whether it is covering up sexual abuse, clamping down on dissent, or perpetuating the image of its saintly public figures like Merton. Secrecy and denial still exist, causing concern as to whether incidents of sexual or mental abuse continue to this day, because few safeguards are in place to prevent reoccurrence, which is based on a code of silence. Lack of candor, together with secrecy, are the bywords in what author Russell Shaw calls "clerical elitism," triggering a belief among bishops and priests that they are "intrinsically superior to the other members of the church and deserve automatic deference." Shaw traces this disease back to days before Vatican I on through Vatican II, where openness and honesty were replaced with deception and cover-up, resulting in scandals caused by the church's "attempting to control access to truth." Nowhere is this more evident, Shaw believes, than in the sexual predations of priests that caused the dam of secrecy to break. This was due to the church's placing priests on pedestals, causing an atmosphere similar to the one where portions of Merton's book were censored in what may be characterized as a rather usual course of doing business, never give it a second thought–type of mindset.[10] Shading the truth was necessary to keep Merton's pre-monastic "dirty laundry" from view with nary a concern for readers who deserved to know the truth for a book promoted as true, with no disclosure otherwise except for a notation opposite the table of contents listing John M. A. Fearns, S.T.D., as "Censor Librorum."[11]

The fact that *SSM* was heavily censored is a given. Its editor, Robert Giroux, admitted it; official Merton biographer Michael Mott corroborated it; and fellow monk Father Basil Pennington, with apparent direct knowledge, confirmed it. Most important, longtime Merton friend and confidant Edward Rice, author of *The Man in the Sycamore Tree: The Good Times and Hard Life of Thomas Merton,* the first biography of Merton, criticized the publication of *SSM* by questioning its legitimacy when he exposed the cover-up in 1970, two years after Merton died. He reported that after Merton's draft was submitted for publication, "Then came the immense job of editing—and castrating—the manuscript. During the year before publication a large portion, perhaps as much as *one third,* was either seriously altered or literally thrown away on the insistence of the Trappist censors."[12] Whether this meant two-thirds of the book was more fiction than fact is unclear, but regardless, the book presented only part of Merton's pre-monastic story. This prompts the view that while the book is regarded as a classic, all copies should be recalled until a disclaimer is included indicating to readers that the book they are reading is less than truthful.

SSM's trail from manuscript to publication tracks past Merton having gained permission to write his autobiography subject to certain restrictions. Once it was written, the book had to receive "the *Nihil obstat* [official approval stating the work did not contradict Catholic teachings] of the two officially appointed censors of the Order of the Cistercians of the Strict Observance (the Trappists), as well as *Imprimi potest* [a second approval] of Merton's own Abbot."[13] The next step: "Having been approved in the order, it then had to be submitted for *Nihil obstat* to the *Censor librorum* of the Church for a given area (usually an archdiocese) before receiving the *Imprimatur,* the final permission to publish from a designated high official. In this case . . . it was Cardinal Spellman, Archbishop of New York." Based on this hierarchical precedent, how did Merton react to the censorship? Though his actual words about the subject were, amazingly enough, censored from the published version of *SSM,* he appears to have rationalized the process in the original typescripts by deciding "there would certainly be no point whatever in embarrassing other people with the revelation of so much cheap sentimentality mixed with even cheaper sin. And besides, I have been told not to go into all that anyway. So that makes everything much simpler."[14] Simpler, yes; completely truthful, no.

The perspective of Merton's official biographer, Michael Mott, is loaded with qualifications: "There was a censor in Merton who was perpetually at war with the writer who saw everything he did (and everything he had done) as important and in urgent need of being recorded." The result: "Merton never quite resolved this. [His] journals later became a sort of compromise, yet even they were often 'coded'—to be read one way by him, and another way by others." The bottom line: "The autobiography [Merton] wrote . . . was [meant] to emphasize, glorify his liberation and his Liberator, yet it had to begin in enslavement, and, if in enslavement, then bondage to specific sins. Merton says enough to let us know that one of these was pride and the other fornication."[15] Insightful words, but none excusing the fact that *SSM* was less than truthful. Books are either true or they are not; there is no in between, as some wish to believe, especially when censorship prevents the truth from being told. Mistakes may be forgiven, but intentional disregard for the truth must be condemned.

To be fair, the other side of the argument is that *SSM* told "enough" of the truth so as to be substantial. Edward Rice, while pointing out that Merton had originally included much more of the real, true story in the manuscript since it was "worth including," felt readers must have wondered "what kind of neurotic Merton had been, to find himself such a sinner on the basis of reading Freud, Hemingway, and D. H. Lawrence, some Italian pornographic novels, and a series of mild flirtations." Rice thus surmised that what was required by readers was "a careful reading between the lines" since "one doesn't have to prove Merton was a bad boy as a teen-ager; he says he was, and obscures the details, and that is enough."[16] Is it?

If *SSM* were published today, those intent on assessing its accuracy and truthfulness as a work of nonfiction, as it was presented in 1948, would examine it carefully. Based on less than full disclosure, the book would most likely elicit screams on review pages and Internet blogs by those investigating whether Merton's story was a truthful work of nonfiction. Witnesses to his pre-monastic behavior would emerge from every direction with differing accounts, some true, some fabricated, from those presented by Merton. Unlike books such as James Frey's purported memoir *A Million Little Pieces,* where outright lies infiltrate the text, or others of a similar nature where untruths are mixed with factual text and yet promoted as a hybrid labeled "creative nonfiction," Merton's autobiography would be judged before a jury of critics as, at the very least, a watered-down version presenting Merton in a much better light than he deserved. And he knew it.

Fortunately, Merton told what was promoted as his own, "uncensored" story, presumably the truth, at least through his eyes and his editors', in seven volumes of journals finally released over several years in the 1990s. At Merton's request, the journals could not be published until twenty-five years after his death.

The historical importance of the journals cannot be underestimated: the entries were apparently written as events unfolded, or within close proximity, unlike *SSM* text written many years after those events occurred. The journals are thus the best primary source for chronicling Merton's life through unvarnished accounts of his thoughts and impressions of what he was experiencing. Without years of reflection to ponder his actions and their consequences, as was the case with *SSM,* Merton wrote his account spontaneously, unblemished by the fear of repercussion for his unsightly deeds, seemingly free of the censor's scissors.

These journals may be supplemented by Merton's own words and voice in private letters and taped lectures, once again providing firsthand accounts of what was occurring in his life. Holes may be filled, and inaccuracies corrected, through a multitude of biographies and other accounts written by those who have researched Merton's life *ad infinitum.* Woven together, they present for the first time, in this book, a complete portrayal of the true Merton, at least as true as is possible based on the most reliable sources. Through a lens that much better explains his life journey pre-Gethsemani, his 27 years there, and the inner struggles that no one knew existed, there will now be an unbiased account of his dedication, based on numerous references to it throughout his life, to one important goal: true freedom that would permit him to be with "God alone." Using Merton's own words to trace this journey presents the story he wanted to be told, the story he knew would be told at some point after his death.

This story, presenting the human side of Merton and the true depth of depravity he experienced during early adulthood, is actually (as he may very well have predicted) much more compelling than the censored text depicting him, as the Catholic Church desired, in some fabricated, Teflon-coated, holier-than-thou image. It chronicles the life of a tormented man who became a brilliant visionary and prophet, a man who climbed the mountain of purgatory once, and would have to scale another mountain, one more challenging than the first, again late in life, when everyone believed he was a peaceful, contented monk. All this occurred when he was experiencing normal reactions shared with all humans by being troubled, frustrated, neurotic—and yes, at times, even depressed, despite days when he enjoyed life. And like millions of people in similar straits, his anxieties and times of turmoil may be traced to one important factor: an inability to understand what loving, and being loved, was all about. It is thus critical, as the true story of Merton's life unfolds, to keep an eye on his various relationships with women in view of what occurred when he fell madly in love with Margie Smith in 1966.

To those who believe it is sinful to taint the Merton image by digging into his past in search of skeletons, one must recall that he purposely and meticulously recorded pages upon pages of personal information in a diary. He would never have done so if he had not intended for these pages to be read and reread by those searching for insight into how he led his life. This includes the many journal entries regarding Margie Smith, ones that are of the utmost personal nature.

While *SSM* was less than truthful regarding transgressions in his youthful days, Merton presumably did not lie about his spiritual journey, and thus what he wrote is a useful account of his pre-monastic years. The book's value is enhanced by realizing that much of the text has been corroborated by objective minds intent on securing a factual basis for Merton's disclosures. It is thus critical to probe what Merton exposed in *SSM* and *what he did not*. We begin with the former so as to contrast it with disclosures later revealed.

The book's first words were strong and decisive: "On the last day of January 1915, under the sign of the Water Bearer, in a year of a great war, and down in the shadow of some French mountains on the border of Spain, I came into the world." Then Merton warned of unrest since he relished his freedom in the image of God but felt he was a prisoner of violence and selfishness akin to that of the world into which he was born. Merton then clarified his remarks by noting that this world he was born into was hellish and packed with people like himself who were destined to love God, but lived in fear and self-contradiction.[17]

Merton was born of artistic parents, Owen and Ruth. He compared his father's talent to that of Cézanne, and thanked him for being religious and a man of integrity. He noted his mother's versatility and dissatisfaction with a confused world. To both he showed appreciation for teaching him a good work ethic, vision, and artistic expression that should have made him royalty.[18]

Owen Merton was a New Zealander, and Ruth, American. His parents had met in Paris, where both were studying art. Their marriage resulted in Thomas' birth of Bohemian cloth in Prades, France. Merton described his mother as "a rather slight, thin, sober little person with a serious and somewhat anxious and very sensitive face." She was "worried, precise, quick, critical of me, her son." His mother painted in the shadows of the hills while his father preferred working in the sunlight. Merton, ever self-critical, called himself "nobody's dream child." His mother was not interested in churches or any sort of formal religion, but his father was a devout believer, in accordance with the doctrines of the Church of England. After Merton was baptized, he was skeptical of its result, believing the waters did not "untwist the warping of my essential freedom, or loose me from the devils that hung like vampires on my soul."[19] The book did not explain who the devils, or vampires, were.

As World War I raged, the Mertons left for the United States, where the youngster met his maternal grandparents, "Pop" and "Bonnemaman." His grandfather was an exciting man who exhibited authority. His grandmother was more low-key. Merton's first home was in Douglaston, New York, where his father was a landscape gardener. Merton's brother John Paul was born when Merton was three years old. He was more tranquil than Merton. He said John Paul, who lay in his crib and sang, was less impulsive, and people were impressed by his happy tone. At this age, Merton admitted to having an imaginary friend named Jack whose companion was an imaginary dog called Doolittle.[20] In a diary she kept, Ruth said Merton played with little boys and toys and screamed a lot, mainly at women.[21]

In 1919, Merton's grandmother on his father's side, Gertrude Hannah Merton, arrived from New Zealand. Accompanying her was Merton's aunt, Kit. Merton loved both women, but especially Granny, whom he recalled sprinkling salt on her breakfast oatmeal. She taught Merton the Lord's Prayer. Nevertheless, Ruth did not believe organized religion was dignified enough for her children.[22]

Without warning, Ruth developed cancer of the stomach but kept her illness to herself. After she was hospitalized, Merton admitted he did not miss his mother very much; he never cried when he was forbidden to see her. Merton learned of his mother's terminal condition not through loving ways, but when his father gave him a note from her explaining that she was going to die and would never see him again. He read the letter in the backyard under a maple tree and felt that "a tremendous weight of sadness and depression settled on me." He compared the grief to that experienced by an adult instead of a child.[23]

It was 1921, the same year Albert Einstein won the Nobel Prize for physics and Adolf Hitler's storm troopers began terrorizing political opponents in Germany. Thomas Merton was six years old and motherless.

Suddenly a widower, Owen Merton was free to paint wherever he chose. Best of all, his son was old enough to tag along. At age seven, in 1922, Merton traveled with his father to the "curious island" of Bermuda. The experience caused Merton an uneasy adjustment, since he was often left alone with strangers or different sets of friends when his father traveled.[24]

Merton's main home was a boardinghouse. He was, in essence, a parentless, tender-aged, impressionable boy with a dead mother, and a father who traveled as far away as Europe to paint and sell his art without taking the young boy along. Most of the time, Merton was alone and felt abandoned. When his father left for New York to exhibit his paintings, Merton was passed on to some of his Bermuda literary and artist friends. When Owen's exhibit in New York was successful, Merton returned to Douglaston, where he learned that his father was leaving for France with close friends. Merton remained in the United States.[25]

Merton's "parents" were now his grandparents, Pop, who worked for the publishing company Grosset and Dunlap, and Bonnemaman. During the summer of 1923, they left with John Paul to visit Hollywood, where Pop knew people in the movies. Thinking back on their trip, Merton recalled his brother as a humble youngster full of love. This contrasted with Merton's own descriptions of himself as hard-hearted.[26]

When John Paul returned, he watched Merton and his friends build huts in the nearby woods. When young boys like his brother came too close, they were chased away with stones. John Paul did not understand the abuse when he thought his brother loved him. Merton's dismissal of the brother he did love suggested to Merton that felt people separated themselves from love through rejection when the real reason was that being loved did not please them.[27]

Pop believed the Catholic Church was wicked, causing young Merton to hate and be suspicious of Catholics. He decided Catholicism should be kept in the dark areas of his brain, with ghosts and dying and such. Regarding the devil, Merton believed Pop could persuade people to feel the same about heaven as they did about hell,[28] an indication that Merton felt people were easily swayed since their beliefs weren't solid.

In 1925, Owen became seriously ill, and Merton was afraid he would never see his father again. But the illness passed, and Owen returned to Merton with the news that they were headed to France.[29] Merton was startled, since he had become quite fond of his surroundings in Douglaston.

In August of that year, Merton returned to France, the land of his birth, which he described as "the intellectual and spiritual life of the world to which I belonged." Soon thereafter, Pop, Bonnemaman, and John Paul visited. Sightseeing was the order of the day, with trips through England, Switzerland, and France. When they left for the United States, puppy love engaged Merton. Nearly 12 years old, he fell for a "mousy little girl with blonde locks called Henriette." He called the experience "a rather desultory affair."[30] Henriette told her parents the son of an Englishman loved her. When he saw her soon thereafter, she was quite friendly, and during a dance party she permitted Merton to chase her around a tree.[31]

Merton enrolled at the Lycée, a school in Montauban, where he wore a blue uniform. Lying on his pillow at night in a large dormitory with only "a hoot owl" to break the silence, he expressed "for the first time in my life the pangs of desolation and emptiness and abandonment." An assignment at school to write a novel involved Merton in a vocation that would render him famous in the future. His was a great adventure story located in India and inspired by French writer Pierre Loti. During this time, Merton lived with M. Privat, who had no neck, and Mme. Privat, who reminded him of a bird. He remembered their kindness and their devout Christian ways.[32]

Soon Merton was on the move again, this time to 18 Carlton Road in Ealing, near London, where he resided with Aunt Maud Pearce and her husband, Ben. Merton appreciated Maud, calling her an angel. He discussed his future with her, explaining that he might consider writing novels or becoming a journalist and writing for newspapers.[33]

Ripley School Court was the next point of entry for Merton's scholastic endeavors. He later dubbed this early time in his life, "my religious phase." Fourteen years of age in 1929, the year the American stock market crashed,

Merton enrolled at Oakham in the English Midlands, and was again living with his father. But any sense of wellness he may have had was interrupted by news that Owen was ill. Young Merton was perplexed, disbelieving the news. He could not tell from his father's appearance how ill he was, but knew he was in pain. The son asked the father what was the matter, but the answer was vague.[34]

News that his father was leaving for a London hospital shocked Merton. When he asked the status of the illness, his father revealed that he would not be getting better. Disturbed, Merton sat alone in dark room pondering his fate. Grief enveloped his being as he realized he had no home, no family, no true country, and few real friends. Uncle Ben delivered the bad news that Owen had a malignant brain tumor. When Merton visited him, he recalled leaving the hospital and understanding that his father would be ill for a year, or two, or perhaps more, and then would die either by natural causes or during an operation.[35]

Merton realized he would soon be an orphan, and he was now, like it or not, independent. This triggered pangs of egotism, and he separated himself from everyone and went his own way. He was bitter and resisted most everything, including connecting with ordinary people he encountered. But one bit of news cheered him up: he was now financially secure, thanks to a fund Pop had set up for him and John Paul. Better still, a new influence entered Merton's life when he stayed in London with Dr. Izod T. (Tom) Bennett, an old friend of Owen's from New Zealand and Merton's godfather. Visits to the hospital where Bennett was treating his father were common, but Merton cried when he realized his father would not live much longer.[36]

The predicted death occurred in 1931. Merton recalled his father as a man with a wonderful mind, a great talent, and a great heart, and the man who had brought him into the world. Merton gave his father credit for nourishing him and shaping his soul.[37]

Owen's death left Merton saddened and depressed. Sixteen years old and an orphan, he imagined himself free, so as to become "the complete twentieth-century man."[38]

CHAPTER FOUR

VISIONS *of* MERTON'S FATHER

"I do think my love for William Blake had something in it of God's grace."

—*Thomas Merton, 1930*[1]

Merton's admiration for the London-born writer William Blake, who was influenced by a fascination for mysticism and the unfolding of the Romantic movement surrounding him, did not mean Merton understood the poet. In fact, quite the contrary, because while he read Blake at age 16 with focused attention and patience, he could not understand his ideas.[2]

If Blake was a mystery, Merton's intentions on a gray spring day in 1931 were clear. According to the *SSM* account, he accepted his grandfather Pop's invitation to visit the United States after his father's death, purchasing a new suit for the occasion. Before the ten-day sea voyage, Merton predicted he would meet a beautiful girl on the trip and fall in love.[3] He did.

After spending time in a deck chair reading Goethe and Schiller, Merton was introduced to a girl by a Catholic priest enjoying shuffleboard on the ocean liner. She was traveling with two aunts, and the threesome did not mingle with the rest of the passengers. Merton's first believed she was older than he was. The girl was "small and delicate" and looked as if she was "made out of porcelain." She had "wide-open California eyes," and her voice was "at once ingenuous and independent." Merton kept looking at her, dazzled by her beauty. As he flung himself toward her affections, he decided she was the lead female character in every novel he had ever read. As the ocean liner approached Nantucket Light on a Sunday afternoon, Merton was not shy about telling this girl of his feelings, of his undying love, or that he would never love anyone but her. He felt such love was timeless.[4]

The girl did not share Merton's amorous feelings. She talked to him with a kind tone but the message was quite clear and not what he wanted to hear: "You are a nice kid. But for heaven's sake grow up before someone makes a fool of you." Merton meekly left her side and then withdrew to his cabin, where he cried for a bit and then went to sleep. This occurred after he had taken a photograph of her that was blurred.[5]

The impact of love gone astray caused him to remark, "You will never be 16 again and you will never be in love again for the first time." Probing deeper, Merton related that what he experienced was "that devouring, emotional, passionate love of adolescence that sinks its claws into you and consumes you day and night and eats into the vitals of your soul!" He decided a love affair like this one could only occur once in life and after that the man was calloused, unable to recover since he could never love so completely in such a surprising fashion.[6]

Back at Oakham, Merton edited the school magazine, read T. S. Eliot and Homer, listened to Duke Ellington records, enjoyed arguments about religion and politics, wrote about Gandhi, and became enthralled with the poetry of Gerard Manley Hopkins, a strong influence years later. Another budding romance occurred while Merton was visiting Bournemouth, England, with Pop, Bonnemaman, and John Paul. As Merton approached his 18th birthday in 1933, he exchanged confusing letters with the Bournemouth girl. Then he headed toward Beaulieu, where he attended a horse show so that he might meet someone more lovely than this girl who he could not forget.[7]

When he completed his Oakham studies, Merton celebrated with a trip to France and Italy. Traveling through Marseilles, Saint Tropez, and the hills overlooking Cannes, he finally landed in Genoa. A great boil on his elbow accompanied him to Florence, but it was too frigid there, and Merton traveled toward the holy city of Rome. Here, Merton was surprised to be more interested in churches than temples but spent time wandering about in museums, libraries, bookstores, and among the ancient ruins.[8]

Within the churches, Merton discovered holy masterpieces where he found refuge from the fast-paced Italian lifestyle. During his pilgrimage, he viewed ancient relics such as "Christ's cradle and the pillar of the Flagellation and the True Cross and Saint Peter's chains." He was somber as he witnessed the tombs of the great martyrs, of the child Saint Agnes, and of Saint Cecelia. He stood before a statue of the deacon Saint Lawrence, who burned on a gridiron, and gazed upward in awe. He concluded that the objects did not directly speak to him because he wasn't listening.

This holy experience triggered a transformation in Merton that was like unlike anything he had ever experienced before. As he walked among the religious shrines of Rome he witnessed "for the first time in my life . . . something of Who this Person was that men called Christ." To gain a deeper understanding of what he was experiencing, he had to focus, to concentrate, because to him at the age of 18, the meanings were obscure and yet some days they were so very real, even more so than he wanted to admit. Overall, the time in Rome permitted him to formulate his initial conception of Christ. Reflecting later on the special meaning of his Roman journey, he realized that "It was there that I first saw Him, Whom I now serve as my God and my King," and "Who owns and rules my life."[9]

Unable to completely grasp what he had seen, but nonetheless inspired by what he had witnessed, Merton began to read the Gospels as his love for the thread of Catholic treasures expanded. And then, as he sat quietly in his small *pensione*[10] room at the corner of Via Sistina and Via Tritone, one featuring windows so guests could look down at the sunny Triton Fountain in the middle of Piazza Barberini and see the Bristol Hotel, the Barberini Cinema, and Barberini Palace in the background, a mystical experience occurred. During an ensuing revelation as clear as the sunny sky outside, "Suddenly, it seemed as if Father, who had now been dead more than a year, was there with me." Merton sensed his presence as if his father were touching his arm or speaking to him.[11]

The collective nature of Rome's mind-rending experiences caused him to look deep within and question the misery and deception of his soul. He felt a bright light piercing him, triggering a sudden ugly reflection on his current condition, and his eyes were filled with the horror of what he saw. Reacting immediately to the impact of his father's presence, he revolted against his inner self as his dented soul screamed to be liberated from the person he had become. Tears filled his eyes as the intense nature of the moment impacted his brain and he talked not only to his father but to God acting as an intermediary. The whole experience, he decided later, was a true blessing, a grace, but he was not mature enough to recognize it as such. Instead, he missed the chance to alter his thought pattern right there in the *pensione,* recognizing later that if he had followed through, his life path might have been altered and less miserable in the years to come.[12]

Heartened by letters from the United States, Merton left Rome, returned to England, and sailed for New York, where he lost his temporary interest in religion.[13] In October, he re-crossed the Atlantic to enroll at Clare College, Cambridge University. The year was 1934, and world war lurked offstage.

To hear Merton tell it, his first year of college was a mirage of unforgettable memories as he attempted to live life full bore. To do so, he ran wild with a pack of crazy school chums who would have stayed out all night if they had not been required to head for home at a decent time.[14]

As Merton acclimated himself to his new surroundings, he was shocked to learn his beloved Aunt Maud had died during an early English winter. Attending the funeral, he saw the officials commit "the thin body of my poor Victorian angel to the Clay of Ealing, and [bury] my childhood with her." Lamenting the loss, he recalled it was Maud who had stood by him during his days of innocence.[15]

Despite being enrolled at one of the most prestigious universities in the world, Merton was restless and unhappy. To locate the source of this sad condition, he became obsessed with the writings of Freud, Jung, and Adler when he wasn't too hungover. Their writings about sex repression caused him to decide this was the root of his problems.[16]

Subsequent irreverent conduct, including heavy drinking at noisy bars and taverns on seedy streets and back alleys, where temptation lurked at every turn, earned the Cambridge student an order to report to London for a meeting with his godfather, Tom Bennett. Merton's memory of the meeting was unpleasant because the short time the two spent together was quite painful. Merton admitted he made little sense in explaining his conduct. But he did not take Bennett's warnings about his conduct to heart, and Bennett later ordered him out of Clare and off to America. Later calling his mindset a result of "a moral fungus, the spores of which floated in that damp air,"[17] Merton, the Cambridge dropout, visited England only once more, briefly in November, to gather the required papers in order to apply for permanent U.S. residency.

Closing this chapter of his life in late 1934, Merton summarized what had occurred to him with a curious phrase: "There has never yet been a bomb invented that is half so powerful as one mortal sin."[18] Later, this language, this clue as to understanding how Merton viewed a certain act during his days at Clare, would be fodder for interpretation when details were revealed as to what the mortal sin actually involved.

Merton's ensuing interest in Communism epitomized a 19-year-old's curiosity about anything, and anybody; he was a true seeker, and he knew it. Crossing the Atlantic in 1934, he enjoyed the peacefulness of the snow falling on the ocean liner. It triggered new thoughts and ideas causing him to conclude that he might be in the midst of a conversion of sorts. Recalling his days at Clare, Merton understood that his conduct warranted a change of behavior. Looking in the mirror, he saw someone miserable, a selfish person. He admitted an obsession with the pleasures of life, causing everything he had coveted to turn sour. He felt he had become "vain, self-centered, dissolute, weak, irresolute, undisciplined, sensual, obscene, and proud." The very reflection of his face disgusted him. Regardless of the tough self-evaluation, the 19-year-old pointed fingers and did not assume total responsibility for his actions. Yes, he had made bad decisions, but contributing to the unhappiness, he imagined, was society in general. Causes were plentiful, and they included greed, lust, and self-love. These existed, he decided, in every age and in every class.[19]

Merton's probing, questioning mind, his searching for answers but finding few, and an apparent desire to devote his life to contributing to the good of society, led him to the gates of Columbia University in New York City in 1935, the same year the Nuremberg laws against Jews were instituted as a prelude to the darkness of war. Merton, still the sassy, immature youngster with the smart mouth and little direction, called Columbia a "big snooty factory . . . full of light and fresh air," in comparison with Cambridge. After noticing the intellectual atmosphere surrounding the campus, he began to study Plato, Plotinus, Daniel Defoe, and T. S. Eliot. Columbia, compared with Cambridge, was a more friendly place, he decided.[20]

Merton's mind was active during this time. Attempting to discover someone he could look up to, Merton met Mark Van Doren, a symbol of "heroic humility." He noted the professor's love of teaching and his love for the subjects he taught: literature and poetry. His admiration for Van Doren, who also taught Jack Kerouac, coincided with Merton's sudden interest in Communism. He attended a gathering hosted by the Communist Party, but was disappointed no alcohol was served. One of the partygoers finally encouraged him to buy bottles of rye at a nearby liquor store. Stoked by a few drinks, he was escorted into a room where he signed up as a member of the Young Communist League. His cell alias name: Frank Swift.[21]

When Merton's exams at Columbia were completed, fraternizing with his brother, John Paul, was a welcome relief. They swam and attended so many films that Merton became bored with the activities. Regardless of efforts to lift his spirits, Merton's downturned attitude prevailed, causing discontent.[22] Something was missing, he surmised, and he could not figure out what it was.

Working on Columbia publications—the yearbook, *The Spectator, The Columbia Review,* and the humor magazine *Jester,* as the art director—provided writing and drawing experience, but Merton was admittedly still a confused man with little direction to his life. An attempt to join the cross-country team was unsuccessful, since Merton never trained and would not give up smoking and drinking or get adequate sleep. The latter was impossible, because Merton was a night owl who rode the subway with fraternity brothers during the wee hours of the morning so they could party at expensive nightclubs.[23]

Hungover nearly every day, Merton became depressed. He had feelings of shame and despair early each morning, when he saw laborers headed for work who, unlike him, had some sense of purpose. He was humiliated and felt worthless, triggering him to remark, "I was spiritually dead. I had been that long since."[24]

Death once again knocked at Merton's door when first grandfather Pop died, followed shortly by Bonnemaman. Merton was left, at age 21, with no mother, no father, and no grandparents on his mother's side to guide his path, or provide family support. Except for his brother, John Paul, grandparents far away in New Zealand, and Tom Bennett, now a distant memory in England, Merton was alone, without anyone to act as his moral, ethical, or spiritual compass.

Merton's agony surfaced while traveling on a train through the freight yards in Long Island City. Suddenly he was scared and woozy. Confused and disoriented as vertigo possessed his body, Merton stumbled off the train and into a hotel in Manhattan, where a house physician was called. The recommendation was to rest and sleep, but when Merton lay prone in the streetside hotel room, he could not escape continual fascination with the window he felt consumed most of the wall facing him. Frightened, and in a disoriented state, he wondered whether the force of gravity might carry his bed into an abyss of some sort, into emptiness. Worse, a voice within enticed him to throw himself out of the window. He concluded that perhaps he was having a nervous breakdown.[25]

Because of this bizarre experience, Merton's life was now dominated by one striking emotion: fear. As he walked the busy streets daily, observed commuters, and watched schoolkids scamper off to waiting buses, he realized this emotion was not altogether new, since fear was connected to pride and lust and inattention to "moral laws," conditions he could no longer hide.[26]During times of drinking coffee, having a smoke, or enjoying the fresh aroma of pastries at an outside café, Merton wrestled with who he was and why his attempt to steal pleasure and satisfaction from life caused him to feel empty. Assessing his plight, he connected these pleasures with what tormented him: distress, anguish, and the aforementioned fear.

As the calendar turned toward the second half of the 1930s, a spark of renewal occurred when a girl who lived nearby interrupted his misery. He fell into a "love affair" and was treated better than he had treated others in recent years. He downplayed the woman's affection by pointing out that love interest number four—after Henriette, the girl on the ocean liner, and the girl at Bournemouth—refused to date him until he charmed the girl with his sense of humor. Ignoring any sense of pride, Merton acted like a dog begging for affection. The affair was fleeting, another rejection by a woman who apparently sensed his confusion and shallowness. This state of affairs led Merton to believe he had hit a dead end, but that hope existed. Instead of wallowing in self-pity, he recognized many of his problems were self-inflicted, but that "my defeat was to be the occasion of my rescue."[27]

Is 1937, the year after elections in Germany gave Adolf Hitler 99 percent of the vote and China declared war on Japan, Merton was confronting a true paradox. He believed man could not deal with important problems if his own nature, philosophy, and ethics were the guideposts. If this route were followed, man would end up in hell. But the saving grace was the proposition that while this scenario was abstract in nature, some higher power must intercede to avoid damnation. Armed with these new insights, he suddenly turned to God for one simple reason: he decided man was created with a soul that was not self-serving, but required divine intervention so that it was possible to reach beyond human powers.

Merton believed this type of potential transformation occurred through God's free gift, His sanctifying grace. Its significance, he told himself one day while returning from Van Doren's class, was "perfecting our nature with the gift of a life, an intellection, a love, a mode of existence infinitely above its own level."[28]

Addressing the meaning of grace, Merton knew it was shared with God, because God was all about selfless love. He believed that by grace, those dedicated to God shared this proposition. Using the metaphor of a ray of light striking crystal and giving it a new ambiance, he described how God's infinitely disinterested love played upon a human soul. Merton called this new life one of continual grace. It was, he realized, a transformation of sorts, where he would stop loving himself and instead know what it was like to be loved by God.[29]

In February 1937, when chilling winds and ice stretched naked Central Park trees toward breaking, Merton, approaching the age of 22, four years short of becoming a monk at Gethsemani, braved the cold and walked down Fifth Avenue. Glancing sideways, and realizing he had a few dollars in his pocket to spare, he spied a copy of Etienne Gilson's *The Spirit of Medieval Philosophy* in the window of Scribner's Bookstore. Later, as he rode the Long Island Railroad and munched on a sandwich, he opened the copy only to be shocked to learn it was a Catholic book. Resisting the temptation to throw the book out the window because he thought its message might be dangerous or unclean, Merton realized his reaction was due to his always having been fearful of the Catholic Church. Despite this reservation, Merton, between puffs of his cigarette, read the book, which introduced him to a brand-new concept of God. More important, he concluded that Catholic belief was not left behind in the Dark Ages or a product of any unscientific theories. The impact of Gilson's words was immediate, with Merton deciding he felt an immense respect for Catholic philosophy and faith.[30]

His faith-based mind stoked with new ideas, Thomas Merton continued to admire classes taught by Mark Van Doren while striking up a special friendship with Robert Lax, a creative sort who would significantly influence Merton's spiritual journey. Lax was balding and had a ready smile; his face featured a chiseled bone structure and curious eyes. He liked to sport a beard, one that would turn snow white in later years, when he lived on a Greek island and wrote acclaimed poetry. Jack Kerouac called Lax "one of the great original voices of our times," and the *New York Times Book Review* wrote that Lax was one of "America's greatest experimental poets."[31]

Anticipating graduation, Merton chatted with Lax about subjects of mutual interest, debated writing a novel, and gathered another friend, Edward

Rice, into the fold. He was thin of build with ruffled hair, short sideburns, and prominent nose. In May 1953, his noted magazine, *Jubilee,* debuted. Later, despite happy times with Lax and Merton, marital woes, financial problems, and depression infiltrated Rice's world. He contracted Parkinson's disease.

A Columbia Bachelor of Arts degree earned, Merton pursued a further degree in the graduate school in English. The poetry of William Blake reentered his life, and Merton gained a greater appreciation of it, especially in comparison with the work of other English writers. Blake's nuanced views of faith strongly influenced Merton, and, as he read late into the night and the wee hours of the morning, he realized during the hot summer of 1937 that he did not want to live without God in his life. The illumination was steadied by his acknowledgment that "the life of the soul is not knowledge, it is love, since love is the act of supreme faculty,"[32] a prophetic statement in view of subsequent events in 1966.

A friendly encounter with Mahanambrata Brahmachari, a poor Hindu monk who had traveled to Chicago and the World Congress of Religions in 1938, spurred Merton to read Saint Augustine's *Confessions* and *Imitation of Christ.* Then Merton ventured to upstate New York with his friend Lax, a trip interrupted briefly due to a new, fleeting love affair. Shortly after, the two men headed for nearby St. Bonaventure, a college operated by the Franciscans. But Merton resisted taking a good look at the college, as he was more interested in a nearby Indian reservation.[33]

By the fall of 1938, the year Adolf Hitler appointed himself Germany's war minister in tandem with his plan to rule the world, Merton admitted the "groundwork for conversion was more or less complete," triggering a dedication to a life with God. He recognized that while his belief was unsteady, and the journey from atheist to "one who accepted all the full range and possibilities of religious experience" had been a short one, he was willing to obey God's law instead of moral law.[34]

Steadfast in his intention to attend a Catholic Mass, he informed a girlfriend that he would not be traveling to Long Island for the weekend. Sober for the first time he could recall on a lovely Sunday afternoon in September 1938, Merton, who had visited many Catholic churches and cathedrals over the years but never attended Mass, entered the brick Corpus Christi Church. Stuffed between two high rises, it was located behind Teachers College on West 121st Street, just east of Broadway. Upon hearing a sermon focusing on, among other topics, the grace of God, Merton was inspired and walked with a fresh sense of purpose when he left the church. The impact was immediate, and even the ugly buildings at Columbia appeared to be transformed.[35]

Soon Merton, his step a bit livelier as he walked toward a neighborhood café, decided to read several Catholic publications. He reacquainted himself with James Joyce by reading *A Portrait of the Artist as a Young Man* and instead of being disinterested when the famous author wrote about his spiritual crisis, Merton smiled as he read a sermon on hell. This stimulated a new interest in preaching. Aglow with spiritual direction, Merton shared his bliss with his girlfriend while visiting Union Theological Seminary. She did not share his enthusiasm about his possibly enrolling there.[36]

A sidewalk newsstand's display of newspapers announcing the start of World War II stunned and depressed Merton. After pondering the uselessness of the conflict, Merton discovered a book detailing the discernment of Gerard Manley Hopkins at Oxford and his interest in becoming a Catholic. As he sat at his apartment desk and read while New Yorkers buzzed along the wet streets below, Merton, inspired by Hopkin's spiritual journey, asked himself: "You know what you ought to do. Why don't you do it?" Unable to contain his excitement, he stirred in the chair, lit a cigarette, looked outside the window at the raindrops, and tried to quiet the voice. The effort was useless. Merton had truly experienced an epiphany.[37]

Unable to resist the call to action, Merton laid the Hopkins book down, grabbed his raincoat, raced down the stairs, and ran into the street toward Corpus Christi. Standing in the doorway after ringing the bell, he told the maid who answered that he wanted to see Father Ford. Disappointed to learn that he was away, Merton retreated to the street only to face the priest, returning at a good clip, deep in thought, from around the corner. After asking to speak to him, Merton sat down in a small parlor inside the church door and pronounced pivotal words that would change his life: "Father, I want to become a Catholic."[38]

The blazing colors of fall brightened the city landscape as Merton, bundled up against the chilly air, began his instruction from Father Joseph C. Moore. Merton was serious about his new leap of faith, never missing an instruction, even when he had to give up many of his previous amusements, ones that had strangled his progress as a Christian. A sermon on the consequences of hell by Father Moore caused Merton to reflect on his own conduct and the impact of sin on his soul. As thoughts about his mental condition swarmed through Merton's brain, he sought not only baptism, but conjured up a brand-new idea: becoming a priest.[39]

Deciding one day that thoughts of the priesthood should be separate from his conversion, Merton contented himself with being baptized so he might enter into the supernatural life of the Church. His hope was that God's mercy would swallow "up all the guilt and temporal punishment of my twenty-three black years of sin in the waters of the font, and allow me a new start." Despite good intentions, he warned himself of future temptations, noting his human nature, his weakness, and other evil desires that he would have to battle.[40]

As part of the ritual of baptism, on November 16, 1938, the still-complicated, still-searching Merton entered a confessional at Corpus Christi, where he exposed his past conduct to Father McGough, a young, innocent priest. "One by one," he later admitted and "species by species, as best [he] could," tore "out all those sins by their roots, like teeth." As Merton sat quietly on the church steps oblivious to the cold temperatures and swirling wind, he noted, "I had come, like the Jews, through the Red Sea of Baptism."[41]

Having received the sacrament, Merton promised to avoid past pleasures and passions. Punctuating the fear that he might not do so since he was weak, Merton admitted that the spiritual experience of baptism and confession only caused him to join millions of people who were "tepid and dull and sluggish and indifferent Christians who live a life that is still half animal."[42]

After lamenting his failure to pray and a lack of devotion to the Mother of God, Merton pondered his ability to avoid mortal sin if he backslid into what he knew was the sinful life he had lived before. Immersed in thinking about God each day, he decided anyone who was selfish and loved themselves over God in fact hated God. His mind ripe with new thoughts by the second, he realized his addiction to lust and the flesh was caused by trying to please himself, something obstructing and deadening any grace within his soul. Noting true conversion of the mind was not conversion of the heart and soul, he admitted to be being "blinded by my own appetites. . . . The evil tree brings forth evil fruits, when it brings forth fruit at all."[43]

After Merton completed a thesis focusing on William Blake, he rediscovered his childhood days while visiting Bermuda during a warmer-than-normal January. He then moved to 35 Perry Street, in Greenwich Village, where a bath, fireplace, and French windows awaited him. He began to pursue a PhD. During subsequent days, he used the apartment telephone to woo a nurse who was working at the 1939 World's Fair, opening that year on Flushing Meadows.[44]

Ever curious about sinful conduct, Merton purchased the first volume of the works of Saint John of the Cross. As he turned the pages while sitting lazily at his desk, he was fascinated with the mysticism but could not understand its true meaning, since his complexity and perverted appetites blocked clarity.[45]

After staying out until 4 A.M. one morning, Merton returned to his apartment with friends. He slept for a few hours as they talked, smoked, and listened to a Bix Beiderbecke record. He then left to pick up a breakfast of scrambled eggs, toast, and coffee, before settling on the floor to chat away. Suddenly, he announced as a matter of conscience, "I am going to be a priest," startling his friends. But his mind was clear in lieu of a clear conscience. Resolved beyond doubt, but deciding he was still in crisis, Merton immediately ambled down the darkening streets to the Jesuit church of St. Francis Xavier on 16th Street. Dodging passersby as he quickened his pace, he felt as if he were perched on "the edge of an abyss: but this time, the abyss was an abyss of love and peace, the abyss was God."[46]

Was Merton ready to step into this abyss, ready to become one with God? His answer: "Yes, I want to be a priest, with all my heart I want it. If it is your will, make me a priest—make me a priest."[47]

CHAPTER FIVE

FRANCISCAN DENIAL

At a men's bar in New York City's Biltmore Hotel in September 1939, while string music played in the background and New Yorkers enjoyed the remnants of fall, Thomas Merton and Dan Walsh, a forceful man whose short stature and square jaw made him resemble a likeable prizefighter, met to discuss Merton's future. Walsh was a part-time professor of philosophy at Columbia, and the two discussed what alternative religious orders might be possible for Merton, the aspiring priest. Among the candidates were the Jesuits, the Franciscans, the Dominicans, and the Benedictines. The last, Merton realized, were under the direction of the Rule of Saint Benedict. Merton believed he needed an order where he could become detached from the world and thus one with God. The Dominicans were dismissed because Merton had read that they all slept together in a common dormitory, an arrangement he disliked. Specifics about the other orders were debated, with the final focus on the Franciscans, who Merton favored, because their lives appeared to be quite simple and basically informal, akin to what he had witnessed at St. Bonaventure. He believed the Franciscan atmosphere was more free, with less spiritual restraint, and absent extensive rules and regulations.[1]

Although the Cistercian order did not appeal to him at the time, Merton listened with interest as Walsh shared his retreat experiences at Our Lady of Gethsemani, the Trappist monastery in Kentucky. "Trappist" was the common name for the Order of Cistercians of the Strict Observance. After Merton heard of the silence imposed, the denial of meat, fish, and eggs, and other such details, Walsh asked whether Merton would like that type of life.

His answer: "Not a chance. That's not for me! I'd never be able to stand it. It would kill me in a week."[2]

The Cistercians dismissed, Merton decided to visit the Franciscans. Walsh gave him a note addressed to his friend Father Edmund, and Merton left to visit him at the monastery of St. Francis of Assisi on 31st Street. Mixed news awaited Merton when Father Edmund told him the order could accept him, but not until the following August. Merton was pleased with the potential to apply, but disappointed with the time frame suggested. But Father Edmund reconsidered, and informed that he might apply earlier, Merton bounced down the steps of the monastery with happiness in his heart, believing God was guiding his path.[3]

Merton's spiritual journey received a boost when he discovered the Spiritual Exercises of Saint Ignatius. To read them in silence, he escaped to his apartment, which was away from the noisy streets. Then Merton the aspiring priest became Merton the teacher when he instructed first a class in English composition (English 201–202) and then one on grammar, at the Columbia School of Business. He also studied Saint Thomas Aquinas in a seminar course taught by Dan Walsh.[4]

Attacked by a bout of appendicitis, Merton slinked into Saint Elizabeth's Hospital, where he had his appendix removed. Recovering, he sipped liquids, read Dante, and chatted with an Italian fellow, telling him he was going to become a priest. This fresh mindset caused him to feel a new sense of spiritual freedom, since he realized he had not committed a sin in months.[5]

Merton viewed his Franciscan path clearly. First, he would begin his retreat, and then dress in the brown robe and white cord of the friar as he walked in sandals with a shaved head, the monks' symbolic crown. At the chapel, he would find his God and belong to Him.[6]

Before his short stay at St. Bonaventure, Merton paid a visit to his brother at Cornell and made a trip to upstate New York to see his college friends. Summer school at St. Bonaventure had begun, and he regularly attended communion but no classes. As colorful flowers lit up the campus grounds, Merton was happier than he had ever been, sitting in the quiet library where he made notes on his newfound dedication to the love and wisdom of God.[7]

Ever the spiritual wanderer, Merton discovered that his bliss was short-lived. This negative attitude was triggered by the realization that many of his old, sinful habits ("natural tastes and fancies") were still alive, and that God did not want anything to do with him until he had completely purged sinful conduct from his soul. He knew it was not enough that he saw no sacrifice in what he was doing, despite avoiding pleasures of the flesh that could consume his existence. Unable to convince himself that he was sin-free and had replaced self-love with God's love, he woke up one morning and discovered the peace he had felt had expired. Experiencing a revelation of sorts, Merton felt his face stiffen as he suddenly remembered who he was, and what he had been. He was amazed to realize how easily he could forget past sinful conduct. Immediately, he recognized a certain truth: no one he had spoken to about his intended vocation, including Dan Walsh and Father Edmund, knew the real truth about his past sinful deeds. Having admitted to himself the incomplete nature of his disclosures, whether intentional or not, Merton realized the men had only accepted him because he was suitable on the surface.[8]

As the train to New York City swiftly crossed the tracks and station after station disappeared in the background, Merton, on his way to see Father Edmund, saw a boy run from the river where he had been swimming along some tall grass as a thunderstorm was about to break. Ahead, a worried mother awaited her son with loving arms. The experience caused him to become aware of his own impending homelessness, since he was certain the Franciscans would reject him. When the train came around a bend and he saw the seminary stone tower in the distance, he said to himself, "I will never live in you; it is finished."[9]

With this somber thought in mind, Merton met with Father Edmund and provided details about a past filled with sinful potholes. The conversation with the priest was cordial and understanding. Merton did not disclose to anyone how much of the truth he told; he was asked to return shortly to learn his fate. The confused would-be-monk attended Communion and prayed as he awaited the decision. Nervous as he sat alone in prayer, Merton's mind was full of strange ideas as he questioned his own conduct, past and present. The whole experience, he decided, felt like a nightmare.[10]

The edict was unfavorable. Father Edmund reminded Merton that he was only a recent convert with but two years as a Catholic. The priest had decided that Merton led an unsettled life filled with confusion. He then informed the dour would-be monk that the novitiate was now full and intimated that when this occurred, he had to be careful not to admit people who didn't measure up. Told that he should withdraw his application, Merton left with a heavy heart, realizing that his vocational dream had been shattered.[11]

Merton was confused and dazed as he walked across Seventh Avenue to the Church of the Capuchins. There, in the dimmed light, he attempted to disclose the source of his furrowed brow in confession to a "thin, bearded priest who looked something like James Joyce," but his jumbled words caused him to mix up the facts. Halfway into the explanation, he felt the hopelessness of the moment, and cried so hard he couldn't speak. The priest was direct and forthright, telling Merton his past deeds did not warrant the monastic life, let alone the priesthood. Before Merton could escape the wrath, the priest told him he was wasting his time and insulting the sacrament of penance through self-pity. Having been thumped severely about the head, Merton slowly walked out onto the slippery sidewalk a broken man. Tears flowed down the fingers of his hands covering his face. The realization kept hitting him—he would never become a priest.[12]

Later, the downcast Merton spent considerable time walking down Church Street amid the hustle-bustle of buses, taxis, and heavy trucks. He found himself before the post office, and as if by divine intervention there appeared his brother, John Paul. He had been inside signing up for military service. The two brothers chatted before Merton showed him four books, bound in black leather, marked in gold. They were breviaries,[13] just purchased, Merton told his brother, because if the powers that be said he wasn't monastery material, he had decided to live his life as if he were a monk. Intent on joining a Third Order,[14] Merton also envisioned teaching at a Catholic college where he would be close to the Blessed Sacrament.[15]

Despite his setback, Merton was resolved to permit no subsequent compromises with a life that "tried, at every turn, to feed me poison." Deciding he was indeed a new man and that his quest to be close to God was worth it, he swore he would avoid the sinful desires that disgusted him. His objective was to climb the hill before him one step at a time, begging God to drag him along.[16]

Certain of his purpose to live a sinless life outside the monastic life he coveted, Thomas Merton turned his attention to a teaching position at St. Bonaventure. Wearing his favorite blue suit and sporting the killer smile that had charmed the ladies for years, he hitchhiked to a meeting with Father Thomas Plassman, president of the college. Success was immediate, and Merton was hired to teach English starting in September 1940.[17]

Under the umbrella of the friars, inspired by the enlightenment of Saint Francis, and dedicated to God, Merton flourished. He was especially proud of his conduct, having left the old Merton behind, the one who, like many others, was glued to enjoyment and amusement. He stopped smoking, avoided irreverent films, and threw away the naughty books he believed were soiling his heart. Expressing hope that his will and his soul were now in complete harmony with God, Merton began to write a book. It was written while teaching English literature focused on such subjects as Beowulf and the Romantic Revival to more than 90 students, a mix of football players and seminarians.[18] He was earning $45 per month plus room and board.[19]

In cold, snowy November 1940, Merton lined up with students and secular professors to provide names to the military draft board. American armed forces needed bodies to fight the Germans and Merton was age-eligible. In February 1941, Merton considered whether he might travel to a monastery retreat during Holy Week and Easter. Despite having shunned the Trappists for the Franciscans, Gethsemani, the monastery in Kentucky mentioned by Dan Walsh, popped into his mind since he wanted a week in total silence where he could pray together with the monks. But his dream was put on hold by the news that his number had been called for potential induction into the army. Deciding to leave the matter entirely up to the God he loved, Merton was shocked and then relieved when, after a complete physical, an Army doctor informed him he was ineligible due to a lack of the requisite number of teeth.[20]

Momentarily freed from being drafted, and more excited each day about his trip to Gethsemani, Merton examined the *Catholic Encyclopedia* for information about the Cistercian order. Impressed, Merton boarded a train for Kentucky, stopping in Cincinnati for Mass. In Louisville, as snowflakes danced in the frosty air, he boarded a slower train headed through the hilly country toward the monastery. Soon he saw the outlines of the buildings, crowned by a tower, steeple, and cross.[21]

When Merton arrived, he noticed a sign bearing the poignant words that would guide his journey from the moment he stepped into the monastery: "God Alone." When the brother who greeted him asked whether he had come to stay, Merton quickly replied "No." Once in his room, Merton sensed the silence of the night, the peace, and the holiness he was looking for. More enamored by the moment, Merton was captivated as the silence spoke loudly and clearly. Standing in the middle of the clean-smelling room as the moon poured its rays in through the open window, Merton knew he was in the House of God.[22]

At Mass the next morning, Merton was enlightened as never before. While bells clanged in sequence, he celebrated a true oneness with God, noting that the symbolism of the Cross and how love was within it. Suddenly inspired by the passion of the Holy Spirit, Merton reflected on his own limitations, asking himself whether he knew what love was. After a few brief moments, the answer was apparent: "[I] have never known the meaning of Love, never," since "[I] . . . have always drawn all things to the center of [my] own nothingness." After Communion, his heart was pounding.[23]

As Merton's Holy Week progressed, and he ate, prayed, and slept among the friendly monks, he felt the sense of belonging with the Trappists. He realized that a man who withdrew from the world was not less a man, but rather more of a person, since the monk's individual strengths were bonded in a union with God.[24]

Back at St. Bonaventure, having truly felt the presence of the Holy Spirit during his retreat, Merton pondered whether to write the abbot at Gethsemani and tell his story or consult Father Philotheus Boehner, a wise counselor at the college. Then he was mesmerized by an inspiring speech presented on campus by Baroness Catherine de Hueck, a cheerful, stout, dedicated, Russian-born woman who had founded Friendship House among the Black community in Harlem. It was located on 135th Street, in the space behind a window imprinted with the words, "Caré d'Ars, Friendship House, Clothing Center." Merton was most impressed, calling the Baroness strong in foundation yet calm and peaceful, with full confidence in God. Before she left St. Bonaventure, Merton asked whether he might visit and spend time working with her cause.[25]

During his visit, Merton soon became distraught over the filthiness of the slums and the plight of the children living in poverty. He believed that Harlem was where God intended him to be. When the baroness visited St. Bonaventure again as snow covered the rooftops and students bundled up against the cold, Merton pledged to live at Friendship House once the semester was over. But it was a good-faith promise made in vain, and Merton decided he had a stronger calling to Gethsemani. As he told Robert Lax one day in New York City, "The time has come for me to go and be a Trappist."[26]

Merton explained his thoughts to Father Philotheus, who encouraged him. Acting quickly, Merton wrote to the Gethsemani abbot, requesting permission for a Christmas season retreat. After receiving acceptance, matters became confused again when a draft board notice required him to report for another physical examination. Merton's chances of being drafted increased when the Japanese bombed Pearl Harbor on December 7, 1941.[27]

Merton contacted the draft board and was able to postpone the examination for a month. Without awaiting a final verdict, he quickly gathered his belongings and headed for Kentucky. As the thought of being in either the army or the monastery bounced about in his head, Merton reflected on the freedom he felt now that he believed he no longer belonged to himself, but God. This, in turn, resulted in his feeling free, freer than ever before.[28]

Praying for guidance, Merton enlisted help from, among others, Christ, Mary, Saint Bernard, Saint John of the Cross, and Saint Francis of Assisi in his quest to be accepted at the monastery. On December 10, 1941, Merton arrived at the gatehouse, where Brother Matthew was standing guard. He looked out between the bars, and with "clear eyes and graying beard" heard Merton say hello before asking him if he intended to stay. Merton smiled and nodded while replying, "Yes Brother, if you'll pray for me."

"That's what I have been doing," Brother Matthew said with a wink, "praying for you."[29]

When the Gethsemani gates closed behind him, Merton tasted freedom even though he was within four walls. Once inside the monastery, Merton approached Father Joachim, the guest master, with the request to become a novice. To his delight, Merton was allowed to stay. He talked to the Master of Novices, a monk who impressed Merton with his kind and simple manner. Merton decided a full confession of sorts was appropriate so he could unload "the big shadowy burden that still rested on [his] conscience." After Merton divulged his sins, the Novice Master monk paused, and then asked how long it had been since Merton was baptized. When Merton told him it had been three years, the monk appeared undisturbed by the news.[30] In February 1942, as war in the Pacific theater continued, Merton was received into the novitiate. If there was a final resolution to his avoidance of the draft, Merton never mentioned it.

To lose any sense of previous identity, novices had their heads shaved and received a new religious name. Merton's was "Frater Louis." If he hoped to wipe away the sins of his previous life, and start anew, it would be an uphill climb, since he admitted that "all my bad habits . . . had sneaked into the monastery with me." But one blemish on his prior record was corrected when his brother, John Paul, arrived for a visit. Merton believed he had treated his brother badly in the past through neglect, but this time he showed him true feelings of love and caring. Merton felt cleansed, and nearly 20 years of guilt were washed away.[31]

As Merton looked on, John Paul was baptized at the parish church in nearby New Haven. He received his First Communion during a private Mass at Gethsemani. John Paul then communicated through letters with Merton from an army base in England where he was stationed. His previous letters had come from Bournemouth, a site whose postmark must have reminded Merton of the long-ago love affair gone awry—especially since his brother later told him of meeting a girl and intending to marry.[32]

On Easter Sunday 1943, the year the Allied forces landed at Salerno and invaded Italy, Merton read a letter from John Paul informing him of his marriage to Margaret May Evans, a typist who had enlisted in the British armed forces. He also mentioned bombing missions, causing Merton to worry about his brother's safety.[33] Buoyed by the news of the marriage, Merton composed a letter to cheer his brother up. Before it was mailed, Merton was called to the abbot's office, where he was told John Paul was missing in action. Days later, the terrible news arrived—Merton's only brother was dead, killed when his airplane engines failed while flying over the English Channel. He was buried at sea after lingering in pain for five days or so.[34]

Yet another family death having hit Merton, he brushed away tears and tried to fill the hole in his heart by writing a loving poem for John Paul, lamenting his loss. Merton was visited by his friend Robert Lax, recently baptized in New York. He provided updates on many of Merton's friends and then returned to New York with poems Merton had written, some at Gethsemani, others earlier at St. Bonaventure. Lax forwarded the poetry to Merton's old professor Mark Van Doren, who sent it to James Laughlin at New Directions, a New York City publisher. Just before Lent, Merton was notified the poems would be published. The book, released in 1944, was titled *Thirty Poems,* and was the first of many to follow.[35] Gethsemani, not Merton, received a $25 advance, and book royalties were set at five cents per copy.[36] But the author was listed as Thomas Merton, not Frater Louis.

Having taken his sacred public vows, Merton struggled to find his true identity. Despite the glee at being at Gethsemani, Merton admitted that a shadow, Merton the writer, had followed him into the monastery. Merton felt as if the writer were beside him "[riding his] shoulders, sometimes, like the old man of the sea. I cannot lose him." Merton believed he wasn't really Frater Louis, he was Thomas Merton, an enemy who was supposed to be dead. Describing the Merton of old, the writer and perhaps more, he believed this shadow was everywhere, even in church. Like a Judas, this shadow talked to him through the voice of a businessman full of bad ideas and schemes. Apparently scared of this shadow, Merton concluded, "Maybe in the end he will kill me, he will drink my blood." Worse, Merton decided that Church superiors were on the side of the "shadow," and he believed fervently that either he or the shadow had to die. Which one would it be: Merton, or the shadow haunting him?[37]

BOOK III

the
THOMAS MERTON
JOURNALS

"[It is] crazy . . . trying to live up to an image of yourself you have unconsciously created in the minds of others."

—*Thomas Merton, Palm Sunday, 1958*

CHAPTER SIX

SEARCHING *for the*
TRUE MERTON

Because Thomas Merton's words in *SSM* were heavily censored, discovering the complete truth about the man who met Margie Smith in 1966 must be approached from all directions, using every source available. This includes the primary source: the seven volumes of private journals released in the mid-1990s. Editor Patrick Hart, Merton's longtime secretary, emphasized their veracity: "[Merton] was expressing what was deepest in his heart with no thought of censorship . . . with their publication we will have as complete a picture of Thomas Merton as we can hope to have."[1] Brother Hart's statement is appropriate based on the rich nature of the journals, but two caveats must be noted. One, there is information from a reliable source that what was deemed to be "irrelevant material" was excised from the original Merton journals before their publication in the mid-to-late 1990s. This decision was apparently made by certain editors who decided Merton's actual words were either repetitious, potentially scandalous, or offensive and harmful because of their off-color nature. Since permission to view the original journal entries is rarely if ever granted by the Merton Legacy Trust, only the trustees know exactly what was censored. Any form of censorship is distasteful, but the editing is believed to have been limited, and thus the journals are arguably the most accurate source for Merton's version of portions of his life story.

Second, and perhaps even more important, to compile a complete, authentic Merton portrayal, one must connect his *SSM* story and any chronicle of undisclosed pre-monastic conduct with the journal entries, biographical data, and book text Merton wrote prior to, and during, the Margie affair. Once this connection is made, it is clear why the romance, one unveiling a struggling, tormented Merton seeking love, is so critical to understanding all that Merton wrote and all that has been written about him, especially regarding the subjects of love and freedom.

But first the journals, and their contribution to the authentic Merton story. Paying close attention to his description of the two years prior to becoming a monk provides contrast with the censored *SSM* account.

In 1939, as Merton pondered his future two years before entering Gethsemani, he admitted the poet Dante was on his mind. He noted Dante's obsession with running "to the mountain" so as to "shed scales" from one's eyes. These were the scales, Dante believed, that hindered one from seeing God.[2] Merton's attempts to shed those scales that were preventing him from seeing God appears to have begun in earnest in the middle of 1939, in his New York City Perry Street apartment. He met the nurse Wilma Reardon, and she became a favorite companion.[3] But as September dawned, he was more concerned about his personal habits, including smoking and drinking. On the radio, Merton listened carefully as the commentator announced that Great Britain had declared war on Germany.

Reminiscent of his party days at Cambridge, one evening he and some friends celebrated into the wee hours of the morning. The next day he recalled the event: "Missie. Some girl, like [Ginny] said . . . The party Sunday night—'scotch-type whiskey.' Swimming in the creek 3 A.M. Everyone furiously drunk."[4] In the following days, he criticized such behavior, acknowledging temptation was still winning the battle with virtue. He knew courage and humility along with love and patience could save him, but only if the Holy Spirit entered.

Ever introspective, Merton recalled how Saint Francis had lectured the birds about being grateful to God for their beautiful feathers and the air they breathed. He decided he was like the ungrateful birds, betraying God's grace and sinning despite having acknowledged the presence of Christ in his life. He called this "terrible damnation," and a worse act than Pilate's sin or that of the executioners who pounded the nails in Jesus' hands. Justification, he believed, was tantamount to Judas' betrayal. Such conduct was dark and hopeless, symbolic of a world gone mad due to anger, lust, and violence. He then went so far as to connect his own conduct with that of Hitler and Stalin, blaming himself and everyone else who was "violent and lustful and proud and greedy and ambitious."[5]

Disgusted with the present, Merton could not forget the past. As New Yorkers scampered along the streets toward work and play in anticipation of Halloween, Merton was enticed into a cozy restaurant by the aroma of roasted potatoes. He was led to a back-of-the-room seat next to a girl whose scent and complexion brought back memories of a "whole class of girls I [had] been in love with from fourteen on." The girls, "rather thin than plump, rather blonde than dark," seemed to him sad in nature; the sadness mysteriously causing them to appear intelligent and good.[6]

Recalling the woman he had known on the ocean liner crossing the Atlantic to New York City, Merton decided any thoughts of making love were pointless without intent to marry. But he had told the woman, whom he admitted was married, that he loved her and gave her a kiss. She told him to grow up, causing temporary misery. He swore never to let such a stupid event occur again.[7]

As the brisk New York days began requiring sweater, scarf, and raincoat, Merton was consumed with thoughts of relationships with females. He examined the sin of lust, and decided that the idea of sleeping with a woman because of it was "ghastly, ugly heresy." He knew man and woman were supposed to love each other with body and soul, and either be married or deny physical pleasures in the name of Christ, who was love. As he passed through the daily rigors of life during the third week of October, Merton, his mind conflicted by the meaning of love and sex but trying desperately to turn the corner from being sex-starved to learning to love for love's sake, suddenly had a change of heart. He decided chastity was a blessing; that not having sex for the love of God made more sense that doing it simply for himself.[8]

When Merton informed Father Ford at Corpus Christi Church in mid-October 1939 that he wanted to be a priest, he was discouraged when the priest told him Orders were the source of evil infesting the churches. Disregarding the advice, Merton concluded the behavior expected of him was to imitate God by following Christ's example. Not doing so, Merton thought, created unhappiness for anyone who served God and failed in his service.[9]

As he scratched out journal entries deep into the silent night with a burning candle to illuminate his writings, Merton considered the seven deadly sins and how they prevented love with God. He decided pride, covetousness, lust, gluttony, envy, anger, and sloth caused one to abandon God. He concluded God's love was a light within, and that sin darkened that love. This allowed the devil entrance, resulting in being unhappy, angry, fearful, and unable to pray.

Becoming even more reflective, he warned that happiness earned through a mind filled with lust turned the person away from the love of God.[10]

As he continued teaching his Columbia English class, his mind was immersed in debating conduct. One evening he pondered how pleasure was the enemy, burdening people with the sins of desire and lust. One could not walk two steps with them in tow "without trying to be a camel getting through the eye of a needle." What was required, he mused as he walked toward a late-night café around the corner, was to rid oneself of these twin sins.[11]

The first week of cold, snowy December 1939 found Merton immersed in the writings of Saint Teresa of Avila, the 16th-century Spanish mystic and author of the acclaimed *The Interior Castle,* described as a "masterpiece of mystical literature."[12] Merton was excited by her spiritual wisdom and thoughts about seeking God's love in all things. To do otherwise, he decided, was a dead end. Merton believed this was where he was in his life; due to his own shortcomings, his life was basically going nowhere. Preoccupied with himself, he decided that in spite of having friends and enjoying his teaching, he didn't really understand others' feelings. The revelation catapulted him to the past once again, prompting him to reread collections of letters from girls and women he had known. Warm in a heavy sweater and corduroys, he examined several from a girl who he believed didn't love him, but obviously did, and others from a second girl who he hoped loved him, but did not. Recalling his days at Clare/Cambridge, he decided he had been obsessed with "filthy ideas (elaborately filthy ideas, too) that get mixed up in prayers and torment and confuse us." Shaking his head in amazement, he told himself that after all of his transgression, his head was "full of crap."[13]

Mid-December 1939 drifted into January 1940 as Merton, now 25, debated whether he could continue in the misery enveloping his life by drinking, chasing women, and enjoying the nightlife, or cease to sin in accordance with the only true happiness he had enjoyed during the past six years. This was his belief in, and desire to serve, God.[14]

In April 1940, when temperatures were unseasonably hot, the curious Merton traveled to Miami Beach on his way to Cuba, where he hoped to see Catholic shrines. The shadowy atmosphere at the Leroy Hotel in Miami reminded him of the Savoy in Bournemouth, England, triggering recollections of the love affair when he approached his 18th birthday, in 1933. He recalled being in love with a girl named Diane, but the relationship had dimmed as fall turned to winter. Upset, Merton had tossed the packet of her letters in a fireplace. Now he wished he had them back, despite the quarrelsome nature of the relationship.[15]

Moving on to his days at St. Bonaventure, as the steamy summer months quickly passed by like cards dealt at a poker game, Merton commented to friends about the war and how Hitler looked like "nothing: an insignificant little guy with a pointed nose and dejected mouth, down at the corners, like a tired wash-woman."[16] In November, Merton listed eight examples of his own poor conduct. Number three concerned the telling of dirty jokes in Virginia.[17]

After the remaining days and months of 1940 and the first three quarters of 1941 passed by with Merton continuing his transformation toward the priesthood, the fall of 1941 arrived with a cold wind and temperatures requiring a heavy coat and gloves. In September, just months before his pilgrimage to Gethsemani, he again questioned his mindset, focusing on the belief that his identity, who he truly was, was known only to God. One late night after leaving his friends (who no longer occupied as much of his time as before), he decided the measure of identity, of one's true being, was how much one loved God. Professing clarity on this point, he concluded that love for earthly things, such as pleasure, reputation, and success, was clearly an obstacle to loving God. Pleasures, he decided, were disgusting and stupid, and gave him "a sickness in the pit of my stomach. I want to spit out even the thought of them."[18]

As early-December temperatures chilled the air and other New Yorkers continued to enjoy the sensual pleasures Merton swore he disdained, the 26-year-old transformed man, armed with this new spiritual philosophy of life, arrived at the Abbey of Gethsemani, bags in hand, begging for permission to stay and become a Trappist monk. Based on all he disclosed in *SSM* and what he hadn't disclosed but was in his journal, could Merton truly "spit out" the sins he knew lay deep within him?

From early 1949 until his death nearly twenty years later, Thomas Merton would become a star, a revered, respected monk known throughout the world. His writings, poems, letters, articles, essays, and books were magical, published one after another as the years progressed. He was, despite his disdain for material things, a cash cow being exploited,[19] a poster child, of sorts, for Gethsemani, with publishing advances and royalty checks pumping out streams of revenue. One year, his royalties accounted for more than 16 percent of Gethsemani's income. Owing to Merton's fame, and other associated reasons, the number of monks at Gethsemani increased from 80 in 1941 to 240 in the early 1950s. More arrived each week.[20]

Despite the best-selling success of *SSM,* accounts of Merton's 27-year stay at Gethsemani are much better known than those of his pre-monastic days, when his soul was sin-infested. Slowly, as the days and months passed at the monastery after he entered in 1941, he was molded into the man who would meet Margie Smith in 1966.

As Merton was accepted into the novitiate, initially assigned the name "Brother M. Louis," baptized in a nearby church, and permitted First Communion during a private Mass at Gethsemani, he, according to private journals, continued to seek separation from the old, self-absorbed Merton. As cool spring temperatures arrived in April 1942, he dwelled on the importance of doing things for God's will rather than his own, in the true spirit of love. Hoping to achieve this goal, he cried out, "Jesus, I beg you, let me live for this one thing alone: Your love. Your love is Yourself. You are love."[21] Merton wrote to mentor Mark Van Doren that same April of how he was enjoying the simple life. Later, he realized how dead he had been and how alive he felt,[22] an indication his quest to lose the old Merton, the sinful one obsessed with lust and frivolity, was headed in the right direction. Certainly the primitive nature of Gethsemani, somewhat reminiscent of nineteenth-century French peasant life, contributed to his new psyche. The monastery in the early 1940s was quiet and lacked the mechanization that would propel it into a production factory in later years. Life was simple, and Merton relished the simplicity of God's world.

The spiritual compass guiding his way was the abbot, Dom Frederick Dunne. Merton truly loved the man, one whose character and common sense—a condition Merton noted was true of many saints—he admired. Dom Dunne was indeed a good man with good intentions. He had become, in essence, a blessed substitute father. Here was a role model Merton could finally believe in.

Two years after Merton had taken simple vows, *Thirty Poems* became his first published work. Titles included "Prophet," "The Holy Child's Song," "The Blessed Virgin Mary Compared to a Window," and "For My Brother: Reported Missing in Action, 1943," a reference to John Paul's disappearance and death during World War II.[23]

Impressed with Merton's writing ability, and aware of his fascinating backstory, Dom Dunne encouraged Merton to pen an autobiography. When he completed an initial draft of the manuscript, labored over for many days after he finished his monastic chores, Dunne forwarded a copy of what would become *SSM* to New York literary agent Naomi Burton in December 1946. To Merton's delight, she praised the book and was quite certain she would secure a publisher.[24]

During the creative process, Merton's back ached from sleeping on a rigid board covered only by a straw mattress. He decided he was less than content since, owing to the confusion and noise of working on the book, he was really not the detached person he had hoped to be. Merton's spirits were lifted when, two days before the new year dawned, and during the celebration of Saint Thomas of Canterbury, he received a telegram from Harcourt Brace editor Robert Giroux reading: "Manuscript accepted. Happy New Year."[25]

Despite his delight, Merton still struggled with inner confusion as January 1947 began. During this year, he would be stretched to the limit, with more than 17 writing projects in the works. It must have been this hectic schedule that caused him to wonder whether demons were etching into his mindset, but during confession he apparently straightened his thinking. But restlessness did not leave his side as he considered whether leaving for another Order might be his calling. As he prayed nightly to the God who had brought him to the monastery, he questioned his path, but Dom Dunne assured him he was in the right place. Merton agreed, believing he had been a fool.[26]

Attempting to truly discover the solitude he had hoped for when he entered the monastery, Merton, after enjoying a morning that included singing with his brother monks, was concerned that writing caused him to focus on certain images and ideas long forgotten. He asked to quit since it seemed that writing was a smoke screen to his real mission, simple contemplation. But the request was denied, causing Merton to realize one thing was quite clear—the abbot wanted him to continue writing his books. Acquiescing to the demand of his superior, Merton, his hands trembling as he prayed, his mind buzzing with conflicting thoughts, decided to make a vow in the middle of the crisis. To please God, he decided he must write books even though doing so made it difficult to be the contemplative person he was supposed to be. Regardless, he committed to trusting God, believing He would lead him along.[27]

To encourage himself, despite mid-March concerns over the health of Abbot Dunne, and a steady stream of bad weather depressing the countryside, Merton told himself it would surprise him if he was the same person he had been ten years earlier. Then he concluded he was not really the same person, except in a superficial sense. The key, he noted, was to separate his outer self from his inner self and to be able to love God alone. If he could be successful, Merton believed he would be transformed in God, and there would be no more Merton.[28]

Despite this exalted feeling, and the distraction presented by clearing stumps from a field where the monks would plant oats, Merton's writing continued to plug the past into the present, as memories of the pre-monastic life crept into his mind. In early May 1947, he wanted to stop the confusion and immerse himself in solitude so he could love God alone. Still certain that God wanted him to write, he nevertheless hated interacting with censors and the business side of writing. Irritation with the censors continued, but on the day before a group of priests visited Gethsemani, he had decided the censorship question had been reconciled. Agreeing to the manuscript revisions with little fight, he had been given the *nihil obstat* (approvals). If he was upset at all, he did not show it; instead, he decided *SSM* had needed a great deal of editing.[29]

In late May, as buckets of rain pounded the Gethsemani rooftops and the brothers were forced to abandon their outside chores, Merton believed staying inside the monastery meant giving up his hope of becoming truly contemplative. Struggling with a wandering mind as he tried to focus on meditation, he concluded from deep within he would not discover peace until he compromised his high ideals and aspirations.[30]

Imagining the audience for *SSM,* he concluded it would be made up of a wide variety of people throughout the world, including those riding on railroads, monks in monasteries as far away as Ireland, nuns who lived at convents in England, his relatives, Jewish friends, Communists, and priests who might be offended by his straightforwardness. His only answer concerning the extent of personal information to include in the book was to leave it in God's hands. But he was pleased that Brother Prior, one of the censors, liked the book. Another, Father Gabriel, did not.[31]

In early August, Merton, fighting a terrible summer cold, helped wash the dishes after a retreat and barked about misgivings with the choir when the chanting did not meet his favor. His love/hate affair with Gethsemani continued in late August when he questioned whether he could love God if he despised Gethsemani. A few days later, Merton decided to leave the Trappists for the Carthusians, even to travel to Europe if necessary despite the protestations of Father Anthony. Confused and frustrated that he did not know what God wanted for him, he broke down during prayer about his inability to find a true union with God.[32]

When September and the beginning of fall arrived with an early change in the leaf color, Merton chuckled when a bird visited the sanctuary during Mass. Despite the light moments, he reprimanded himself for being less than spiritual, because his "filthiness and . . . sins" caused him to "feel scabby . . . for I know my inequity, and my sin is always before me." Day after day, he attempted to discover spirit in the virginal sense, where his mind could be clean and truly with God. Two months later, he decided that, all evidence to the contrary for others who saw him daily, he was not living like a monk or a contemplative person, since his actions proved he was afraid of God and trusted only himself.[33]

As 1947 turned to 1948, the year Gandhi was assassinated, Harry S. Truman was elected president, and another confused man, Norman Mailer, hit the bestseller list with *The Naked and the Dead,* Merton focused on the galley copies of *SSM.* Upon receiving them, Merton believed there was more work to be done on a day when deep snow powdered the Gethsemani cedars and a bright stream of sunshine caused the abbey buildings to turn gold. Despite the snowfall, the monks busted up rock on the road leading to the lower bottom past the old horse barn. Later, Merton walked to the cemetery in work boots and read a book about the ninth-century French Bonneval Abbey while noticing caterpillar tracks across the snow. As he read the *SSM* proof pages, Merton was astonished at his nasty tone. He believed the inner turmoil exhibited was caused by him and not by the outside world. Despite a tasty supper of potatoes and sauerkraut, Merton was concerned with the other monks over the behavior of Frater Damian, who, after reading but not understanding the words of Saint John of the Cross, became belligerent, leading two men to handcuff the poor monk after he had run around the monastery half out of his mind.[34]

Awaiting publication of *SSM* a few months later, Merton accepted the censorship of his book. But in mid-June, he was not pleased with himself, deciding his lust for writing and books complicated life and caused him to complain needlessly, since writing was an act of loving himself and not God. This was a sin and resulted in his being useless as a monk. When he prayed, he asked God for mercy and teachings so he might live without pleasure and instead be humble.[35]

When Merton was presented with the first copy of *SSM,* on a day so hot that sweat ran down his back, he seemed overjoyed, especially with the printing. He read excerpts while walking on the new crushed-limestone paths in the gardens. He decided that, along with *Thirty Poems, SSM* was the first respectable book he had written. On the day before, he even dreamed a bit, wondering whether actor Gary Cooper might play the lead if the book was turned into a film. Despite his glee over the publication of the autobiography, Merton was wary of being poisoned by the pleasure he felt. He believed that even though he attempted to keep that pleasure away, "the smell of it goes into your blood anyway. You get drunk by sniffing the cork of the bottle."[36]

As the warmth of the summer months of 1948 turned to fall and the monks began to spend more time indoors, Merton left the walls of Gethsemani for the first time in seven years when he traveled to Louisville. To his great regret and sorrow, a few days later Abbot Dunne died and was replaced by Dom James Fox during a year when Merton enjoyed not only the publication of *SSM,* but also *What is Contemplation?, Cistercian Contemplatives, The Spirit of Simplicity, Exile Ends in Glory,* and the *Guide to Cistercian Life.* When the obedient Merton received a $900 royalty check for *SSM,* he gave it to the abbot and was told to keep writing.[37]

By the end of September, Merton was full of spark and good fortune. He enjoyed praying behind the church, where a steady wind cooled the air and he was alone. He felt love for all things, especially the God who loved him. He called out "Love carries me all around. I don't care for anything but love, love, love."[38]

With notoriety at his doorstep owing to the success of *SSM,* Merton suddenly was consumed with the fear that people would recall "all the nasty pictures I did for *Jester,*" and other shameful sins. Always self-critical, he further decided he would be one of "the ten most abjectly humiliated sinners in the history of the world, but it will be my joy, and it will fill me with love."[39]

If Merton was overwhelmed by the book's success two months after publication, he did not admit it. Instead, after beginning his eighth year at Gethsemani, in 1949, he thought of simplicity, of his continuing quest for the solitude he had sought years earlier. The key was nature, being able to walk in the woods from time to time. During those walks, when he could say hello to the squirrels, and groundhogs, and birds of every kind, he wondered whether he had changed. Laughing as he thought of his becoming balder, he nonetheless questioned whether he had more of an interior life. If he did, he was not certain how it had changed.[40]

The following March, as spring peeked through the Gethsemani windows and into the woods, bringing vivid color to bushes, trees, and flowering plants, Merton's spirits were buoyed by the arrival of his new book, *Seeds of Contem-*

plation. But walks around the Gethsemani grounds did not quell his unease, because he believed that each book published under his secular name was a problem since he wanted to be Frater Louis and not Thomas Merton. He recognized that the books were a reflection of his character and conscience; that he always hoped to find himself agreeable, and never did.[41]

During 1949, Merton's published books, in addition to *Seeds of Contemplation* and *The Waters of Siloe,* included *Gethsemani Magnificat* and *The Tears of the Blind Lions.* In *The Waters of Siloe,* he talked about the Cistercians as men who lived with the secret of God's face and were consumed with love. Proposing a definition of the contemplative life for which he would become a revered expert, he decided such a life was devoted solely to "the knowledge and love of God and to the love of other men in Him and for His sake."[42]

In late May 1949, Merton approached his day of ordination with trepidation. He joked that he would be a priest in three days if he was still alive, and the archbishop did not fall down and break his leg. But he wasn't sure he deserved the honor, since he still felt he was not truly one with God because he was self-centered. In essence, he was doing his will, not God's will. He was sick with sin with the hope of being absorbed in God's purity. The day before, and the day of, his ordination (May 26), Merton reflected on the un-holiness of his life. But nearly a month later, his head clear after a light morning rain had tickled the plants and flowers, he thought he had indeed become a new person with a new identity.[43]

In late June, Merton broke free of the monastery confines when permission was granted for him to wander the nearby countryside. Even though a black sky hovered over the knobs, and thunder beckoned far in the distance, he enjoyed the respite from people and felt God within. He knew when he was with people he felt lonely, but when he was by himself he and God could unite without interruption.[44]

Perhaps more than was visible on the surface, Merton's journals, eight years after having entered Gethsemani, reflected questions about his own mindset in regard to his pre-monastic memories. Although he relished the publication of *SSM,* he later wondered whether anyone was really their own self, or a facsimile. Pondering the question, he decided nobody was who they thought they were, or who others thought they were. He concluded that most people did not know what was good for them.[45]

In mid-September, he read the Book of Job and decided he was going to live it as well as read it. Pensive on the day before the sycamores began to turn yellow and brown, he considered the different types of fear. One of the worst related to the idea that he might become a protagonist in a Graham Greene novel, the "man who tries to be virtuous, and is in a certain sense holy," but nevertheless was overwhelmed by sin, an indication of sins never exorcised.[46]

While standing in a cornfield and watching a new machine that plucked corn, reduced it to tiny particles, and then sprayed it into a truck, Merton felt uneasy about life in general, deciding there was conflict between the spiritual life and the spiritual way of the artist. He decided his heart was "an abyss of self-hatred—waiting for the next appalling sea."[47]

Merton celebrated eight years at Gethsemani on December 15, but while chopping down dead trees he felt lonely and humiliated, that he was not a true person. The same day, he was appointed to a position on the monastery fire department, and asked Dom James to permit him a respite from being a deacon for a week. Later, confused about his plight in life, he felt fearful and dejected, despite recalling a nice walk in the woods on the Lord's birthday where he could see the countryside from the knobs. He chuckled when reminded of the day when he had wrecked a jeep loaned to him by a fellow brother. Wet, muddy roads were the cause of his skid, but the incident served to further his reputation for being a bit of a klutz with mechanical things. The jeep had ended up in a ditch; he thanked God he was still alive.[48]

Time passed quickly for Merton as the calendar moved to 1950, the year the Korean War began, anti-Communist sentiment grew in the United States and beyond, and Jack Kerouac's first novel, *The Town and the City,* was released. Early January brought black clouds and sheets of rain, and Merton pulled on a community raincoat and headed for the woods, where he bounded up one of the steepest knobs. A week later he believed that it was in the silence of the trees that he had discovered solitude for perhaps the first time in his life. In mid-March, after a morning Mass and singing, he wondered if his mind was really progressing in the right direction. Bowing to the God he worshiped, Merton's eyes were moist as he told his Lord, "I want to say over and over again, that I am sorry. I do not know how I can go on living unless I convince You, Jesus, that I am really sorry."[49] Later, he wondered how he could know Jesus if he did not know himself.[50]

In early March 1951, the year China entered the Korean War, Merton glanced at the manuscript of his unpublished novel, *Journal of My Escape from the Nazis,* later called *My Argument with the Gestapo,* for the first time in ten years. He had written it at St. Bonaventure when World War II began. He felt it was symbolic of real moral questions in his life. As he read, he recalled being on a search not only for a catharsis of sorts, but for something concrete in himself. But the more he meditated, the more he realized it was Gethsemani providing the antidote to the old, sinful Merton, since the monastic life had taught him how to live.[51]

In June 1951, on the day before he was named Master of Scholastics, Merton decided the man who was writing in his journal was dead, as was the man who had finished *SSM.* Most important, he concluded that the main character in *SSM,* his old self, was dead, too.[52]

Was he? Or was Merton only kidding himself?

CHAPTER SEVEN

FREEDOM SEEKER

Thomas Merton's journey toward discovering the true gift of love was mixed with his desire to discover his true identity. During the 1950s, he struggled with who he really was: a famous celebrity or a humble monk in God's world. This frustrated Merton, as he faced the feelings that he was not the contented monk he desired to be, nor the one promoted by the Catholic Church to the outside world.

With three years having passed since Merton authored his international best-seller, private journal entries reflected a man who dueled demons that continually prevented him from achieving his goal of becoming a person of solitude. This stemmed, his brother monk Dr. Rudy Bernard believed, from "the ongoing conflict Merton had between the community life and the monastic life and his desire to be alone. It was a conflict between the inner solitude of being with God alone and the demands of fraternal love for the [Gethsemani] community and its needs."[1]

In 1951, Merton became Master of Novices, a position of importance in educating aspiring monks entering Gethsemani.[2] The prolific writer would also publish ten books during the 1950s, including such classics as *The Sign of Jonas; Bread in the Wilderness;* and *No Man Is an Island.* The latter featured 16 essays on a wide array of subjects, including one titled "Love Can Be Kept Only by Being Given Away," a sure sign that the subject of love was on his mind.

In mid-September 1952, on the day after the smell of malt from the nearby distillery infiltrated the monastic valley, Merton had a conversation with a Chicago psychiatrist friend named Phillip Law. Merton believed the Trappists were, by definition, not a truly contemplative order, and Law agreed with the restless monk that he should leave Gethsemani. Merton considered alternative orders, including the Carthusians—monks who lived in individual hermitages and joined for only a few church services. That his inner struggle was close to bursting was evident when he admitted, in perhaps an overdramatic tone, in late October, "I have been having another one of those nervous breakdowns," a reminder, he lamented, of the "old days, in 1936, when I thought I was going to crack up on the Long Island Railroad, and the more recent one since ordination." Continuing days spent in self-reflection, Merton was despondent, deciding that he was not really a monk except in his own imagination. He felt exhausted from "the entertainment of all my illusions." When he prayed, he asked God to help him lose what he called the greatest illusion of all and start to live his life over again, or to die.[3]

Calmer waters appeared in Merton's life at a small, shingle-roofed toolshed located in the woods beyond the horse barn. When weather permitted, he sat at a wooden desk in his robe and sandals, and read or wrote, while gazing out at the trees in front of him as various forest critters scampered by wondering what he was doing there.[4] In mid-February 1953, Merton's spirits were high, since Saint Anne's—his name for the shed—was what he had been looking for all his life: a place to be alone, really alone. Thanking God for the gift during his daily prayers, Merton felt that in the silence of Saint Anne's, he could experience real unity, not his unity, but unity with God.[5]

Merton took a hiatus from writing journal entries from 1954 to 1955 while he was master of novices, but in mid-July 1956 he wrote of traveling along with Father John Eudes and Dom James, to Saint John's Abbey in Minnesota for a retreat. Also attending was Dr. Gregory Zilboorg, "an analyst of wide reputation," who had treated Ernest Hemingway and various other writers and artists. According to Merton, they talked for an hour and a half, and he told Zilboorg about his troubles. The analyst then informed Merton he was in bad shape, and was, among other things: neurotic, a gadfly to superiors, stubborn, and quite afraid to simply be an ordinary monk at Gethsemani. Zilboorg believed Merton and Father Eudes could easily become "a pair of semi-psychotic quacks." He said Merton liked being famous, and enjoyed the spotlight. "Megalomania and narcissism are your big trends," the doctor stated, before adding that Merton's hermit intentions were pathological. He said Merton was the type of fellow who would earn all kinds of money on Wall Street and lose it betting on the horses the next day. Zilboorg added that being forbidden to write was not the answer, because Merton must make the decision not to write for himself.[6]

To Merton's shock, Zilboorg said he had already told *SSM* editor Bob Giroux his opinions. Merton's reaction was to admit he learned "things which I know and did not know. And I suppose that is just the trouble."[7] Lashing out, Merton later decided Zilboorg resembled Josef Stalin. When he returned to Gethsemani, Merton sang with his brothers at Mass and prayed to God to understand what he might do about his shortcomings.

Further details regarding the Zilboorg confrontation would surface later, but for the time being, Merton moved on with his attempt to live a contemplative life in the woods at Saint Anne's. Mark Van Doren visited with news that Merton's friend Robert Lax was ill. As 1957 closed its door, an unsettled Merton lamented on a snowy, quiet Christmas Eve that the manuscript for his forthcoming book, *The Secular Journal,* had been sidetracked by censors who felt his language was too cutting and hurtful. Two days after the holiday, Merton wrote that he had decided his main goals were to promote peace in the world, to be an apostle, to help people understand the truth, and to make his whole life a witness to God's truth.[8] Pondering daily, Merton wondered what love meant in the modern world. He decided there was the need to love with newness before concluding, "I suppose the first thing to do is to admit I do not know the meaning of love in any context—ancient or new," a startling admission for a man who had written about love and how others should love in any number of his books.[9]

Merton experienced another epiphany that broadened his view of love on March 19, 1958, during a visit to Louisville. What he observed and wrote in his journal about his bond with the real world would become a most revered passage, discussed, quoted, and written about for decades to come. One memorable line: "I suddenly realized that I loved all the people [of the world] and that none of them were, or, could be totally alien to me."[10]

A Palm Sunday 1958 worship service caused Merton to consider whether he was worthy of love, and what the obligation to love really meant. After noting that his book *The Secular Journal* had been approved by censors, with publication scheduled for 1959, Merton, bolstered by strong coffee, was concerned with the concept of self. He decided he could finally be a monk when he quit trying to become one. But he concluded it was "crazy . . . trying to live up to an image of yourself you have unconsciously created in the minds of others." Addressing this fact as he walked the path to Saint Anne's, he decided the solution was to destroy the image.[11]

What image Merton believed he had registered in those who knew him both inside and away from the monastery remained undisclosed. He continued to exhibit the mind of a troubled man instead of one at peace with the monastic life and the world in general. Having learned Dom James would not give him a letter from Monsignor Ricaurte, of Bogotá, regarding Merton becoming involved in starting a new monastery the abbot deemed too provocative,[12] Merton was bitter and depressed. He woke up in the middle of the night, frustrated with his ideas and hoping for a more sane existence. He felt he was a "prisoner of *vanitas monastica* [monastic pride] and its crudities, incomprehensions, and falsities."[13] In mid-December, when snowy roads made passage risky, Merton felt alienated.

After ruminating about the complexity and the unhappy state of his monastic life for the remainder of 1958 and the early months of 1959, Merton decided he needed to examine his feelings about being a true Christian. Deep into the night, he wrote and rewrote on the subject, finally concluding that love equaled emotional pressure toward conformity so as to avoid insecurity. To clarify, he concluded there were fundamentally treacherous values behind the backdrop of love. He asked, "When will we ever become Christians?"[14]

During a day in May, when bright sunshine lit up dew on the grass, Merton, appearing to extend his wonderment about the true depth of his Christian soul, was visited by Robert Lax and Robert Giroux. He must have kept his confused mind hidden from them, since after they left he pondered the thought: "The thing is, when people come to see me, they are not really edified." Clarifying his visitors' lack of enlightenment, he decided this was due to his being neither a monk nor a Christian. The confusion, he believed, resulted from his casting an aura of outward calm when he knew there was turmoil within. Such feelings caused him to discuss leaving Gethsemani when his good friend Dom Gregorio Lemercier of Cuernavaca, Mexico, visited. But he concluded that opposition would be strong and he still wasn't sure about leaving. He realized he needed to pray about the decision, holding nothing back from the God he loved.[15]

Merton, who was spending mornings reading in his woodshed, once again blasted the monastery's hierarchy and the monastic life as practiced at Gethsemani. He decided that it "warps people, kills their spirit, reduces them to something less than human." He felt that many of the monks simply parroted the words of superiors, causing a false spirit to prevail. Merton was also frustrated and upset at his own plight. He decided that the monastic life was like

living a lie. Since he felt powerless to do anything about it, he made the decision that he had better leave. But then, as he left the woodshed to walk down
through the brush to the abbey, he had a strange feeling that he later recorded:
"perhaps it is I who am the liar and perhaps leaving would be the greater lie."
This led him to worry about the consequences of his leaving. Questioning his
own motives, his mind whirling in confusion, Merton recognized that while
something was drawing him away from Gethsemani, he could not pinpoint it.
Something was missing, he knew, but wouldn't there always be something
missing for such a restless soul?[16]

During the second week of June, after deciding New Mexico, Arizona,
and the Virgin Islands might appeal to him as new locations, Merton decided
to ask Dom James for permission to become a woods hermit, although he disliked use of the word "hermit," believing it to be a fictitious idea. Predicting
the request would be refused, but still hopeful, Merton attempted to sort out
his feelings, realizing his old enemy, illusion, was complicating matters, because the inner debate over whether he would be happier at Gethsemani or
somewhere else was frustrating and confusing.[17]

Given his quest for freedom, Merton wondered whether finding it would
be possible in lieu of the alternative: committing to be content as a surrendered
captive. Concluding he did not really want to be a hermit, or truly contemplative, he nonetheless wanted a complete break from any fiction or pretense,
any façade or hypocrisy, in connection with Gethsemani. Merton believed God
was calling him to some sort of missionary solitude, the simple life. But it must
have "love in it, and not an abstract love, but a real love for real people."[18]

In late July 1959, Merton's anger was aimed directly at Dom James. He
concluded the abbot was a "good, sweet, and dangerous man because he believes in his own sweetness and does not see the inexorable, self-righteous appetite for domination that underlies it." Tossing more abuse at him, the
frustrated Merton believed the abbot was quite possessive, like a mother who
was moralistic and stubborn. He concluded that he was afraid of the abbot,
who undermined those he believed were more intelligent than he was. The
following month, Merton faced his foe in a conversation about his problems
at the monastery, and his desires for isolation and the simple life. The end result was unsatisfactory: while he had argued the merit of his leaving, the abbot
argued the opposite—he should stay—and no resolution was advanced.[19]

On the final day of August, which was hotter than normal, Merton wrestled with his restless soul. A temptation appeared that added to his continuing

dilemma. He met Father Anselm's sister Carolyn, whom he found charming, intelligent, and honest. Later, he would call her a child. Merton was genuinely moved by her sense of courage and loneliness, and the two comforted each other with spiritual nuances. But he sensed that "anyone with two grains of sense [would] probably detect behind all this a sort of sexual attraction." He concluded that it was instead somehow a companionship of spiritual nature, which justified the encounter and his feelings. When Merton considered this sudden interlude during the quiet of the night as he lay on his straw mattress, he decided he was human, and that humanity was part of the mysterious nature of Christ. Then he took it one step further, concluding that very rarely was there any spontaneous human feeling in which sex did not play a part.[20]

A month later, with Carolyn still fresh in his mind, a second female temptation arrived when Natasha, the wife of his friend Stephen Spender, "blew in with a girl from the Coast, Margot Dennis." Merton envied the two, who were driving across the country, free as birds. The famous monk enjoyed the intellectual banter about such subjects as Zen, Freud, Saint John of the Cross, and his *Dark Night of the Soul,* before leading the two attractive women to Saint Bernard's Lake, where the threesome ate sandwiches and had fruitcake for dessert. They talked about subjects ranging from monasteries and abbots, bishops, and popes to Mexico. The carefree threesome swam and sunbathed, and Merton enjoyed himself immensely. The rest of the afternoon was spent chatting and laughing while talking of Mexico. When he recorded his feelings that evening, he decided that "Margot, once dipped into the water . . . became completely transformed into a Naiad-like [Greek nymph] creature, smiling a primitive smile through hanging wet hair." He admitted that in the future, when he met intelligent women, ones thirsting for lively conversation, he needed to be more careful. Merton realized swimming with the women had been a true act of disobedience of his monastic vows, but one he could not resist.[21]

Still considering leaving Gethsemani, the rebellious Merton began to debate the merits of detachment before spending a fine day walking in the woods. He was determined to pursue more of an interior life in a new direction. Doing so would be in the way God had in mind for him with his job to move forward, to grow within, to pray, and to disconnect from attachments. This, in turn, would help him resist fear, grow in his faith, and change his life pattern entirely. His ally would be the Holy Spirit.[22]

Armed with whatever true intention filled his mind, Merton marched ahead. In October, when pumpkins ripened in fields around the monastery and a train whistle reminded him of his first visit to Gethsemani, he noted that an optimistic letter had arrived from Rome concerning his request to transfer. But only a month later, as he awaited further news, he was certain he was a failure, especially with regard to love. This was due, he decided, to his own weakness and a feeling of alienation from the monastic community, since he did not love it enough owing to his faults.[23]

As cold December 1959 arrived, Merton, his mind complicated and anything but contemplative, discussed his reasons for wanting to leave Gethsemani with Dom James after the abbot had visited Rome. Nervous as he awaited further word, Merton complained of dark days, ones apparently caused, among other things, by the abbot's refusal to give him a letter from his friend, Nicaraguan priest Ernesto Cardenal.[24]

On December 16, Merton received his answer from Rome: "No." Signed by two cardinals, the letter explained that they were sorry, but his departure would upset too many people, both within the order and outside it. The superiors asked that Merton stay where God wanted him to be with the hope that he might find solitude.[25]

As he walked through the woods on the way to Saint Anne's, Merton was not angry, because he believed the decision was God's will. This made him feel as though a mountain had been lifted off his shoulders and that he must surrender himself to the God he loved. But as the calendar turned to 1960, Merton's inner burdens of pride, disobedience, and a lack of true faith haunted him.[26] Did these include the sexual temptations of Father Anselm's sister Carolyn and Margot Dennis?

CHAPTER EIGHT

"PEOPLE THINK
I AM HAPPY"

Thomas Merton's most peaceful days during 1960, the year when he applauded the election of President John F. Kennedy, were spent listening to the sounds of bullfrogs at 2:30 A.M. or the whippoorwill that began his "whoop" a half hour later.[1] Regardless of the solitude Merton felt during the times when nature was his best friend, he admitted tendencies toward escapism, snobbism, or narcissism. As he walked the Gethsemani grounds, he decided the problems derived from a sense of guilt and his desire to cover it up. Despite appearances to the contrary, he knew he was confused. As he scanned the scheme of human ideology and its place in social consciousness, Merton believed the United States was not the democracy it pretended to be. He felt brokenhearted, not only for himself and his sins, but for the rotten flavor of the world infesting all human beings. He wanted to write about his misgivings, but felt the censors would never permit him to speak freely.[2] In early August 1960, Merton was certain a change was necessary. He wasn't quite sure what that change should be, but he believed he needed to obtain a clearer idea of purpose.[3]

In late August, Merton reached into the past to discover clarity for the future. As he continued his daily hours of meditation and fasting with fellow brothers while walking in the woods with his friends, the animals, he decided his current moral problems were ones he had never faced in the past. Thinking had become a delusion, he concluded, and the result was that he could not act, thus rendering him, in his own words, a Gethsemani political prisoner. He blamed Dom James for stomping out any spark of freedom.[4]

During the next month, Merton's spirits blossomed as he watched the building of a retreat center in the Gethsemani woods. In mid-December, when sparkling snow covered the stumps and bushes, and frosty temperatures lit up every breath, he overcame doubts to the contrary and decided he was perhaps stronger than those who knew him well thought he was. But feelings of insecurity made him wonder whether he was somehow afraid of this strength, and whether he used it against himself so as to feel weak.[5]

At the dawning of the new year, 1961, five years before he would meet Margie Smith, Merton was concerned with the public's perception of him and his writings. He decided that people in general used others to create an illusion of how they were supposed to live. Furthermore, he believed, "through my own fault I have become part of too many collective illusions, and have wanted to," an apparent reference to the public Merton, the one immersed in the real world. Connected to these illusions, he felt, was the concept of happiness. He knew people could decide what life they wanted, and that there were many forms of happiness. But he wondered why people forced themselves to experience illusion in order to discover happiness. This, Merton decided, was only a happiness approved by others. He told himself he was happy and that God had given him happiness, but that he felt guilty because he didn't think he deserved it.[6]

At age 46, Merton found himself reflecting more and more on nature's beauty. He watched with curiosity a mid-April thunderstorm, the first he had sat through since being permitted to use the retreat center-turned-hermitage, one originally built to hold some of the ecumenical gatherings Merton was conducting. It was christened Saint Mary of Carmel. Merton called it "Janua Coeli, the gate of heaven," and thanked God for the wonderful gift he had been given. Later, Edward Rice would say Merton used "trickery and pressure and evasion to obtain it." Rice said Merton told him, "Father Abbot thought I was going to build a little wooden hut to sit and think in . . . but I had the novices build a real cement-block house." Dom James was upset, Rice concluded, and "had his revenge" by not permitting Merton to enjoy the benefits of a kitchen, a toilet, or a chapel in the hermitage until shortly before he left for Asia in 1968. This treatment caused one New York friend, Rice noted, to believe that the "abbot had it in for Tom."[7]

In early September, Merton prayed for inner peace, realizing that the selfishness and lack of love within him had caused "bitterness and selfishness." Unclear as to what would cleanse his worried soul, he wondered what he was capable of doing, what God wanted of him, and—if he saw clearly what that was—whether he had the capability to do it.[8]

Despite his early acceptance of Rome's decision to bar him from leaving Gethsemani, Merton anguished over the defeat. He felt there was injustice in the air, and despite Dom James' giving him permission to be at the hermitage, he concluded the abbot was controlling him, being devious and tricky.[9] Just as visits to Saint Anne's had not been enough to soothe his worried soul, Merton's seclusion at the hermitage was failing as well to calm his restless mind.

In late October a fog permeated the cold, wet days. Merton was pleased when an article he wrote, "The Root of War is Fear," was published in Dorothy Day's *Catholic Worker*. He was proud to be one of the few Catholic priests to speak out against the Vietnam War and against violence of any kind to solve world conflict. A month later, buoyed by a visit from Aunt Kit from New Zealand, Merton interrupted writing about his political views to focus on family. He learned from his aunt that his mother and grandmother had disliked each other, and his mother believed that Granny had been too indulgent with him and that he should have been disciplined. His aunt's comments caused him to recall his mother as "strict, stoical and determined. Granny believed children ought to be brought up by love."[10]

In late November 1961, an otherwise confused Merton was certain of one thing: he loved the novices he taught daily. One evening while he was on night watch, he opened the door of the novices' scriptorium, and flashed the light over the novices' empty desks. He felt the warmth and love of his students and the goodness they possessed. He thought of them as his children, and loved them and felt loved by them.[11]

Merton's 47th year on the face of the earth, 1962, the year of the Cuban missile crisis, opened with a January when warmer temperatures caused rain to pour down on the snow. He admitted he was still not the free man he wanted to be, because he blocked himself through a false sense of independence. He questioned motives and the abbot's actions, deciding he made too much of them and that God was not going to use any of this to free him.[12] Regardless, he was pleased when *New Seeds of Contemplation* was published.

When the calendar turned to March, he continued to address his own shortcomings despite the outside world's belief that he was the happy, contemplative monk he projected. As the birds began to chirp in the sunshine and blades of grass crept up from their home in the fertile, half-frozen soil, he was pensive but certain of his foolish sin that had "always nested in my nature," but that grace had not dismissed. He wondered if there was within him "some innate cleverness that will outwit death when it comes, and, of course always with grace, be saved." Summing up a life packed with rollercoaster emotions for a man who was supposed to be peaceful, contented, and free, he decided "It is from this folly that I probably deserve all the bitterness that is in my life." In late March, Merton spent a full day at the hermitage. It was the first time he had had permission to be there for that long, and he noted a sure sign of spring, spying ants leaving their huge anthills. In April, as wildflowers blossomed all around him, he relished the smell of fresh tulips that had survived munching by rabbits.[13] Interrupting Merton's peaceful tone was the sledgehammer of censorship from the Abbot General prohibiting him from publishing any more articles on the Vietnam War. He felt disgust at the restriction and more imprisoned than ever.

In early September, Merton had a dream in which he left the monastery and was in a village near Bardstown with Tony Walsh (his mentor at Columbia), where the two met a pair of young women dressed in white. They were lovely. Deciding to hitchhike with the women in tow, he paired himself with the one who did not look like a nun. With his arm around her waist, they walked down the road. The fantasy woman was "fresh and firm and pure, a beautiful sweet person, a stranger yet freely intimate and loving." She told him he must not kiss her or try to seduce her, and he replied that he had no intention of such conduct. Nevertheless, this did nothing to alter their intimacy.[14]

Suddenly, Walsh and the other woman vanished from the dream, and he was alone with the "sweet person," whom he called "A." Headed to Gethsemani, the pair encountered several people waiting for a bus. All of them knew her because she had preached to them. One was "an Indian" and another said something lewd about her, but Merton defended her virtue. When the bus arrived, Merton boarded and walked to the front but no one was there. A. entered through another door and they met.[15] Then they left the bus.

Merton's dream then traced the pair's movement toward the monastery. Along the way they hoped to get a ride but didn't, before columns of smoke appeared near the town of Bardstown. He knew some sort of test was afoot and noted A. telling him not to kiss her. Monks dressed like soldiers blocked the road and Merton believed he would be captured, but A. concealed what appeared to be a monastic crown of some sort that would protect them. Moving on in the dream, Merton saw himself in a barn without A. beside him. He set the straw on fire to divert the monks who were chasing him. Then, after appearing to be trapped, he was in an open field. In the distance was a Dutch church, and he saw a cross. Then he woke up.[16]

Merton never mentioned the dream or its sensuality again. But he noted turning melancholy in early December as stiff, cold winds whipped around the hermitage and knocked a tin can off of the porch. Merton recognized it had been 21 years since he entered Gethsemani and he wondered if he was closer to his beginning or his end. When a fellow monk left the monastery, it awakened Merton's desire to be free, as well as the belief that he never would be free until he died. As he gathered some firewood and stacked it neatly by the fireplace, he decided his current state of mind was "like standing on the deck of a sinking ship and watching everyone else go off in a lifeboat." The conclusion: "What I am facing is the slow and inexorable sacrifice of my will and my life." Glancing at the naked branches on many of the trees, Merton concluded he was going to die within a few years. Worse, he knew his will was being taken from him, and he hated the thought of this occurring. He would rebel against it, with little hope for success.[17]

Clearly living in a darkened, secret world despite his fame and the permission to live in solitude at the hermitage, Merton's mind often delved into the past, into events that had occurred more nearly 30 years before. In late January 1963, a year in which three more of his books were published (*Life and Holiness, Emblems of a Season of Fury,* and *The Solitary Life: A Letter of Guigo*), Merton decided there was a lack of meaning in his life and that he was still the same "self-willed and volatile person who made such a mess at Cambridge." Walking down the winding path toward the abbey, he felt he had not changed much from those days and was still vain and self-centered. Beneath the mask he wore for others, he almost hoped that he would die of a heart attack.[18]

In late May, when abnormal temperatures still chilled the air, Merton indicated a growing concern over the man he was, or was not. During the day of the 14th anniversary of his ordination, he wished he had truly grown internally in those years but feared he had not. Although he could recall some happiness and productivity during a bout of self-criticism, he realized the depth of his frustration and the likelihood of his ultimate defeat. Exhibiting feelings of confusion over the man he appeared to be, he decided it had all been "some kind of a lie, a charade." He concluded that his life had been full of "repeated failures, failures without number, like holes appearing everywhere in a worn-out garment " . . . nothing has been effectively patched. The moths have eaten me . . ." Sensing the real problem was a semiconscious desire to keep his identity, he called himself a failure, unjust and unenriched. At day's end, he was discouraged and felt the "depressions [were] deeper, more frequent. I am near fifty. People think I am happy."[19]

During a hot spell in July 1963, when short sleeves were the order of the day and he drank cool water from a lake near the hermitage, Merton was determined to lose his old self, to discover true solitude. He wanted a new identity, aside from that of a writer or a monk, but, he concluded it would be like a cocoon, masking any transition stage.[20]

As the sound of chainsaws infiltrated the silent world of the hermitage in mid-July, Merton admitted he was not in good physical shape. The yoga exercises he endured a year earlier were becoming more difficult. As he climbed the hill from the abbey to the stone hermitage, he was short of breath. But shortly thereafter, his spirits soared when he received a personal letter signed by Pope Paul VI, thanking him for a letter of congratulations. It included a special blessing for him and the novices.[21]

Despite feeling blessed to have received the letter, Merton continued to evaluate himself as the month of July emerged. He wondered what the outside world truly thought of him. He had already mentioned illusion and confusion, but now he sensed an element of deception, since people truly did listen to him and accepted his words of wisdom.[22] Illusion, confusion, and deception— hadn't he abandoned these in the outside world?

CHAPTER NINE

DANCING *in the* WATER *of* LIFE

During the fall of 1963, Thomas Merton's body was falling apart. As he considered fresh means to further detach from both the monastic and material worlds, arthritis, cervical disk pain, and possible permanent injury to his vertebrae caused him discomfort. His arm kept falling asleep.[1] Then he was attacked.

The rather bizarre incident occurred just a few days before President Kennedy was assassinated in late November. A woman apparently persuaded Gethsemani officials she was Merton's distant relative. He described her as a "remarkable, beatnik, Charles Addams [American cartoonist], hair in the eyes type who turned out, in the afternoon, to be, he concluded, a nymphomaniac." During their brief time together, she wanted to have sex and the interlude became quite physical. When he finally tore loose from her, his virtue, he decided, was mostly intact. But he was shocked that the deranged woman had come on so strong. Reflecting on the incident, he concluded he was ashamed, bewildered, and amazed at the temptation, even though it was "phantomlike." He said she had an "active, sweatered body" and had arrived and left before he knew what had happened.[2]

Once the shock of the incident had worn off, Merton's interest in photography advanced, and he began enlarging some of the pictures he took. Later, he would use a Kodak Instamatic to capture black-and-white visions of an old cedar root he kept on the porch. Ever curious, he used Naomi Burton Stone's Nikon, a Rolleiflext, and a Canon FX lent to him by his friend John

Howard Griffin.[3] In total, the collection of photographs was quite compelling. In later years, the public's curiosity about his photography would intensify, and many exhibits were presented well into the first decade of the 20th century.

When Merton learned of President Kennedy's death in November 1963, he was overwhelmed with sorrow. He believed Kennedy was a flawed but honest man who was trying to do what was right for the country. He wondered if his honesty caused the assassination.[4]

Three more books, *Seeds of Destruction, Come to the Mountain,* and *La Revolution Noire,* were published in 1964, the same year Merton cheered when Dr. Martin Luther King Jr. won the Nobel Peace Prize. Merton called this a true jubilee year, even though he was not clear as to where he was headed. But there was a new beginning to his life, he believed, as he enjoyed June weather despite one day when cold, beating rain pounded the hermitage rooftop. He admitted experiencing a "mild case of crisis" but believed it was nothing brand new but perhaps intensified by his approaching age 50. This did not keep him from traveling, with permission from Dom James, to New York City to visit Daisetz Suzuki, a leading Buddhist scholar.[5] But it was a short visit; the abbot did not trust him to be absent for long.

Merton, now sleeping at the hermitage as the hermit he desired to be, nevertheless continued to bombard Dom James with ridicule. He viewed him as unreasonable and arbitrary, causing constant frustration and even true resentment. The abbot's favorite statement, one imprinted on a rubber stamp, was "All for Jesus through Mary, with a smile," a somewhat glib reference, some monks believed, to the abbot's desire that everyone cooperate regardless of any objections to the contrary.[6]

In mid-December, when he watched shining stars race across the horizon, frost appear on the coal pile, and birds feast on frozen bread left on the porch, Merton appeared reconciled to never permanently leaving Gethsemani. He concluded he had no desire to pursue another monastery of his own order, or those of the Camaldolese or Carthusians. Despite the decision to stay, Merton continued to feel ill-will toward the abbot and confusion about his true identity. Experiencing the milestone 50th birthday, he concluded the past had included times of embarrassment and others of joy, though in retrospect they all seemed quite meaningless. As he sat on a wooden chair in the hermitage, a wintry and lonely place, Merton compared himself to the lonely boy of 18 who had visited Bournemouth. Walking outside to view the softness of a new snowfall, he decided that what he regretted most was his "lack of love, [his] selfishness and glibness (covering a deep shyness and need of love) with girls, who after all, did love me I think, for a time." This led him to believe his greatest fault was an unwillingness to believe it, because he required proof of love, some sort of perfect fulfillment.[7]

When he sat down to write that evening with only his bird friends as company, he decided to be completely honest, triggering an astonishing admission: "So one thing on my mind is sex, as something I did not use maturely and well, something I gave up without having come to terms with it. That is hardly worth thinking about now—twenty-five years nearly since my last adultery." Adding more details to the wild time of his life occurring in 1940 or 1941, he recalled the summer heat in Virginia and his "moral helplessness" contributing to his feelings of madness. As he thought clearly about the confusing time, he recalled walking on the beach with an unnamed woman. He did not want to speak to her, and did so only with great difficulty. He could not share his ideas or anything he truly loved. Continuing to reminisce, Merton regretted his conduct, especially one incident with a woman named Sylvia at Clare College, which occurred as he sat on a boathouse's steps late at night. Reflecting on the memories, he concluded, "What I find most in my whole life is illusion. Wanting to be something of which I had formed a concept."[8]

As he stood outside the hermitage trying to make sense of his lonely life, Merton was bent on becoming free but knew there was a struggle ahead. Despite mistakes and illusions that had consumed much of his life, he was pleased that there had also been happiness. But he recalled years filled with insincere conduct, mostly when he was younger than 21 and chose his friends poorly. Merton believed the way he led his life had improved considerably after his senior year at Columbia, but before that there had been sporadic happy times at the San Antonin school in France, Oakham, St. Bonaventure, and in Cuba. But he realized that many of the best times—but also some of the worst—had been at Gethsemani.[9]

In May 1965, Merton enjoyed sitting in the hermitage at 4 A.M., his only companion a large cup of coffee as he translated poems. Regardless, stress continued to build in his mind. But he was philosophical about his woody existence, suddenly bringing female companionship into the equation. He told himself that it was necessary for him to "live here alone without a woman, for the silence of the forest is my bride and the sweet dark warmth of the whole world is my love."[10] When dawn arrived that day, he watched a beautiful sunrise and heard the howl of a hound chasing a rabbit Merton knew he would never catch.

In mid-June, Merton understood the dichotomies of his life, especially those concerning obedience and protest, and freedom and imprisonment. He griped about having been banned from personal contact with the world at large by being forbidden from traveling extensively. He saw this solitude as a reward in some ways but a punishment in others. But he was upset that he could not travel to Asia at this point in time since he was curious to learn more about the Eastern religions. Ultimately, this left him with the feeling of imprisonment and confinement.[11]

After Mass one day in late June, he suddenly remembered his boyhood friend Andrew Winser's little sister Ann, whom he had known in the early 1930s. She had been 12 or 13 when he visited the family on the Isle of Wight. Merton remembered her fondly because she was the "quietest thing on it, dark and secret child." He decided that while a person does not fall in love with a child of 13, he realized that he had not forgotten her, and if things had been different, if he had "taken another turn in the road [he] might have ended up married to Ann." He told himself that she was the "symbol of the true (quiet) woman I never really came to terms [with] in the world, and of this there remains an incompleteness that cannot be remedied." Looking within, he acknowledged "the years in which I chased whores or made whores out of my girlfriends (no, that is too strong and also silly, besides there were plenty that I was too shy to sleep with) did nothing to make sense of me on the contrary." Then he recalled Ginny Burton as another girl with whom he could have fallen in love but did not, even though he loved her with feelings not immersed in sex.[12]

Four days later, Merton delivered a revealing audio-taped lecture to the novices. It was pertinent since he turned a discussion of the monk Philoxonus of Mabbaugh, bishop of Hieropolis and one of the fathers of the Oriental Church in Syria (AD 488–518) into a diatribe about love. Merton had begun speaking to his students about Philoxonus in mid-May. He believed man was supposed to love God and be loved by God, who would show the way. Man had a natural goodness, he believed, and despite falling, was never radically corrupted. Merton preached that vocation was interrelated with crisis, and it was through crises that one grew, since the angels purposely tested man by pushing the soul into deeper crisis, where man was completely troubled regarding the choices he must make. Merton believed the deeper the crisis, the better, because it would spur one to overcome it through the "strong fire of love." Advising real Christians living the monastic life, Merton then posed the question: "How do we know our life of prayer is genuine?" He answered by pointing out that man is tested by his willingness to suffer. If he suffered, then God permitted him to grow as part of the test.[13]

Merton explained to the class that any hope must be true hope before he asked what the difference was between true hope and false hope. He concluded true hope could not be deceptive, but must instead be a hope in God. He then asked whether man trusted God or himself. If it was the latter, he concluded, and most times it was, then this person had much work to do. Merton reminded the novices that suffering triggered hope. By suffering and by trial, a man abandoned hope in himself and instead placed his hope in God. This was because he had to be tempted, to have his back to the wall, to understand he could not handle matters himself. Strength to handle the suffering, he concluded, was only possible through God. This was, in his mind, a basic truth.[14]

Deciding to provide testimony, he recalled times in his past when he "didn't do too hot, see." Pausing for reflection as past experiences filled his mind, he decided it was easy to recall times when he lived his life on his own terms with bad results. Homing in on personal experience, Merton told the novices that God reminded those who tried to control their lives by presenting certain temptations or trials. He then offered the novices three questions: "Do you want to be the boss? Do you want to take over? Do you want to drive?" Pausing for effect, he then told them they were free to drive the car over the cliff.[15] Less than a year later, when Margie Smith came along, Merton would be tested, would be asked who was the boss, he or God? Would he drive over the cliff?

In December 1965, Merton hinted at a state of transformation when he wrote that he felt each day that his old life was leaving his being and would eventually be gone. If his mind was ripe for a change, his body was not cooperating. He was experiencing an arthritic hip, a case of chronic dermatitis on his hands, which forced him to wear gloves, and sinusitis. When he had an x-ray, it indicated a puzzling shadow in his lungs. Diarrhea was a constant companion, most of his teeth were missing, he had lost nearly all of his hair, and he had chipped vertebra in his neck. He was anguished by this less than by his whole existence. Worse, his mind was tormented as well with his admitting, on an otherwise sunny day, to "the awful depression that I had a couple of times at Christmas in recent years." He focused on dying and accepting his fate.[16]

On Christmas Day, Merton experienced for the second time "a curious, somewhat sexual dream about Naomi [his literary agent]." He thought long and hard about the significance of the dream before deciding that the two loved each other in some way even though they loved each other in some complicated way. Unable to reconcile his feelings for his literary agent, he decided "to feel it and bear it as another bloody nuisance, like my psychosomatic sickness."[17]

BOOK IV

the MERTON
BIOGRAPHERS

"[The critics] were trying so hard to find pictures of
[Thomas Merton's] halo that they missed his face."

—*Merton's friend, Robert Lax*

CHAPTER TEN

the OTHER SIDE
of the STORY

Having examined Merton's words in *SSM*, and those in the private journals, we now turn to the biographers. Some information may appear duplic-
itous, but it all connects to a presentation of a complete portrayal of Merton
utilizing every morsel of information available about him. What was the root
of Merton's discomfort, his unhappiness, his restlessness, his anger at Abbot
Dom James, and the state of depression he described on several occasions?
What caused him to reminisce about past relationships with women trailing
back to the 1930s and to regret his actions during the dark days at Clare College in Cambridge?

Even when Merton was given the opportunity for solitude, first at the
toolshed and then at the hermitage, it was not enough to calm a restless and
sad soul. Despite outward appearances and his stream of writings, he continued to anguish in a separate world contrary to the one in which close friends,
brother monks, academic colleagues, and millions of readers believed he existed. Why was he suffering so much when he appeared to have been blessed
by a God who had swept him into Gethsemani so he could avoid a world
tempting him left and right? Had he not been saved by grace; had he not been
truly cleansed by ordination as a priest and by a dedication to "God alone"?

Merton's admissions in *SSM* and in private journals regarding such subjects as the disjointed relationship with both his mother and his father (but especially his mother); the orphan years, when he was as confused as he was
excited about new independence; the disappointing love affairs with one girl

and then another; the mess he made of the time at Clare and the disappointment of Tom Bennett; the continued search for both purpose and deeper personal relationships while at Columbia; and even the admitted adulterous affair
months before entering Gethsemani—none alone validates the extreme inner
turmoil blowing through his writings like a winter wind streaking across the
barren plains of Kansas. No, there must be more to explain the anguish, and
of course, there is, much more to assist our understanding of the conflicted
Merton, the one beneath the mask of holiness. What is it? What didn't he tell
us? And how will additional information he never divulged affect the ultimate
decision—Margie or God—he would make as the years flow from 1966 to
1968?

During the past 30-plus years, multiple biographies have chronicled Merton's life and times. Each author researched not only new sources of factual
data about him, but also his writings, carefully sifting through them to separate
fact from fiction. Based on his popularity, Merton must have anticipated this,
realizing people would wish to know him even better than he knew himself.
Otherwise, why would he have taken the time to record nearly every emotion—the good, the bad, and most of the ugly—he had about nearly every subject in which he was interested on nearly every day of his adult life? Such
conduct was especially revealing regarding the love affair with Margie, a topic
he could easily have avoided due to its sensitive nature for him and, perhaps
more relevant, based on privacy issues for her. One indication of how much he
loved Margie and respected her privacy was his decision to prohibit publication
of the private journals, especially Volume VI, which details the love affair, until
25 years after his death. Recall that she was engaged to be married during much
of the affair, causing her to be less than honest with her fiancé who, it must be
assumed, never knew of her love for the famous monk twice her age. The historical significance of the writings is apparent, since the biographies reveal secrets neither Merton nor the Catholic censors wished to expose. Melding what
Merton wrote and said with the biographers' contributions provides a much
clearer picture, the "other side of the story," if you will, of who Merton really
was when Margie Smith entered his life in April 1966.

During his journey, Merton wrote and wrote and wrote some more,
whether it was spiritual books, critical essays, inspiring poetry, pointed articles,
or notes on the back of scrap paper. Is there any doubt that from 1946 until
he died twenty-two years later he was one of the most prolific writers alive? He
ultimately had more than 70 books to his credit. Arguably, his body of work

spread among so many important subjects is second to none during this period and is even more impressive if one includes his writings pre-Gethsemani. If Hemingway revolutionized the novel with stocky prose like that he used in *The Old Man and the Sea,* if Mailer created a whole new language in such books as *The Naked and the Dead* and *Armies of the Night,* if Kerouac added a "beat" emphasis and "spontaneous prose" to storytelling through *On the Road,* and modern writers like Anne Lamott introduced spicy language into spiritual books like *Bird by Bird,* written in the echo of Merton, what of him—where he does he stack up in the history of literature? Each of his books was certainly written in a unique style, characterized by Merton biographer Robert Inchausti as "Joycean." When it came to Merton's novels and poems, Inchausti said they were "more theologically mature than his literary peers Jack Kerouac and Henry Miller," and "more in touch with the realities of his times than those of his Catholic cohorts Jacques Maritain and Jean Leclerq." Amen.[1]

Those who wished to chronicle Merton's amazing life did so whether they knew him or not. One who did was his first biographer, Edward Rice. A longtime friend and colleague of Merton's, Rice captured the essence of his struggles in *The Man in the Sycamore Tree: The Good Times and Hard Life of Thomas Merton,* a revealing title patterned after Merton's unpublished novel of the same name. Released in 1970, Rice's book was mentioned infrequently in later biographies. Some, including Merton's brother monk Paul Quenon and Dr. Paul Pearson, who was director of the Thomas Merton Center in 2009, expressed the belief that Rice's account was "too sensational."[2] Other scholars suggested it was weak in truth, since later research failed to substantiate some of Rice's claims, and he offered no reliable sources. Critics pointed to his use of the words "An Entertainment" below the subtitle, believing this tainted the authenticity of Rice's proclamations about Merton. But to Rice's way of thinking, Merton's life was entertaining as well as inspiring. He was right.

Regardless of the attacks, Rice's account is worthy of consideration because he knew Merton better than anyone (with perhaps the exception of Robert Lax), was a participant in many of the events Merton described, and wrote about Merton within two years of his untimely death. Most important, why would Rice, whom Merton called "my godfather" in *SSM,* have lied about his observations? Merton was his friend; he loved him. There was no cause to badmouth Merton, or even to exaggerate. Robert Lax believed those criticizing Rice's book "were trying so hard to find pictures of [Merton's] halo that they missed his face."[3] Author James Harford said the book "was highly praised by Lax and by friends who had known the monk from before Gethsemani days,"[4] adding credibility to the account.

Subsequent biographies were written by British journalist Monica Furlong, who dubbed Merton "a dynamic, full flesh-and-blood modern man," one committed "to a lifelong search for a meaningful and authentic way of life."[5] Based on meticulous research and a deep interest in chronicling the true Merton, official biographer Michael Mott's *Seven Mountains of Thomas Merton* was nominated for the Pulitzer Prize. Mott believed there was "a special paradox in [Merton]: he had written so much in an effort to reveal himself."[6]

Merton's brother monk, Father Basil Pennington, cherished him as a friend and chronicled his struggle to mature during his days at Gethsemani, with an eye on his quest for freedom. Jim Forest, a close friend of Merton's, wrote of him "having become the most celebrated monk alive, and the most famous Trappist, it was by no means clear to [Merton] that he was in the right place."[7] David Cooper analyzed the Merton who he believed suffered from a tension between art and spirituality—"the two poles around which he plotted his quest for a durable self-identity."[8] William Shannon, general editor of Merton's letters, called him "a lamp lighting the way for many who, without the 'spiritual direction' embodied in his writings, would have found little to illuminate their way along life's journey."[9] Harford, a personal friend of Edward Rice and Robert Lax, wrote a three-pronged biography of Rice, Lax, and Merton titled *Merton & Friends*. He pointed out that Merton's writings "were consumed avidly by members of other Christian denominations, to whom he helped build bridges."[10]

Michael Higgins portrayed Merton's life as emulating that of British poet William Blake, but noted "Merton's life was fraught with contradictions, polarities, and wild paradoxes."[11] Paul Elie, with access to pages in Merton's unpublished *SSM* manuscript because of his friendship with publisher Robert Giroux, documented Merton's lifelong "pilgrimage" in the context of the lives of Dorothy Day, Flannery O'Connor, and Walker Percy.[12] Joan Carter McDonald wrote what she called "the first biography of Thomas Merton that tells us about him as he wanted us to know him," weaving her own opinions with fresh facts about the legendary monk.[13] These were the principal Merton biographers as the year 2010 approached.

The biographers' contributions to the Merton story begins with chronicling the life of a four-and-a-half-pound baby with blue eyes and reddish blond hair born precisely at "9:30 P.M. on January 31, 1915, at 1 Rue du 4 Septembre, at Prades, France, in the Eastern Pyrenees."[14] The Mertons' home was located on a narrow street, and only small cars could park in front of the stone wall hiding Owen Merton's garden. A balcony was shaded by vines, and Owen's studio was on the third floor, where Mount Canigou could be seen clearly in the distance. Merton's full name was Tom Feverel Merton, the "Tom" a tribute to his godfather, Tom Bennett, and because his mother, Ruth, did not care for the name Thomas.[15]

As the savagery of World War I contaminated the world, Merton was born to a woman who was called devoted and obsessional. Like Merton in future years, Ruth kept a diary. Hers was called "Tom's book" and the scribbles noted that he was strong, active, and smart, seemingly well aware of the inflamed world around him. By candlelight and during times when he was fast asleep, Mama Merton wrote that her son disliked strangers, mainly women, and would scream when they were around. But he enjoyed playing with other little boys and with toy soldiers. Perhaps these habits contributed to his later admitting, "I was nobody's dream child."[16]

Owen Merton, who was listed on the 1914 marriage certificate as a "bachelor" and an "artist," passed his fair hair on to his first son. Ruth, depicted in a later photograph with dark hair pinned up with the tips of her ears showing, had the word "spinster" written beside her name. Born in 1887, Ruth's education included study at Massachusetts' Bradford Academy, where yearbook entries described her as the "cleverest" and "most artistic" and having "the keenest sense of humor." After graduating, she studied with other aspiring artists who painted day and night at the École Nationale des Arts Decoratifs in Paris under a Canadian painter, Percyval Tudor Hart.[17]

Ruth's diary indicated a mother's caring for little Merton but also a lingering detachment. Later, when Merton was immersed in a disagreement with a woman friend, he said he found cerebral woman difficult to deal with because his mother had also been cerebral. In *The Sign of Jonas* Merton noted, "perhaps solitaries are made by severe mothers."[18]

An Owen Merton painting of Ruth was described as strangely ethereal and cold by one observer, with her hair color conveying the only warmth. According to various biographers, Owen was an independent thinker with a bit of roamer in him who met Ruth at the French studio where he was also a student. The two must have bonded over their love for art, sparking a sensual attraction that led from chic Paris cafés to an apartment bedroom. Born in Christchurch, in New Zealand, in 1887, Owen first taught school. His education included stops at Christ's College and then the Canterbury School of

Art before leaving for England. During his career, he was reasonably successful, with election to the Royal Society of British Artists in London a highlight.
Merton's feelings about Owen were best characterized by contrasting his father
with his maternal grandfather "Pop," who emerged in Merton's autobiography
as a strong, masculine figure, a description Merton never employed to define
his father.[19]

Upon their return from Europe, Ruth and Owen Merton rented a small
home, not in the best of shape but surrounded by several robust pine trees, in
Flushing, Queens, five miles away from Ruth's parents in Douglaston. There
Merton read, among others, Tom Swift books and watched a movie starring
W. C. Fields being filmed in a nearby vacant lot.[20] Many believed that when
John Paul was born, he replaced Merton as the apple of his mother's eye, with
son number one shoved into the background. This slight caused Merton to
have low self-esteem and a feeling of being less than worthy. When Ruth died
in 1921, Merton was free from being under her wing and began a sort of spiritual journey, the first true liberation of his life.

Merton's days living alone in the balmy air of Bermuda while his father
traveled, beginning in 1922, were far more important to understanding the
man he would become than has been believed. Despite days when he would
swim in the clear, blue-green water and dance in the surf as his skin browned,
Merton was motherless and lonely. In the original unpublished manuscript
for *SSM,* he recalled being eight years old and feeling like the son of divorced
parents. His father wanted to take care of him, but did not really know how
to do so. He thus felt he had no family, no true schooling, no church, no
morals, and no God in his life. Later, he called his childhood days desperate
and despairing, with his mother dead and his father off to France and Alge-
ria. When Owen returned to hug him and announced plans to move to
France, Merton was overjoyed.[21]

Before the move, Owen fell deeply in love—or lust, depending on varia-
tion of the story—with budding novelist Evelyn Scott, who was married to
Owen's friend Cyril Kay Scott. Evelyn, who believed Merton was "un-child-
like," later said, "Little Tom hated me," and characterized Owen as behaving
like a child.[22] Evelyn's own son, Creighton, who shared a bed with Merton
during part of the Bermuda stay, said Evelyn scolded Merton for things she did
not scold her son for.[23]

The love affair flourished during warm nights on the beaches, but it must
have paralyzed Merton's emotions toward a woman who was set to replace his

recently dead mother. Owen had two choices: marry Evelyn and sweep a step-mother into his two sons' lives, or break off the affair. Whether Merton knew his father was contemplating marriage to a woman Merton hated was unclear, but in the end, Owen chose to end the romance with Evelyn. His mindset, revealed in a letter sent to a mutual friend of the couple's, told of inner turmoil since if he married Scott and left the children, he would have been haunted the rest of his life. Later, Owen said he had been acting hysterically during the affair.[24]

Regardless, Merton was under the control of a woman whom he disliked and who threatened to split father and sons. Compounding the agony was Merton's indication that Evelyn was too much like his mother, "cerebral, detached, and cold." Because of Merton's hostility, indeed hatred, the affair was doomed.[25] Regardless, Owen's fling with a woman married to a good friend must have impacted Merton's moral compass years later. If it was okay for his father to be consumed in an adulterous relationship, what prevented him from doing so?

The subsequent move to France did indeed save Merton from Evelyn, but at the Lycee he was the object of ridicule, insult, and obscenity since he did not fit in with the other students. To the rescue came Merton's Aunt Maud, a positive female role model in his life. He later described her as "tall, thick, gray-haired, given to wearing old-fashioned clothes and large floppy hats." Merton admired her innocence.[26]

When Owen moved the family to England, and Merton attended Oakham, he drew cartoons, and wrote various articles, parodies, and some short stories. Schoolmates recalled Merton as bright but a bit of a loner who stayed in his room with books as best friends. In an indication of the moral compass Merton lacked then and in future years, he thought it was perfectly fine for a married woman who visited Oakham to be alone with one of the adolescents she fancied—in fact, he thought it was "funny, terribly, hilariously, ridiculously funny."[27]

In admissions recorded in an unpublished journal, Merton, attempting to sort out his pre-pubescent emotions at Oakham, spoke of the "pain of his nascent sexual longings in a world that seemed to him to have been shaped in its attitudes by the woman-hating Plato." Romantic interaction with females was limited at the all-boys school since town girls were taboo in the eyes of the boys. Merton realized his inability to discover any young women to romance caused an absence of love more serious than any absence of sexual expression.

That Merton, whose body was maturing as fast as his mind, desired female companionship was natural for a motherless child. But he appeared to be obsessed with finding someone to care for him, deciding he wanted to be in love, despite the fact there was no one around Oakham to love. To substitute for a lack of girls, Merton, ever the seeker even at a young age, chose to admire movie stars. His favorite: Greta Garbo. But Merton admitted he was sexually frustrated, being encased in a boys' school three-quarters of the year. He wondered what romance was really like and how he might prove himself through larger-than-life acts to impress women.[28]

Merton was indeed consumed with discovering love in his life as he neared the end of his days at Oakham. He was intent on gaining a scholarship to Cambridge and then finding someone special at popular bars or other places where good music was played, because this was where he believed beautiful women hung out.[29]

Merton crossed the ocean in 1931 for a visit to America on the ship *Minnetonka.* As the eclectic passengers roamed the decks with tales true and false, and sipped exotic-looking drinks served by uniformed waiters with accents from near and far, he smoked Craven A cigarettes and enjoyed his pipe, a gift from Pop. One day when the ocean was steady and the sun illuminated the shiny surface of the ship's stern and bow, a Catholic priest with an Irish accent introduced him to some older women from Cleveland accompanied by a younger woman named Norma Wakefield and her two aunts.[30] Merton, smartly dressed and intent on romance as mentioned in *SSM,* did not know until the end of the trip that the younger woman with "California eyes" he encountered was twice his age. Although he realized she was not as intelligent as he was, not really his type of girl, he was blown away by her beauty and nevertheless declared his love for her. They were an intriguing pair—he was trying to look older; she was trying to look younger. But Norma was married, a fact Merton ignored in *SSM,* and on was her way to Australia via New York City. But she broke his heart, causing him to have a bewildered look about him when his grandparents met him as the boat docked.[31]

Merton's 1931 love affair on the beach at Bournemouth was distressing as well, but then he joined his friends the Winsers on the Isle of Wight, an island in the English Channel five miles from the south coast of England. While Merton was living with the Winsers, a visit not well explained in *SSM,* in a home filled with the scent of homemade pies and delicious dinners, he became smitten with Andrew Winser's 13-year-old sister, Ann, when she applauded a painting Merton had created of "The Fall of Lucifer." Later, she appeared as a character in his novel *My Argument with the Gestapo,* where Merton wrote of respecting her even though she was young and never said much.[32] This was the same girl he mentioned in his journals, the one who was quiet and gentle and who he might have married if things had turned out differently. Would Merton ever find another Ann Winser?

CHAPTER ELEVEN

CALAMITY *at* CAMBRIDGE

Biographer Paul Elie wrote of Thomas Merton's days at Clare College at Cambridge: "[Later Merton] would be set free. But he would not be set free yet. First he would bottom out, first he would become a father himself, and would feel the stern gaze of Christ the Judge upon him."[1] What did Elie mean when he said Merton would become a "father himself," a notation other biographers had mentioned dating back to Edward Rice's book in 1970? No incident about fatherhood existed in *SSM* or Merton's journals. What were Elie and the others talking about?

Framing Merton's fatherhood requires portraying it in the proper context of knowing more about who he was when he entered the hallowed university. Despite having been basically on his own since the age of 16, the Merton who entered Clare in 1933 was well traveled, experienced in the ways of social mores, and overall as mature as most 18-year-olds. Unlike many young Englishmen attending single-sex schools, he appeared to be uninhibited regarding women and sexual matters.[2]

Consensus appears to conclude that Merton was quite likely a virgin upon his arrival at Cambridge. As he roamed the grassy lawns at Clare, founded in 1326, and marveled at the famous gardens encircled by dykes and the river Cam, Merton was part of a prurient society in which class made a difference and discretion was essential if one were to date a nice girl who attended one of Cambridge's two women's colleges. The student who became involved with the wrong type of girls—the unapproved—was "likely to see himself as a sort of hero-outlaw, certainly living dangerously." This fit perfectly with Merton's wide-eyed fantasies about movie stars and beautiful women, but it complicated his life since he wasn't one to be discreet.[3]

Describing Merton, armed with good looks and an ornery smile that appealed to girls interested in a Cambridge lad, unnamed school friends[4] used phrases like "[Merton] went right off the rails," was "like a ship without an anchor"; he "mucked in the wrong set," he took up "drinking," and "debauchery is not too strong a word." The rowdy crowd Merton joined (one friend he partied with committed suicide), drank excessively, roamed noisy bars with such names as the Lion and the Red Cow, and pursued women at every chance.[5] Merton "threw a brick through a shop window, got arrested for riding on the running-board of a car, cut lectures, and climbed in and out of his own and other colleges [rooms] and helped various girls do the same."[6] Despite the comfort of his trust fund, Merton owed more money than he had. The result was predictable; the drinking and womanizing causing him to fall behind in his classes.

Chasing girls was a young man's fancy, but Merton's girls, according to school buddies, were often shopgirls, girls not of his class. A popular conquest for Merton was one known as the "Freshman's Delight," a reference to a loose party girl easily bedded. Biographer Monica Furlong believed what Merton regretted most about his youthful days was a lack of true love and the selfish attitude he had shown toward girls, both a result of some shyness but more in tune with longing "for love with a dismissive glibness."[7]

Merton, when he wasn't carousing, looking for women, and drinking himself silly, had a passion for 19th-century French literature and Italian subjects; he also took an interest in Eastern religions, including Buddhism. But frequenting pubs was more important than being stuck in the classroom studying English literature, and Merton frolicked with many women, including ones named Joan and Sylvia. He tried to be an adventurous, out-of-bounds, renegade lover who cared little for the identity of the woman next to him in bed. Furlong's assessment of this mentality: "[Merton] regretted the way he had tried to live up to an illusion of the person he ought to be, instead of simply trying to be himself,[8] a characteristic foreshadowing future conduct.

The downhill slide of Merton's morals while at Clare culminated in a mindboggling event on November 14, 1933. The circumstances, based on the facts known: a gathering of drunken students on a cold, blustery evening when snow may have been falling. At the party, as the students drank themselves into a frenzy, Merton must have either suggested the crazy idea, or found himself with a dare he could not refuse. Regardless, the partygoers talked of staging a "mock crucifixion." Before long, as alcohol displaced good judgment, and shouting and hand-clapping rang throughout the pub, Merton permitted himself to be tied to a wooden structure serving as a pseudo-cross. Before he knew it, he was actually affixed to the structure with either nails or another fastener, turning the mock crucifixion into something close to a real one. When he sobered up the next morning, Merton must have been aghast at the marks on his hands. He later revealed the scars to his literary agent, Naomi Burton Stone, and called them his "stigmata." He also acknowledged at least one as a "Scar on palm right hand" on a government application.[9]

One piece of evidence that the event occurred: The near-complete typescript of one draft of Merton's 1939 book *The Labyrinth* was missing a number of pages from the chapter titled, "The Party in the Middle of the Night." Written in 1939 in the upstate New York cottage he shared with Robert Lax and Edward Rice, *The Labyrinth* was a work of fiction, but Merton wove names of real people into the text. He also included the date of the party and its location, The Rendezvous, a popular hangout at Cambridge.[10]

In unpublished manuscript pages from *SSM,* Merton admitted facts about the night in question by noting his desire to "hesitate even to talk about the truth of this crucifixion, because that statement has at least a certain dramatic character about it, and therefore makes the affair sound interesting."[11] Like a forsaken Jesus, Merton had been crucified, perhaps just as a frivolity, perhaps with some deeper meaning even he did not realize at the time. Regardless, the bizarre evening served notice that Merton's mindset was confused and irrational, reflecting an out-of-control 18-year-old looking for trouble. He would find it in spades soon thereafter.

From the first chilly September days of the 1933 Michaelmas term, when mother nature lit up the countryside with a canvas of red, green, and yellow leaves, Merton's time at Cambridge, as noted by biographer Michael Mott, was disastrous. He believed that for Merton this was "the lowest circle of the Inferno. It is also personified into something like an animal." The result: "[It] gored him so deeply he felt that he would never entirely recover from the wound. What the wound was he never quite tells the reader."[12]

Certainly there were plenty of wayward experiences to choose from. If being crucified, even in jest, wasn't enough to suggest a confused and irrational mind, Merton compounded the craziness in his life by impregnating a young shop girl. Whether Merton was drunk during the escapade is unknown, but lust consumed his mind as he enjoyed the lush warmth of a girl succumbing to his considerable charm. How often he had sex with the girl is a mystery, but the result was predictable. Monica Furlong reported: "One day [he] came to friend Andrew Winser and told him that he had 'got a girl into trouble'; he was deeply distressed by this."[13] Another source of proof of the pregnancy was a letter sent to the bishop of Nottingham from the headmaster at Oakham in early March 1942 suggesting there were two rumors regarding Merton's leaving Cambridge: "no funds, untrue, and a threatened affiliation order (a paternity suit) against [Merton], from which he escaped by leaving Cambridge."[14]

With Merton bedding women at the pace of a Le Mans race driver, the pregnancy was certainly no surprise. He boasted of having sex with "all kinds of girls, English, American, and Middle European." No one knows for certain where the sex took place, but speculation surrounded a boathouse used by the Clare College racing team, where the two lovers, Merton and the woman, apparently Sylvia, sat by the edge of the water with sculls racked in the distance.[15] Whether abortion or marriage was ever contemplated is doubtful, but how to handle the situation became priority one. Help was required and he sought it from his godfather, Tom Bennett.

Regardless of whether there was actual threat of filing of a paternity suit, a legal settlement of some sort was completed by Dr. Bennett. Money changed hands, with a promise to young Merton that those in charge of his trust fund would not be told of the unhappy circumstances under which he was leaving Cambridge. Later, Merton would admit lawyers had been called into the fray.[16]

When Merton mentioned the incident to friends at Columbia, he told them the girl eventually bore his son, but that both were killed during World War II London air raids. In *SSM,* Merton noted women in general, and his poor treatment of them while at Clare, but never went into detail, except for mentioning his commission of a "mortal sin," nature undisclosed. Was the crucifixion what he referred to? Or the unwanted pregnancy? Nobody knew, because mention of both was censored.

In February 1944, more than a decade after he fathered the illegitimate child, Merton must have believed mother and son survived the war since he "left his shares in the Optional Saving Shares Account [his trust fund] to be divided equally between his sister-in-law and 'my guardian T. Izod Bennett,' Esq., M. D., of 29 Hill Street, Berkeley Square, London, W.1. this second half to be paid by him to the person mentioned to him in my letters, if that person can be contacted."[17] "That person," Merton scholars believed, was the impregnated woman.

When Merton was told of his banishment to America, perhaps he sat in his apartment, textbooks unopened, and realized he had blown a good thing. He had been given money, permitted to study at a great university, and provided support from his family. But the pregnancy was the final straw; Tom Bennett had had enough, and Merton was issued his walking papers. Whether this was a good thing, to be able to walk away from responsibility for a woman he had impregnated and a child soon to be born, is debatable at best. But the irresponsible Merton could walk away, and walk away he did. Such behavior caused biographer William Shannon to observe: "It was during the year at Clare College, Cambridge . . . that [Merton] reached the nadir [lowest point] of his life. Spiritually and morally, and to some degree even academically, he touched bottom."[18]

Merton, with time to reflect, referred to his days at Clare as "the damp and fetid mists of Cambridge." Leaving, Monica Furlong believed, left a "sour taste of unredeemed failure and disgrace, a miserable inheritance at nineteen." The result: "he had longed for love but had found instead how easy it is to father an unwanted child."[19]

At the final "sit-down" with Dr. Bennett, Merton must have realized the free-swinging sexual conduct of his heroes, such as Ernest Hemingway and D. H. Lawrence,[20] caused hurt and sorrow for everyone involved. Instead of being a character in a novel, this was real life, and in real life, people hurt others and were held accountable for their actions.

Merton's reflections about his days at Clare were apparent from the gifted wordsmith's prose in *My Argument with the Gestapo*. Bitterness bled through the pages where Cambridge cried out from the past "like the waiting rooms of dentists:"

> Oh, peering Cambridge, I taste you in the broken skin of my lips like the bloody leather of twelve-ounce boxing gloves. I constantly hear the dried scraps of putty falling from your windows onto the linoleum floor; I smell the awful cleanness of soap in the dank showers underneath the College Buttery, where the soccer player hung himself. The thought of you empties like old gin out of a glass that has been standing several days, among the clean plates . . . Cambridge you are as

restrained as postmarks on a letter, but you are as disquieting as syphilis or cancer.[21]

A failure in so many ways at Cambridge, Merton crossed the Atlantic unaware of what the future held for him. Michael Mott believed that "in a sense this *was* a liberation."[22] Such may have been true, but the Merton who left England behind had more than a scar on the palm of his hand. Mott was right in recognizing Merton had been gored and wounded with the potential never to recover. The man who had abandoned a pregnant woman and never checked on her condition, or that of their child, had scars, deep, emotional, psychological ones embedded in his heart, ones that would not completely surface until many years later.

CHAPTER TWELVE

the RESTLESS MERTON

Those who met Thomas Merton when he entered Columbia University in 1935, the year he turned 20 years of age, did not know of the wild, rambunctious, over-the-top youth who had left behind piles of broken hearts, disappointed family members, and a pregnant woman carrying his child. Thirty-four-hundred miles plus and an ocean away from England, Merton had a fresh start, a chance to reform his immature ways and become a serious student. Would he do so or backslide into the sinful Merton of old?

When Merton first arrived at Columbia, Edward Rice said his friend was "full of energy . . . cracking jokes, denouncing the Fascists, and squares, being violently active, writing, drawing, [and] involved in everything." Others called Merton "merry and sober," "witty," and "charming." He hung out at fraternity house parties where he drank a great deal and "sang bawdy songs," with "The Bloody Great Wheel" and "The Good Ship Venus" being favorites. Muscatel and beer were among his beverages of choice. This conduct was in keeping with Rice's observation that Merton had become a big man on campus.[1]

For those who later wondered when Merton began to consider Eastern religions, Rice decided it was in the mid-thirties, when Merton first read Aldous Huxley's *Ends and Means*. Merton also examined a series of Buddhist writings in French edited by Father Léon Wieger. Rice believed Merton recognized Buddhism as not a substitute for Christianity, but instead as an enriching and fulfilling spirituality, one Christians could embrace without compromising certain beliefs. Rice noted that Merton dressed like a businessman during this time, wearing a smart suit and "a double-breasted chesterfield topcoat." He carried a leather briefcase packed with drawings, articles, books, and papers. He was confident and talkative, but appeared restless in search of his true self.[2]

Anyone curious to know who Merton really was during his days at Columbia has only to read excerpts from *My Argument with the Gestapo.* Sprinkled with true-life experiences, it included a scene where British officers were questioning the main character, who Merton had obviously patterned after himself.

> If you want to identify me, ask me not where I live, or what I like to eat, or how I comb my hair, but ask me what I think I am living for, in detail, and ask me what I think is keeping me from living fully for the thing I want to live for. Between these two answers you can determine the identity of any person.[3]

After settling into student life and having chewed his first bite of Columbia, Merton pledged a fraternity and gravitated to Columbia's humor magazine, *Jester,* in 1936. If he had lost the obsession with sex that dragged his morals to a new low in England, his drawings as the magazine's art director showed little proof. Left out of *SSM,* and never mentioned in any of his journals, was the soft pornographic nature of his work at *Jester.* Why Merton decided to draw nudes is unknown, but his disorientation with sex continued to infiltrate his mind as he sat at his desk, cigarette smoke filtering through the air. Instead of pouncing on women with the prowl of a predator as he had done in England, he saw fit to draw them in various stages of undress in a sort of humorous but demeaning manner, thereby extending the ladder of depravity for a man who was only a few years away from becoming a monk.

Rice's book included a photograph of Merton, clad in tweed coat and tie, with Robert Lax and Ralph de Toledano at the *Jester* editor's desk. Some pages later, Merton's drawing of two lovely women, expensively dressed and sitting on a bed, one reading what might be a Bible, was introduced. The caption read in part, "Merton was an accomplished and witty artist: he drew with facility and speed. The cartoon above was one of a number in *Jester;* he had a similar series, slightly more risqué, in a magazine published by the Dixie Cup Company."[4]

Eight pages of Merton's drawings—the first of two women, totally naked, one with slightly larger breasts than the other, each with nipples and pubic hair fully exposed—were included in the exposé. One woman had her hand raised to her head while the other appeared to be excited, dancing in place with arms raised toward the sky. She had no eyes, in contrast to the other woman, whose eyes were blackened. The next drawing, titled "Primavera," featured three nudes, two dancing and one turned away, buttocks in view. "The Foot Race" followed with five nudes racing across the drawing. Underneath the pictorials were five more women scampering away, each appearing to have a beard and two covered with bathing suits. Below this drawing were the initials "tm."[5]

Merton's drawings supplemented his reputation as a jokester. One drawing, made over his passport picture, depicted himself with full beard, a long, curly mustache, round horn-rimmed glasses, and parted-in-the-middle frizzy hair. He wrote below it that no one would recognize him since his hair treatments. In three other drawings, instead of simply sketching the border of the women's frame, to shape their bodies he cleverly used tiny, handwritten words like "Zowie! I'm rich! Have a cigar, I'll spend it on candy and hats . . . Now I can go to college! A million intellectual zizz! Zippy! Ziggy! Zowie! Zam!" to form their bodies. One was called "The Soldier's Girl," the second, "Dame Winning a Lottery," and the third, "Patriotic Singer." Each of these women was clothed.[6] Based on chats with Merton, Father Basil Pennington believed that "If some of Father Louis's admirers were shocked when his friend Ed Rice later published some of Tom's unseemly cartoons from Columbia days, Tom himself was later disgusted by them—both for their moral content and because they were such poor art, slavish imitations of what others were doing."[7]

Did Merton really have regrets about drawing the pornographic nudes or any of his other indiscretions? Apparently at some point he did, deciding, "Nothing so completely blinds a man, morally and spiritually, as slavery to the appetites of his own flesh." He admitted it took five or six years to understand what a frightful man he had become. During this time he felt as if he were "being turned on like a pinball machine" toward understanding what a nasty person he was by such influences as Thomas Aquinas, Augustine, Meister Eckhart, William Blake, and the sacraments of the Catholic Church.[8]

Additional influences at Columbia included Mark Van Doren, whose belief in Jack Kerouac led him to send the talented writer's first novel to Merton's publisher, Robert Giroux (it was rejected); Aldous Huxley, author of *Ends and*

Means; and Étienne Gilson, the early 20th–century French Thomistic philosopher. Merton was captivated with Gilson's view that "the notion of God was neither vague nor superstitious nor unscientific." Huxley's work taught Merton that prayer, faith, detachment, and love were the keys to reaching beyond the materialist word into a world where spiritual values reigned.[9]

At Columbia, Merton the braggadocio never hesitated to shout out his sexual proclivities. While drinking and smoking at one of New York City's watering holes, as jazz exploded in the background, he talked freely of his teenage conquests, telling his friend Rice, as noted, about an active sex life, the first experience one with a beautiful Viennese whore he met in Hyde Park. He also boasted of learning Hungarian while in bed. Rice's perspective: "[Merton] had an endless number of nubile, compliant girls, about whom he was very cagey and reticent. The one he talked about, half-boastfully, half-regretfully, was the girl in Cambridge,"[10] a reference to the woman he impregnated.

One perplexing encounter occurred in New York in June 1938, when Merton met a girl from Chicago named Pat Hickman. He recalled arriving home to a cool temperature and a refreshment. Later, he had trouble walking to bed since his limbs, back, and groin ached. He recalled "many carnivals with my Chicago girl [Pat Hickman], all kinds of festivals I did." In an August 1938 letter from Merton to Robert Lax, never mentioned in *SSM* or any journal, he wrote: "Listen, for Christ's sake, why don't you go to Boston to N. Flagg [Nancy Flagg, Lax's girlfriend] and I'd go up to Boston and stay with some people and then we'd all get drunk. Except the fool girl I would be staying with has got a fallen womb or some beetles in her cunt, and so she doesn't drink or laugh much."[11] Use of such filthy language was certainly at odds with the man who finally decided to become a Catholic priest. But many believed Merton's religious leanings at 24 were genuine, although Merton scholar Anthony Pavadono was certain Merton was on the verge of a nervous breakdown and that Catholicism came to the rescue.[12]

Merton's graduation from Columbia and his move to Greenwich Village were followed by the confirmation at Corpus Christi. Then he spent the summer of 1939 at the Olean cottage in upstate New York. Owned by Robert Lax's sister's husband, Benjamin Marcus, and located in the Allegheny Mountains, it was a dark-shingled structure with a small windowed back door. It had two brick chimneys and a screened-in porch with an entrance up some steps.[13] Edward Rice told Merton biographer William Shannon the cottage where they stayed was akin to a hippie colony, where the gang wrote, drank, read books of all kinds, sneaked into movies, and enjoyed jazz. All the while Merton was reading religious books, ones detailing the lives and ideas of Saint John of the Cross and Saint Teresa of Avila. Merton also read the Bible. His readings of these books, in addition to William Blake and Plato, paralleled those being consumed by Merton's contemporary, beat poet Allen Ginsberg.[14]

Rice said the cottage was messy, with dishes in the sink for days on end. The friends bought food at the nearby A & P store and enjoyed graham crackers and hamburgers while drinking Jim Beam bourbon in the balcony at the movies. Rice had a girlfriend but noted that Merton and Lax were rather anti-woman, even though Merton was sexually active despite speaking derogatorily about women. Merton wrote a novel, drank at Lippert's Bar, and joined his friends as they picked up girls from the nearby tuberculosis sanitarium. He grew a beard.[15]

The cottage looked down on a series of hills and valleys where pine trees flourished. The air was clear, with hot, sunny days and cool evenings. Rice mentioned a trapeze they installed on the porch and a collection of controversial literature smuggled out of France, including *Tropic of Cancer, Lady Chatterley's Lover,* and *Vile Bodies.* He said Merton had more money than anyone and bought bottles of scotch. The trio began a contest to see who could write the first novel. Life was simple, but all three were restless. Merton cooked scotch-soaked hamburgers, but they were so bad he threw them over the roof like an outfielder tossing baseballs. Rice said the trio was arrested,[16] without a clue given as to what for.

A second summer at Olean was even more enjoyable than the first. Another "novel-writing race" was begun; a cat from a supermarket became a pet; they ate pork chops for several meals in a row; the housemates were drunk for three days or so on wine, beer, or gin; and Merton made two tea bags last through the summer. Rice said the house resembled a rural slum in Mississippi, and even the huge fireplace couldn't keep it warm. In August, Merton sat peacefully on the porch, gazing into the valley, or heading into the woods to ponder his future.[17]

In New York Merton had been courting a new girlfriend, Wilma Reardon, a nurse who worked at the World's Fair and lived in Forest Hills, Queens. Merton, drink in hand, cigarette at the ready, enjoyed her stories, one involving a Seminole Indian who was bitten by an alligator. Merton listened intently as the two cuddled and whispered during cozy interludes at outdoor cafés where soft music serenaded the couple.[18] During the fall days of 1939,

Merton also "loved" two women, Pat Hickman and Doris Raleigh. He enjoyed the nightlife, spending time at a lively gathering place, Dillon's Bar and Grill, on the corner of Sixth Avenue and 48th Street. Along with a friend, he waited until the performance at the nearby Center Theatre was over so that the two swingers could drink with some of the women who were in the show.[19] One night, a woman named Ginny Burton showed up. She had "brown curls and . . . lively eyes," and the "same looks and qualities as Giulietta Masina in the early films of Fellini."[20] Burton was witty and popular with many of Merton's friends. Robert Lax recalled her as "really cute, a dark-haired, dark-eyed Barnard girl, very funny: she wanted to be a stage comedienne, like Imogene Coca, whom she loved."[21]

After some discussion, Burton invited Merton to join her and a friend when they returned home to Virginia for a house party the next day. Once he had attended Mass the next morning, Merton accompanied the girls on the train, where they sipped Tom Collins drinks and enjoyed sardine sandwiches. At Burton's, Merton drank, played, and struggled to keep up with the young people's party mood. He enjoyed having drinks at the ready, and even made a night run when liquor supplies dwindled. The drunken crowd "sang an exaggerated and slurred 'God Bless Ameri-cuh!'" as the car raced in the dark through Saluda, Virginia. Despite the fun, a vicious toothache and news of the raging war in Europe spoiled part of Merton's weekend. Burton was surprised at his demeanor, believing he appeared transformed. She told Michael Mott she had never seen Merton like that before, or in the days ahead.[22]

It was a docile mood produced by drinking for several days as the hot sun tanned their bodies. Deciding this was "*his* party," Merton captivated his audience at the house. His jokes caused the guests to laugh endlessly since he acted like an experienced entertainer. Merton also recited verse after verse of "The Infernal Screwing Machine" while providing a commentary. Back in the city, Merton experienced an awakening, a confusion really, that the Virginia holiday had only served to emphasize—that his life was going nowhere. He slept on the floor, had little use for breakfast, and even lacked desire for his first cigarette of the day. He felt disgusted about the life he was living.[23]

The Ginny Burton romance lasted longer than most, but Robert Lax suggested Merton "rather frightened women by rushing at them: it may have been a way of ensuring that he did not get too involved." The result: "Most of Merton's infatuations tended to be short-lived." Merton said he considered marriage, but Lax and Burton doubted this intention. Interviewed by Mott about her relationship with Merton, Burton said she never considered Merton to be obsessed with women but instead obsessed with his writings. She was surprised he categorized her as a serious love interest and swore the two never talked about getting married. This didn't mean Merton, apparently exaggerating the extent of the relationship, wasn't serious about her.[24]

The relationship with Burton did not quell Merton's distaste for his disconcerting lifestyle. He was still conflicted while walking the streets of New York City or sitting on park benches or in dimly lit cafés, pondering what lay ahead. Father Basil Pennington believed Merton's "vocational struggle was an open one, a struggle for freedom, to be free enough to do what he really wanted to do and do it as his true self."[25]

Merton's rejection by the Franciscans that summer was no surprise because he had served up a false image of himself, "a kind of pseudo Merton."[26] Merton the imposter had not informed Father Edmund that he had been a drunkard and a womanizer to the extent of having fathered an illegitimate child. Instead, the Franciscan friar was presented with a watered-down version of Merton as a newly converted Catholic. When he learned the truth, he threw Merton out the door.

Regardless, after accepting the defeat, Merton bounced back and became a member of the Franciscan Third Order. Mott wrote that Merton walked about in full view of others wearing a scapular and two sections of brown cloth fastened with a thin cord underneath his clothes. This reminded him of his obsession with living as a monk in the real world and how he regretted not being able to do so. Mott said Merton tightened the cord until it cut him when he overate. Merton was feeling blue at the lack of any purpose in his life, and his psyche reached a low ebb as the calendar turned to 1940. Despite his lack of self-esteem, during the Christmas holiday, Merton accepted Burton's invitation to visit her in Virginia. There he hung out at a New Year's Eve party with two blondes, but they flirted with Edward Rice after learning Merton intended to become a priest.[27]

Merton had glimpsed his mood and the extent of romantic interludes while writing *My Argument with the Gestapo* during the summer months at the Olean cottage. There, day after day, Merton scribbled words on the page in the quiet of the countryside where the chirping of birds was many times the only interruption. He had used the name Thomas James Merton for the main character, a man who was roaming through London during the Blitz. An old girlfriend, "B.," was introduced in what Monica Furlong called "a profoundly unhappy book."[28] The character B. was the true love Merton lost only to discover her again, but there was little time for love since any chance was "defeated by the squalor and cruelty and lust and falsity of war." Describing her, Merton noted she was wearing a dress instead of a uniform, and she stood with folded arms in Queen's Hall when he visited to see a promenade concert. He had described her with elbows leaning on the tablecloth at a favorite restaurant called Pagani's, the way she smoked, and how she curled up her legs when she sat in a chair and read *Vogue* magazine.[29]

Merton's, the character's, love for B., he had written, was genuine, but she felt the war had caused all love to be lies. They had been in love, but it was too difficult to be in love and he had to leave anyway. Speculation as to who B. was centered on a composite of all of the women he had known, including Ann Winser and Ginny Burton.[30]

In late November 1941, just a month short of deciding to enter Gethsemani, Merton was suffering. After returning from a trip to New York City, he decided he was not physically tired, but filled with "a deep, vague, undefined sense of spiritual distress, as if I had a deep wound running inside me and it had to be stanched." Without specifying exactly what the wound was, again, he believed it was just another indication of his being an exile on earth, and the wound bled inside him like a hemorrhage.[31] These dark words recalled Merton's mood in *The Secular Journal*, where he had admitted "besides the spiritual anxieties, a tremendous physical restlessness." But Edward Rice concluded that the true sense of Merton's conflicted mind had been unleashed in *My Argument with the Gestapo*, because unlike any of his other writings, in this book fear and alienation were alive and well. Such fear was paramount to the story, Rice said, but it was a metaphysical fear, not a physical fear. Overall, Rice characterized Merton's life as one of nostalgia and alienation. He also believed his friend was lonely.[32]

Merton's initial reluctance to become a Trappist, he later realized, had been based on misinformation. This included the belief that Trappists slept in coffins and prayed nonstop about death. He also had heard that many of the monks were seeking penance for crimes, including murder.[33] But Merton kept most of his inner thoughts to himself about this and other matters since he was a very private person, one who, if troubled, appeared more occupied than distressed. An exception was a letter he wrote while attempting to decide whether he should keep his commitment to Friendship House in New

York or pursue his dream of a solitary, monastic life. This letter to Baroness de Hueck in Harlem revealed that a new, more forthright, more honest, Merton was emerging.

While he had previously withheld information about his sordid past, this time he was upfront, perhaps to a fault, by warning the baroness about the man she was asking to aid her effort on the streets of Harlem. One imagines Merton writing this letter, alone with this thoughts, admitting perhaps more than ever before what was in his heart and soul—a giant step forward for a man who had either denied immoral conduct, lied about it, or rationalized it. After asking her if she was worried about the past conduct of people who worked for her, he wrote, "I got into some trouble once which I don't particularly want to tell anybody about." He then mentioned the potential for scandal or a negative reflection on the baroness if the truth were known. He told her the severity of his offense demanded a full life of penance and self-sacrifice. Merton noted the past sin had "spoiled my last vocation," a reference to his Franciscan rejection, before admitting, "I am no white-haired hero, no model of self-sacrifice of holiness either." Concluding, Merton added, "you are getting no bargain . . . I am not only not a saint but just a weak, proud, self-centered guy, interested in writing, who wants to belong to God, and who incidentally, was once in a scandal that can be called public, since it involved lawyers. So that's the dirt. Never forget me in your prayers."[34]

This confession did not mean his decision making was any easier. In *The Secular Journal,* reflecting on the path God wanted for him, Merton recalled pondering whether he should be going to Harlem or to the Trappists. He asked, "Why doesn't this idea of the Trappists leave me? Perhaps what I am afraid of is to write and be rejected." He decided living in Harlem made good sense as a reasonable way to follow Christ, but that becoming a Trappist was exciting, filling him with a sense of awe and desire. He decided the end goal was to give up everything.[35]

Having opened his soul to the baroness, yet having decided Gethsemani was really where he believed God wanted him to be, Merton fell to his knees under a clear, blue sky in the grassy grove at St. Bonaventure and prayed to know whether there was some chance he might become a priest.[36] Hamstrung by insecurities based on the feeling that he was unworthy of proceeding directly to Gethsemani, he heard in his imagination "the grey bell of Gethsemani ringing in the night—the bell in the big grey tower, ringing and ringing and ringing, as if it were just behind the first hill." Believing the bell, tolling at the same time as it did every day at the monastery, was calling him home, he was determined to join the Trappists, where he belonged.[37]

Merton met with Father Philotheus, who suggested he leave for Gethsemani when the Christmas vacation began so as to tell the abbot his story. This, Merton apparently decided, he could now do, since the confession of past sinful conduct to the baroness had helped wash him clean, even more than the confessionary tribunals at Corpus Christi had during his baptism. But then the sin of Satan inflicted Merton once again. Exactly when he fell prey to the temptation of sexual passion and committed the adultery he admitted in his journal is unclear, but even this sin could not misdirect the ship he had boarded toward Gethsemani. Circumstances as to how the New York City adulterous affair occurred, and with whom, were not disclosed, but Merton's choice of words, indicating the transgression had occurred "twenty-five years nearly since my last adultery,"[38] confirmed similar acts in the past. Now Merton must have been even more determined to enter the monastic life, where there was no chance of repeating such a mistake.

Worrying about being a foot soldier at the European front was also on Merton's mind in late November, since all men 21 to 28 years old were subject to the military draft. But Merton's recollection of the process conflicted with the surface account in *SSM*. Whether he purposely left out details, or whether the censors excluded them is unclear.

In his journals, Merton acknowledged that he realized he could avoid the draft and that this played a part in his becoming a Catholic, and in turn, a priest. He denied that it was the true motive, but it was on his mind. If he was drafted, he decided, he would become an ambulance driver to avoid fighting on the front. Flip-flopping, he decided becoming a Trappist was not a decision connected to the war, but then admitted he had a selfish attitude, but hoped that entering the Trappist world would heal this disturbing character flaw. He noted that he knew he would "get out of the draft—useless to deny I thought of this; it was the war that drove me, in one way, to decide about becoming a Catholic, and it helped me to decide quick that I wanted to be a priest."[39]

On December 2nd, bad news arrived: his 1-B status (Available; fit only for limited military service) would be reviewed. He was ordered to appear for re-examination at the draft board since the rule about teeth (his having too few had exempted him before) had been revised. The realization hit him that if he passed, he would be classified "1-A" and could be inducted into the army as soon as January, despite his claim: "I have no interest in human wars. Wherever I am, I am a citizen of the Kingdom of God and fight only as a soldier of Christ—killing nobody."[40]

While millions of others, including his brother, John Paul, had volunteered to fight for their country and given their lives in the process, Merton decided to, in effect, dodge the draft. Rushing to avoid any notice, he forwarded copies of many of his writings to trusted friends and allies, such as Mark Van Doren, Father Fitzgerald, and Baroness de Hueck. Then, he "packed a small suitcase with a few clothes, his Vulgate, his breviary, *Imitation of Christ,* his Hopkins, his Blake, and two half-filled notebooks," and headed west on the train toward the mountains of Kentucky.[41]

Merton's acclimation to Gethsemani was not an easy one. His health was not in the best of shape, he cherished privacy, and the smell of straw disturbed his senses. But having escaped the draft and knowing he would also escape the temptation of women he might desire, he suddenly had a good feeling, "a feeling of freedom."[42] Key to this new existence, he realized as he prayed quietly, was to be disciplined, and thus to be with "God Alone," the Trappist motto painted above the door at the entrance to the guest quarters.[43]

A letter (Trappist monks were permitted to write only four letters a year, two at Easter and two at Christmas) sent to Edward Rice dated December 26th, 1941, sixteen days after Merton entered the monastery, explained his thoughts: "This is the one place where everything makes sense . . . Everything that was good when I was a kid, when I was in England, when I was anywhere, has been brought back to life here." He told Rice that all the things he hoped to do, the things he wanted most out of life, were now possible with no interference. He said he was at peace because God was everything to everybody, and the only thing preventing a closer relationship to God was one getting in God's way through his own dumb will.[44] From the upbeat tone of the letter, Rice concluded anything bad for Merton—any sense of pride, vanity, selfishness, or showing off—was absent in the monastery. Merton was truly experiencing a religious euphoria, feeling the presence of God at every turn. He could function better and turn his thoughts to nothing but this God who was saving him from the destructive capabilities of the outside world.

For the next few years, Merton continued his spiritual recovery, reading and learning and watching fellow monks who provided daily words of wisdom. Slowly, the past was disappearing from his mind, triggering a true cleansing such as he had never experienced before. Slowly, the sins he had committed seemed far, far away, almost as if someone else had committed them. There was no more Thomas Merton, but instead Frater Louis, free from the soiling misconduct during his Cambridge and Columbia days. There appears little question that Merton's bliss would have continued ad infinitum if the real world and all its confusing elements had not seeped into the monastic world when Merton began to write his life story. Doing so caused him to revisit old times, resurrecting distasteful feelings, emotions, and conduct nearly buried.

Merton must have sizzled at the initial suggestion that he was not a good enough writer when a censor decided that *SSM* was unworthy of publication, but not for theological reasons. Instead, the reason was Merton's lack of "present literary equipment." The censor suggested that Merton enroll in a correspondence course in English grammar. Writing ability aside, the censors' major criticism was the book's frankness. Rice, who must have heard Merton's objections to the objections, said Merton had to clip whatever bothered the censors and tone down the manuscript so as to not shock people.[45] It was Rice who also reported that nearly a third of the original text had been excised.

The story Merton told in *SSM* protected the good image of the Trappist order, certainly an issue if Merton's fathering an illegitimate son was exposed. Father Basil Pennington apparently had direct knowledge of the censorship in action. He described a scene where Merton was writing *SSM* at a small desk in a dimly lit room, as Father Anthony, one of the Catholic censors assigned to oversee the writing, hovered. When a page was completed, Merton handed it to Father Anthony, and according to Pennington, "When Tom's unfolding story told of the pregnancy, Father Anthony, a gentle, pastoral priest . . . was not particularly surprised." Next, "Father Anthony, without raising any objections, sent the material on to Father Gabriel [another censor]. Gabriel's reaction was quite different from Anthony's. He felt that it would not be edifying for the faithful if they learned that a monk had one time fathered a child." Father Grabriel wrote Frater Louis that he must delete the passage.[46]

Father Pennington made an important observation in view of later comparisons of *SSM* with Saint Augustine's *Confessions*. According to Pennington, Merton, "fairly new at the censorship game, wrote back that if it was all right for Saint Augustine to be known to have a son out of wedlock, he didn't see why it was so scandalous in his case." The response, Pennington noted, was terse, with Father Anthony stating, "You're no Saint Augustine," with the "emphasis on the word *saint.*" Father Anthony's putdown notwithstanding, Pennington was intent on providing readers with a more positive personal opinion of his friend: "Thomas Merton was a man. Much of his attractiveness lies in the fact that he was, indeed, a person of flesh and blood, body and feeling, time and place."[47] Obviously, the Catholic Church and their censors did not agree. The "good image of the order" had to be protected at all costs. The result: for the enlightened, disciplined and peaceful monk the world perceived, the sinful demons of youth and early adult conduct festered beneath the surface, ready to spring to life as Merton's tormented nature expanded through the years. Biographer David Cooper realized this when writing about Merton's shocking love affair with Margie Smith. He noted "the doubts and misgivings" the monk experienced "were further exacerbated by sensual undercurrents which eddied within Merton."[48]

Regardless of the less-than-truthful nature of the book, "the autobiography of a young man who led a full and worldly life, and then, at the age of 26, entered a Trappist monastery,"[49] caused "a quiet revolution among American Catholics."[50] The *New York Times Book Review* applauded the book in a section including reviews of books by Henry David Thoreau and Irwin Shaw (*The Young Lions*). Among other notable quotes, the reviewer said that Merton's writings had an "urgent and phenomenal quality," one "nervous in texture [and] rapid in movement." Bottom line: the book was Merton's "story of conversion," one arriving "at precisely the right moment, its critical edges, its spectacular discontent with the immediate past" [ones that did] not cut against the grain of the present hour, but resolved smoothly within it."[51] Subsequent reviews also praised the book.[52] Within a year of publication, *SSM* had sold 600,000 copies, promoting it to the best-seller lists, where it finished third one year, between *The White Collar Zoo* and a book on the card game canasta.[53] When the Signet Triple Volume mass-market paperback was released, at 75 cents a copy, the text above the title read, "A Widely Acclaimed Bestseller—The Revealing Experience of a Man Who Withdrew from the World."[54]

Edward Rice assessed the substance of the book: "It was essentially the story of a modern intellectual from a secular, artistic, vaguely leftist background who found his way into the Church, and happiness."[55] Rice said Merton sensed more of a beginning than an end, a comment echoing one offered by Father John Eudes. Some years later, he said Merton told him "*SSM* should be rewritten, but it does not belong to me anymore." Merton also told Father Eudes, "I wrote it to convince myself to stay [at Gethsemani]."[56] Later Rice decided to paint Merton standing outside Gethsemani. Using several vivid colors, including gold, off white, green, light green, and a grainy black for Merton's robe, Rice left Merton's face blank, because he was disgusted with those portraying Merton as a plastic saint, believing that he was much more human than people wanted to believe. If anyone could dissect Merton, it was Rice, who knew him from the party times in New York to the moment he entered Gethsemani and beyond. He had listened to Merton describe in detail the sinful days at Cambridge and the lengthy trail of women he had romanced, observed his heavy drinking and passion for the night life, and watched him draw the soft pornographic characters at *Jester.* He knew the true Merton, warts and all.

From the rest of the story provided by astute biographers and other sources, detailing, among other things, the mock crucifixion, the illegitimate child, the latest adultery, and the possibility that dodging the draft impacted Merton's decision to enter Gethsemani more than previously believed, it is much easier to understand Merton's confused, tormented, angry, and suffering mindset when he met Margie Smith in 1966. He did so with knowledge that previous relationships with females had caused him heartache and pain to an extent no one fully understood.

CHAPTER THIRTEEN

the HAREBRAINED NEUROTIC

By the mid-1960s, Thomas Merton's life was consumed with frustration. He felt compelled to write book after book, his health was poor, he lamented his advancing age, and he was restricted from traveling any long distance from Gethsamani. Rome had long ago denied him the request to leave the monastery for another order, and the curse of fame prevented the true solitude he coveted. He also continued to experience feelings of persecution from Abbot Dom James, whom he had called "stupid" and a "dangerous man."

This groundswell of disillusionment occurred at the same time Merton had endured several rather puzzling interactions with women: Father Anselm's sister and his "sexual attraction" to her; the outlandish nymphomaniac who apparently attacked him; and the day at the lake with Margot, the "girl from the coast." He also experienced sexual fantasies in his dreams, including ones featuring "the two lovely young women dressed in white," and his own literary agent, Naomi Burton Stone. She was described by Merton biographer Joan C. McDonald as "a young career woman, just four years older than Tom . . . an attractive girl with beautiful green-blue eyes much like Tom's, and short, curled brown hair."[1]

Occurring in tandem with this unrest was Merton's tendency to revert more and more to memories of past love affairs and to lament his less-than-satisfactory conduct with women prior to entering Gethsemani. His mindset reflected feelings of guilt and remorse for having treated women without courtesy or respect, especially those he believed really cared for him, even loved him, despite his inability to realize it at the time. Regrets abounded, indicating that the middle-aged Merton was sad that he had missed out on true love and even sadder that it would never present itself again.

Adding to his inner tension was Merton's admitting as early as 1957 that he had never known the meaning of love. But through the many books he read and his experiences at the monastery, he had learned enough about love— both of God and, more important to him, of others, women in particular— to recognize how much he desired to love, and be loved. This, he realized, was not the sexual, lust-driven love he had coveted pre-Gethsemani, but real, true love, the pure kind he now knew existed but was forbidden to him under his monastic vows. This added to his feelings of vulnerability in 1966 when he met Margie Smith.

Clues to Merton's disconcerted mindset first appeared in the later pages of *SSM,* where he referred to uneasiness with the shadows of the old Merton following him into Gethsemani. But then he seemed to have abandoned this point of view, deciding that writing the autobiography chased away many of the demons pursuing him. Any spiritual decay or nameless terror was thus stripped as an illusion, with the old Merton buried among the skeletons in the monastery graveyard—that is, until Merton's disenchantment with his keeper, Dom James, surfaced. Edward Rice confirmed its existence by recalling a poetic, if somewhat confusing, quote from Merton to an acquaintance: "I'm in jail and sitting on the faggots while the head Inquisitor fumbles with the matchbox which is luckily in his other pair of trousers."[2] This was the man who replaced Dom Frederic Dunne, who was perceived as something of a benevolent dictator by monks who loved him as a father figure.[3]

Merton hid his discontent from those closest to him, but outside observers knew of his unrest. Black Panther activist Eldridge Cleaver was "particularly touched by Merton," but believed he was "alternately confused, transpired and 'some kind of a nut.'" Another friend called Merton "a kind of free-lance monk, because he was growing so independent of the monastery."[4]

Another source of conflict was the fact that from the start, Merton had requested his books be written under his monastic name, Frater Louis, to erase the Thomas Merton of his pre-monastic days. But this request was refused. This must have confused Merton, because monastic life was supposed to be all about brotherhood and community, and now he was separated from his brothers like an outsider. In effect, he was two people, two versions of himself, split as he was between writer and monk, causing the prediction he made in

SSM to come true: he had not lost the writer side of Thomas Merton when he entered Gethsemani. Worse, this Merton was not free but was under the control of Dom James, the aloof, arrogant, business-oriented adversary, one who recognized Merton's potential as a continuing revenue source for the monastery once *SSM* was a smash hit.

Instead of blending into the monastic community as he had hoped, Merton had in essence become "the chosen one," the famous monk who was making Gethsemani famous. When Bishop Fulton J. Sheen spoke at the 100th anniversary of the founding of Gethsemani in 1958, reporters in attendance surprised the abbot by requesting that Merton be at the press conference. He was also given special privileges to write in the rare-book vault. Five monks received and answered Merton's fan mail.[5] Dom James looked on in awe at the celebrity monster, the star that he and the Catholic Church's powers that be had helped to create.

At one point, Merton, having become public property and a cash cow for the monastery, described himself "as a duck in a chicken coop." Merton began to distrust Dom James and even his literary agent when he learned they were speaking about business decisions behind his back. This must have infuriated him, as his books generated revenues in excess of $20,000 to $30,000 a year from 1949 to 1951, a huge sum in those days.[6] Some of that money was used to buy a circus tent to house 50 of the 270 monks, some as young as 15, who had overcrowded the monastery.[7] Many of the novices were World War II veterans.

Gethsemani's enhanced visibility is documented in early 1950s photographs showing a buzzing atmosphere, with many buildings surrounding the abbey. At one time, to earn revenue in addition to Merton's contributions, the monks produced cheese, bacon, smoked ham, and bourbon-flavored fruit cakes. One "factory" was called "Little Pittsburgh," where alfalfa pellets were manufactured and sold as feed for turkeys and racehorses. One of the horses who ate the alfalfa won the Kentucky Derby. Coincidentally, the wise businessman Dom James had invested Gethsemani funds in Churchill Downs, where the race was run.[8]

Merton was infuriated when the Gethsemani gift shop began selling a religious medal imprinted on a cigarette lighter with a photograph of Saint Christopher on one side and the monastery on the other. To promote sales of monastery products, the great wordsmith was reduced to being a Madison Avenue ad hack. One ad he wrote proclaimed, "Many porkers are called but few are chosen to produce our luscious hams." Such work was beneath a man who had sought an atmosphere of solitude and silence when he entered the monastery years before.[9] A monk of distinction, he was now simply a tool in the hands of enablers who immersed him in the commercial world. Ever obedient, he certainly played the "good soldier" by acquiescing to their demands, but he must have been embarrassed at being manipulated at every turn.

The more Merton was promoted, the less he liked it, and depression began to eke into his private thoughts as he sat alone in his tiny quarters. He was asked to consult a psychiatrist in Chicago. The advice: leave the Trappist order to gain the solitude he desired. But Dom James wouldn't let him. The Trappist was trapped, as evidenced by the abbot's 1955 letter to Archbishop Montini, in which he agreed that while Merton was a genius when it came to writing books and quite a dynamic fellow with endless energy and a vivid imagination, he had no idea what a public figure he had become, for both Catholics and non-Catholics. But his leaving, the letter continued, would cause a huge scandal. Others within the order, and within the Catholic Church, would wonder why, if Merton couldn't cut it at Gethsemani, if he could not become one with God, how they could expect to do so themselves. Perceptions of how one might lead the contemplative life would suffer as well, with Merton joining Mother Teresa and Saint John of the Cross as one who tried to inflict absurd ideas on people.[10]

In a 1955 letter Dom James wrote to Jean Leclercq, the abbot declared, "Father Louis [Merton] should give up writing for five years, [he] has worked himself into a great brain fever, and he is blaming everyone else and his surroundings for his lack of peace which is common to neurotics." Biographer Monica Furlong's observation: "After fourteen years of patient effort at Gethsemani, Merton was seen by his abbot and described to others as a harebrained neurotic, with perhaps a touch of con man to him. Dom James was clearly very angry at the nuisance Merton had caused."[11]

With the fuse burning on Merton's ability to cope with stress at every turn, a blowup was bound to occur. It did in July 1956, when Merton was at a conference in Minnesota, where the noted psychiatrist, Dr. Gregory Zilboorg, a bushy, mustachioed gent with rosy cheeks, wire-rimmed glasses, and balding head who relished bow ties and sharp suits, awaited him. In his journals, Merton only summarized what occurred but Michael Mott told the rest of the story. Prior to the conference, Merton's mind was aflame with the knowledge of a letter Dom James had sent to Rome protesting any consideration of Merton's leaving the Cistercian Order. The substance of the message: "that Father Louis was temperamentally unstable, [and] too artistically volatile to be entrusted with determining his own spiritual destiny."[12] With this put-down on his mind, Merton rose during the question-and-answer session following Zilboorg's address and asked, "How do you define the dysfunction of a neurotic?" Zilboorg's answer: "Science does not start with its definition but ends with it." A private meeting with Dr. Zilboorg followed the conference, and Merton admitted learning "things which I knew and did not know." Zilboorg had delivered several verbal punches straight to the chin, including calling Merton narcissistic and accusing him of enjoying his fame. Regardless, Merton later told Naomi Burton Stone that Zilboorg "had been terrific . . . as for my own personal problems—clearly Zilboorg is the first one who has really shown conclusively that he knows exactly what is cooking."[13]

Michael Mott reported that Zilboorg with Dom James present, began to discuss "the case of Father Louis," leaving out no details of their previous meeting, where he had singed Merton with the verbal tongue lashing. The reaction: "[Merton] was not ready to be exposed in front of Dom James. He flew into a fury and cried tears of rage." Mott's observation: "Only two people—Merton's mother Ruth, in the distant past when she had insisted on such things as the correct spelling of *which,* and the Capuchin [priest confessor] in 1940 after Merton's escape from the interview with Father Edmund—had ever seen Merton behave in such a manner."[14]

Reacting to Zilboorg's harsh comments, Merton "saw himself trapped, and . . . sat with tears streaming down his face, muttering 'Stalin! Stalin!'" Mott believed that "These were the most damaging ten minutes since [Merton] had left the world for the monastery." When Zilboorg visited Gethsemani a few months later, he and Merton chatted again, and Merton poked fun at himself, telling Burton Stone later, "it transpires that though I am indeed crazy as a loon I don't really need analysis."[15] But he sought it anyway after giving himself the Rorschach test, leading to more consultations with another psychiatrist, Dr. James Wygal. These meetings were necessary, Monica Furlong suggested, because by 1959, seven years before he met Margie Smith, Merton was in crisis due to his "longings for solitude" as "his exhaustion [grew] more intense, and he [felt] himself near a breakdown."[16]

Whether Merton was more distressed by his incapacity to discern between the famous writer who flew in the winds of the real world and the monk immersed in a monastery where God prevailed, or simply with his inability to escape Gethsemani, is debatable. But there is no doubt both contributed to unhappiness and torment. His failure to become a solitary figure contributed to his feeling that the real world wasn't much different from the monastic world. *SSM,* a true blessing and a curse, but in retrospect more of a curse, had killed any chances for anonymity or to be with "God alone." Now he was just a monk attempting to fight his way toward some sort of freedom wherever he could find it, while the old Merton chased him down the hall like a forgotten relative.[17]

In *The Sign of Jonas* (published in 1953), Merton wrote, "They can have Thomas Merton. He's dead. Father Lewis—he's half dead too. For my part *my* name is that sky, those fence-posts, and those cedar trees."[18] But was it? A year later, he wrote to Dorothy Day, his friend and the founder of *The Catholic Worker:* "The problem that torments me is that I can so easily become part of a general system of delusion . . . I find myself more and more drifting toward the derided and possibly quite absurd defeatist position of a sort of Christian anarchist."[19]

One indication of Merton's mindset and desires may be found in his words in the poem "Fire Watch," first published as an epilogue to *The Sign of Jonas.* Its value may not be underestimated, as noted by biographer Paul Elie. He believed it is "perhaps the purest expression of [Merton's] spirituality of places and spaces. In it he is the monologuist, the secret sharer, investigator, tour guide, and the fire watch is a stage of his pilgrimage . . . it shows how he and the Abbey of Gethsemani have changed since *The Seven Storey Mountain* made them famous."[20]

The story was based on Merton's assignment to check the dark and silent monastery. He wore tennis shoes and carried a flashlight, keys, and a timepiece. Merton took the duty seriously, and while walking alone through the halls he could stop and think about past and present and who he really was at the age of 35. Merton visited "the 'catacomb,' the scullery, the cloister, the tailor shop, the furnace room . . . the choir and novitiate chapel," and suddenly realized that this was the solitude he had sought for so many years, that he truly was alone with God.[21] Within the confines of the dark and silent monastery on this special evening, there was no writing to do, no censors to confront, no letters to answer, no literary agents to deal with, no publishers to satisfy, and no abbot with whom to quarrel. He was truly alone with God. The next morning, Merton must have wondered how he might continue this sense of solitude, this freedom, and he decided he would seek it whenever possible in the months and years ahead. Anything, he must have realized, to lose that shadow, that "old man of the sea" following him that he wrote about in *SSM.*

In effect, Merton was trapped by his own international reputation, which he believed was a figment of his followers' imagination. Michael Mott believed that by the end of 1959 and the beginning of 1960, Merton's "life at Gethsemani was like Don Juan's in prison no existence—but in despair,"[22] a fair comment based on Merton's inability to discover the freedom he was seeking at a monastery that was suddenly just as renowned as he was.

If Merton was a prisoner, Dom James was the warden, and Merton thumbed his nose at him whenever possible. When Merton received an autographed portrait of Pope John XXIII after Merton sent him a congratulatory letter following his election in 1960, Dom James was shocked and apparently jealous to boot. Even more accolades came Merton's way when Lorenzo Barbato, an Italian architect and close friend of the pope, visited Gethsemani and presented Merton, in appreciation of his contributions to the church, with "an ornate gold brocade stole worn by the pope at his investiture, and in addition, some medals he had blessed." Despite requests from the abbot to the contrary, and in direct defiance of a superior, the rebellious Merton wore the stole during prayer days each month.[23]

Such conduct crystallized the unhappiness Merton felt with a life of good intentions gone sour when he entered Gethsemani. Everyone else applauded his books, everyone was in awe of his achievements and his contribution to the library of inspirational books for millions around the world, but it was not enough. And he knew it, writing in 1963 to Father Chrysogonus Waddell in Rome: "If there is such a thing as 'Mertonism' I suppose I am the one who ought to be aware of it. The people who believe in this term evidently do not know how unwilling I would be to have anyone repeat in his own life the miseries of mine." The result: "That would be flatly, a mortal sin against charity . . . anyone who imitates me does so at his own risk. I can promise some fine moments of naked despair."[24] Perhaps these comments were dismissed as humble assertions on Merton's part, but they were air-raid warnings to which nobody was listening. These same people also did not understand that although his discontent was aimed at Dom James, the arrow pointed straight at Merton himself, because he knew the root of discontent lay in one important factor: he had never learned the true meaning of love.

BOOK V

MARGIE *or* GOD

CHAPTER FOURTEEN

QUESTIONS *and* ANSWERS

As Thomas Merton's love affair with Margie Smith intensified during the latter half of 1966, he expressed his feelings for her in a poem called "For M. in October," referring to his hope that their being together might be "possible." Written for her with all the literary skill he could muster, and later published in *Eighteen Poems,* this poem captured the essence of his yearning for a woman he truly loved.[2] As the day of reckoning, the real moment of truth, approached, when he had to decide between her and God, more questions existed than answers. Some questions relating to Margie are impossible to answer since she has insisted on privacy and never addressed in full her relationship with Merton. What were her motives? Was she simply starstruck? Was she interested in the "idea" of falling in love with a famous monk instead of the man himself? Was Margie the "seducer" rather than the seduced? Did she live the fantasy of some women, to taste the forbidden fruit by coaxing a man of the cloth to break solemn vows? Or did Margie really love Merton, in spite of the fact that the chances of an extended relationship were little or none? In the end, would Merton hurt her emotionally, causing her to suffer, or would the experience of loving Merton be a positive, defining moment in her spiritual journey? Perhaps in the future through her writings, or an interview, she will provide her side of the story.

One must ask why Merton, during his 51st year on the face of the earth, and his 25th as a priest and monk at Gethsemani, was suddenly vulnerable to the temptation of a woman half his age. What was his true motive for pursuing her despite his perceived obedience to God and monastic vows? Did Merton fall deeply in love, or was it simply lust and an obsession with eroticism propelling his inner feelings? What was the rebellious monk trying to prove, to himself, and to those who knew him best that he trusted with knowledge of the affair? Was he really "this close" to leaving the monastery and living with or marrying Margie, a decision certain to cause a scandal for Gethsemani and the Catholic Church? Or was he simply using her, at least at the beginning of the relationship, perhaps subconsciously, in an attempt to reconcile guilty feelings simmering ever since his ill-treatment of women during his early adult years? Pondering these questions and beyond would appear to many unnecessary, unfair, and off-limits. Throughout history, mankind's inclination has been to treat heroes with kid gloves, to avoid their humanity, to disregard any blemishes or flaws—anything diminishing their persona. By turning them into sacred cows, by focusing entirely on the positives, by expecting them to be perfect, the idols are given a pass, an aura of invincibility so as to fit the image required by those seeking to protect the value of their beloved symbol of excellence. This is especially true where enablers exist, such as a Catholic Church bent on protecting its own image despite its knowledge of improprieties.

Only when tough questions are asked, only when a fresh lens is used to peer beneath the obvious, does a new perspective appear, one that may initially taint the heroic image before a new one rises to the surface, permitting a more complete appreciation of the hero, warts and all. Oftentimes, this new human being is more revered than the old, because there exists a deep appreciation for the suffering sustained, the obstacles overcome, and the resulting growth. People can relate to sin and to failure. They just don't want to be lied to about it, or told half-truths. Ask Bill Clinton.

Thomas Merton's saga, strongly emphasized by his struggles during the mid-1960s, fits within this framework. Based on his writings, as 1966 proceeded along toward the day when he had to either leave Gethesemani or abandon Margie, with apparently no in-between decision possible, there was little doubt he was not the person he appeared to be. Instead, he was a tormented monk seeking salvation. Merton was truly in pain; he was the baby, the orphan who never grew up, attempting to battle the reptiles of sin consuming him.

Most important to understanding whether Merton might leave the priesthood for Margie is the fact that he had never taken responsibility for his actions, never been called to account, never been forced to totally admit his sinful ways. His guardian, the rich family friend Dr. Tom Bennett, had bailed him out of the pregnancy mess at Clare; he walked away from the adulterous affairs in New York with no regrets; and he avoided the duty to serve his country in the military by entering Gethsemani. In effect, Merton, the "trust-fund baby" who had never been forced to make a living with any full-time job, exhibited characteristics that would disappoint any parent—he was spoiled, morally weak, ethically handicapped, narcissistic, deceptive, secretive, independent to a fault, and by all accounts, irresponsible. Whether his assets outweighed his liabilities is subject to conjecture, but one thing stands out: he was human, and not the near goody-two-shoes projected by his Catholic superiors for all the world to see and idolize. In effect, Merton became the abused spouse in a marriage to Gethsemani and the Catholic Church. Regardless, he must be appreciated for his enormous contribution to the world of inspirational writing. Who else in the history of literature may lay claim to such an outstanding body of work, especially one compiled during a time when he was so confused and tormented? Viewed in this light, Merton's achievements are all the more impressive.

Analyzing any academic whys and wherefores of Merton's romantic interlude is best left to clinical experts, who might dissect it using high-flung psychological principles. But doing so may very well disregard what is most important: the humanistic aspect of what occurred, a wondrous, magical story about two people, whatever their motives may have been, who fell madly in love. At times, Margie might have felt like Cinderella, plucked from obscurity by a man whom she regarded as her true Prince Charming. Age made no difference when the glass slipper fit perfectly.

Understanding Merton's conduct with Margie permits, in turn, a better understanding of who he was, and why his inspirational, encouraging words about love, and freedom, are relevant today. Merton may be better known for his dedication to the contemplative way of living and his belief in the inclusion of all religions and spiritualities, but his thoughts about love and freedom are the common denominator binding all he wrote and taught.

By examining Merton's surprising behavior with Margie through the lens of his total life experiences, we may gain insight as to what decision he would make, Margie or God. This examination also shows that Merton was seeking out what nearly every person, regardless of sex, age, race, or socioeconomic standing, aspires for in life—to know the true meaning of love by loving and being loved. Love often leads to a sense of freedom from loneliness, heartache, depression, and misery. Merton's story is thus a story for everyone who seeks something to dearly cherish; if it is attained, they must decide whether it was truly what was desired. But first it must be attained, and for Merton, this meant finding someone to love.

One important passage that provides significant clues to how much Merton knew about the quest for love appeared in the 1961 book *New Seeds of Contemplation.* Reading it carefully, one begins to understand Merton's insight into any projected unity with God. Merton wrote that one of the paradoxes of any mystical life—and Merton was certainly a mystic—was that a man was never able to enter into his deepest center and pass through this center to God unless he could pass out of himself, become empty, and give of himself to others in selfless love. Merton thus believed no one could possess God until God possessed one's heart and soul. When one was isolated and didn't love, he asked, "How can fire take possession of what is frozen?"[2]

In *No Man Is an Island,* Merton touched this subject again by suggesting that people do not exist only for themselves. When they realize this, then, and only then, they may love themselves and love others. Loving oneself properly, he concluded, meant "desiring to live, accepting life as a very great gift and a great good, not because of what it gives us, but because of what it enables us to give to others."[3]

The catalyst for Merton's final steps to truly loving God, and God alone, was the gift of Margie, but before this could occur, Merton realized he needed to cast away the dark side that had been shadowing him before and, most surprisingly, *during,* his days as a monk. Few had any idea such a blemished, flawed Merton existed since, as biographer Michael Mott noted, "[Merton] had always kept, and was always to keep, his inner turmoil from others. At most, they would notice that he seemed preoccupied." Father Basil Pennington called Merton "a very private person," and fellow monk Father Timothy Kelly agreed. After reading portions of Merton's private journals, he noted "[I never knew] the amount of struggle he was going through . . . none of this came through in a personal relationship. I had no idea all that was going on."[4]

What was before their eyes, but what they were unable to see without clear-lensed binoculars into Merton's past, was a logical connection between Margie Smith and Merton's inability to love during his formative years. The trail to discovering this obvious link begins with examining what Merton wrote about the subject of love. Through his writings, lectures, and articles, clues appeared as to how much he yearned for someone to love and to be loved by. This, in turn, strongly impacted the decision-making process when he was forced to choose between Margie and God.

That Merton sought love in his life during his teenage years (Henrietta, the girl at Bournemouth; the woman on the ocean liner; the women at Clare College), and through early adulthood (Wilma, the nurse; the girl on his New York street; Ginny Burton; other New York City romances), is apparent. During his first days at Gethsemani, he wrote of being healed into the likeness of God only through one inlet: learning to love.[5]

As early as 1951, in *The Wisdom of the Desert,* Merton had praised the Desert Fathers, the first Christian hermits who migrated to the deserts of Persia, Egypt, and Palestine to live in solitude. He admired their abilities to rise above "all passion and become impervious to anger, lust, pride, and all the rest." Merton learned of the hermits' feeling that love was more than just sentiment, or token favors, but experienced on the inside with a spiritual identification. He admired how they concluded that love was about bonding with another self, with humility and reverence. This required total inner transformation so the person loving was in some sense the person they loved. This was only possible when someone, figuratively speaking, died, losing sight of his own self.[6]

Four years later, Merton's evolution toward understanding what love was all about triggered more revelations, which he wrote about in *No Man Is an Island.* The book's prologue was filled with words of wisdom, beginning with Merton's devotion to capturing the essence of love. Working feverishly when time permitted him to write during a year in which fame brought hundreds of letters to the monastery each month, he decided to inspect "the antithesis between love of self and love of another."[7] Alone with his thoughts, he concluded there were several types of love, but the end result to be valued was knowledge that one had to love oneself in order to love someone else—so one discovered one's self by giving oneself to others.[8]

Merton's yearnings were evident across the spectrum of his writing. He talked about the need to consider the true welfare of the other person and how one must agree to be loved.[9] In 1965, Merton addressed that subject, and the subject of marriage, by writing "All monks, as is well-known, are unmarried, and hermits more unmarried than the rest of them . . . but I see no reason why a man can't love God and a woman at the same time." He then added, "If God was going to regard women with a jealous eye, why did he go and make them in the first place?"[10]

A year later, Merton would admit feeling a "deep emotional need for feminine companionship and love."[11] In 1968, after having experienced Margie's caring ways, Merton was even more certain, deciding that any sense of man without woman was ludicrous, causing no completion in either one. He also concluded that the point of being married was not simply sexual fulfillment, but a true communion between people. He even compared men's and women's ability to complete each other with how Christ and the church were joined together as one.[12]

Merton's notions of love, and his continuing education on the subject, had certainly been influenced by the teachings of Saint John of the Cross, the Spanish Carmelite friar, poet, mystic, and author of *Dark Night of the Soul.* Both Saint John of the Cross, whose verse was replete with "romantic, erotic, and sensual imagery," and Saint Teresa of Avila, another Merton influence, believed that life was a love affair, "a romance between God and the human soul that liberates us to love one another."[13] Saint John advocated the idea that "the soul *arrives* with perfect union with God through love," with love being "at the core of everything."[14]

Such influences indicated the mindset of a man who had finally put it all together. After years of learning about love and yearning to love and be loved, Merton appeared to get it. During the early days of the Margie affair he admitted "one thing has suddenly hit me; that nothing counts except love . . . that a solitude that is not simply the wide-openness of love and freedom is nothing. . . ." Merton concluded love and solitude were the "one ground of true maturity and freedom."[15] Of all the words he had written during 25-plus years at Gethsemani and even before, these words may be the most important. At age 51, it appeared Thomas Merton had finally grown up, matured, and become a man who would welcome a chance to love if one appeared, an improbable event, if not completely impossible.

When Merton met Margie, the realization of there not being any chance at a long-term, loving relationship forced him to admit: "I do feel a deep emotional need for feminine companionship and love, and seeing that I must irrevocably live without it ended up tearing me up more than the [back] operation itself."[16] Here was a man who could write beautiful prose describing how *others* should love, or perhaps illuminating how *he* would love if he ever had the opportunity. He thus must have been quite disappointed knowing that while he learned about loving and being loved enough to write poetically about them, there was no opportunity to put into action anything he had learned. It was too late.

Merton's confidant and brother monk Father John Eudes agreed: "Merton struggled with love precisely because he had such a deep need for it, had invested so much early in life in seeking it only to be frustrated. Because he never gave up the search for the real thing and because he was truth at a deep level, he was able to discern the various qualities of love at different levels of the psyche and spirit." The result: "He could write about what he had very concrete ideas of."[17]

If Merton prayed for a companion, a woman to come into his life, maybe God answered those prayers by introducing him not to a woman his age, not an academic or fellow spiritualist, not a Protestant, a believer in Eastern religions and spiritualities, or an atheist, not a plain Jane with little sex appeal, but a twenty-five-year old beautiful, sensual, loving Catholic girl who shared his passionate ways.

And maybe God told Merton, "Okay—here she is, what you have always wanted, the chance to truly be *in love*. Now show me whether you have really learned the true meaning of loving, and being loved, and the difference between true love and love of the flesh. In the end, the choice shall be yours: Margie, a woman who loves you dearly despite your flaws and limitations, or me." Margie Smith thus became not simply a temptation, or even a gift, but a true test of Merton's capability to discover whether what he apparently coveted—a loving, lasting, sharing relationship with a woman—was what he really wanted. Or whether he would instead resist this longing, and be obedient to "God alone."

CHAPTER FIFTEEN

MERTON *the* CHRISTIAN

FAMOUS MONK MERTON LEAVES
PRIESTHOOD TO MARRY PREGNANT
STUDENT NURSE HALF HIS AGE.

I magine if this had been the newspaper headline around the world in late 1966, 1967, or 1968. Imagine the shock that would have prevailed among millions of readers of Merton's books, among his followers, and especially among those in the Catholic Church who viewed him as a near-saint. The scandal embarrassing the Vatican would have been news fodder for weeks, especially if Merton had impregnated Margie and actually become father to her child, a possibility he kidded Dom James about.[1]

Many of Merton's followers would certainly have felt betrayed by him and his holier-than-thou writings. Here was a self-professed contemplative monk who insisted mankind obey the highest moral and ethical standards, with God, or another higher power, at the center. He would not only be disobeying the monastery that had welcomed him despite his sinful flaws, but apparently doing so for selfish reasons—reasons few would have understood because of his incomplete disclosures about his pre-monastic life.

Most fascinating about this scenario is that it was not far-fetched. Obsessed with his new love, Merton seriously considered forsaking his sacred vows and dashing off with Margie. Exactly why he might have chosen to do so has been debated for years. Theories run the gamut from his disenchantment with the domineering Dom James and the church hierarchy he felt censored and imprisoned him both body and soul, to his inherently independent, wander-lust nature.[2] This propelled Merton, the argument might be, to decide his love for Margie was more in keeping with the true nature of his tormented soul than continuing to hide behind a mask that portrayed him as the peaceful her-mit of solitude and silence.

Certainly Merton's love affair with Margie must be placed in context with his disenchantment with Dom James, the "dangerous" superior who labeled Merton everything from hare-brained to neurotic. If one takes Merton's tirades against the abbot at face value, it would be tempting to think he might have left Gethsemani solely because of his distaste for and frustration with the abbot. But Merton may have been more vehement with his words than his actions, and he never appeared to be wholeheartedly determined to leave the monastery solely because of the abbot.

Another factor that may have led to Merton's dissatisfaction with Dom James was simply his restlessness. Merton was a wanderer like his father, who took him from France to the United States to Bermuda to the United States and back to Europe. Merton was always restless to move on whether to a new location or a new woman. Being restricted to Gethsemani meant he was un-able to wander, and for a time he wanted to leave this monastery for another far away. When his request to move was denied, Merton appeared to accept the decision despite some grumbling, and decided his wandering had come to an end. A letter he sent from Asia shortly before his death to Brother Patrick Hart confirms the decision to remain at Gethsemani despite the opportunity to leave. In part, it read, "I think of you all on this Feast Day and with Christ-mas approaching I feel homesick for Gethsemani."[3]

Merton, as evidenced by Dr. Gregory Zilboorg's toxic findings, was cer-tainly a rebel and an egotist who relished fame for a time. He enjoyed those who joined the "Merton cult" in Christ-like admiration for every word he spoke or wrote. But showing the Catholic Church and the world how inde-pendent he really was, how much of a rebel he had become, does not seem to be enough impetus for Merton to leave behind his vows and scamper away into the night with his student nurse.

Father John Eudes added to the doubt as to whether Merton would have left Gethsemani over his disgruntlement with Dom James and the Church fa-thers, or because of his independent nature. Father Eudes cautioned those who read Merton's scathing words about every frustration in his life that Merton

had a "talent for satire and he cultivated it assiduously" because it comple-
mented his temperament and massaged his "quick and perspective mind."
Eudes traced Merton's satirical style to "the influence of his suave and polished
guardian, Dr. Bennett," whose example taught him that "perhaps the most effective criticism of all is a light superior mockery, the urbane and gentle murder of pretense and genius alike."[4]

Father Eudes cautioned readers to be wary of interpreting Merton's criticism literally, and in turn from "unfair or biased opinions of the victims of
such treatment." He believed this was especially applicable when Merton
used satire to air ill feelings about superiors, the Catholic Church, the
monastic community, and some individuals, since Merton had also written
about them more positively elsewhere. Misinterpreting Merton's views could
be difficult if care is not taken to closely inspect the true meaning of his
words.[5] But this doesn't mean Merton's writings should be disregarded;
whether about himself, or others. He is the primary source for his feelings
with interpretation a risk at best. The risk increases when paraphrasing occurs, a necessary evil in this book that the author wishes he could have
avoided, since Merton's writings, especially about the Margie affair, are the
result of his gift as a true wordsmith.

The more likely reason for Merton to potentially turn his back on sacred
vows and leave Gethsemani with Margie may be because Merton knew for
certain he was not the man he appeared to be to friends, colleagues, fellow
monks, novice students, and most important, his legion of readers and followers around the world. Through Merton's writings, nearly all believed he
was a true converted Christian, a peaceful and contemplative monk, and a
spiritual guru who knew exactly how one should lead one's life. He was promoted as such by the Catholic Church and did nothing to expose the myth.
If one read his works without any knowledge of the true sense of his sinful past,
it would appear he was writing words of advice for others, and not himself. But
a closer look at what he wrote when one is aware of the languishing sorrow
within him reveals that he was talking more about himself than anyone realized. Certainly one area of interest is to re-examine his lectures to the novices
about Philoxonus, where he clearly indicated questionable conduct in his past
and the need for God to take over one's life as "the boss."

In essence, Merton was an imposter of sorts who put on a good front so
others would not know of his inner agony. Certainly he had flashes of happiness along the way when he wrote, taught, spent time in the woods or bonded

with friends. But it would be 25 years after his death, when his private journals were published in full, before the world had the full opportunity to witness glimpses of the true Thomas Merton even though biographers such as Edward Rice, Monica Furlong, and Michael Mott had paraded moments of uneasiness before readers in early books about him.

Even when the Merton journals appeared—especially volume VI, detailing the Margie affair—it appeared that those who studied Merton missed the obvious: that due to demons deep within his soul, he must have questioned whether he was, by his own definition or standard, a true/authentic/faithful/converted, whatever word fits, Christian. Simply put, Merton questioned, as many Catholics do, his true dedication and obedience to God, when all the world thought this was a given. Merton certainly was not a fraud, but he intentionally concealed feelings and misrepresented facts by shading the truth and rationalizing his behavior. No better evidence exists than permitting *SSM* to be published as true when he knew it was not the whole truth.

Because the original chronicle of his pre-monastic life was tainted by censors who clipped more than a third of the text from the original manuscript, the question exists as to whether fruits of what he later wrote were also tainted since readers never knew the true heart and soul of the man whose words they were digesting. This may also cause some to question whether Merton would have gained such an international following if readers and friends had known that he and his enablers had hoodwinked them in *SSM*. As often occurs in today's confusing world, no one had a clue as to what was percolating inside Merton's soul because outside the mask he wore, a rosy picture was painted for all to see despite the anguish, frustration, and longing for love and freedom that pervaded his years at Gethsemani. Amazingly enough, Merton, the writer, could disengage himself from the false self he promoted to the outside world, and write inspirational books ranking with the finest ever published.

Perception of Merton's state of mind regarding whether he was a true, converted Christian may differ depending on whether someone is a Catholic, whose conversion is viewed as gradual in nature; a Protestant, for whom a defining moment's conversion is the focus; a kindred spirit of Eastern religions, where aspects of conversion are mainly unknown; or an atheist, who could care little about conversion experiences. Regardless, the question of whether Merton was a converted Christian *is* significant since he gave the impression that he was Christ-like in nature through his words and messages, which portrayed someone who certainly *sounded* converted, someone who was one with God.

Like any believer, Merton wrestled with the concept of true Christianity throughout his life. In March of 1959, after ruminating about monastic obedience, he wondered about real and personal values, under the pretense of love, before asking "When will we ever become Christians?" After a scintillating conversation with Robert Lax and Robert Giroux when they visited in May of that year, Merton decided he must face the disturbing fact that he was "not really a monk and a Christian. . . ."[6] even though he believed monastic existence was the life of a real Christian.[7]

By all accounts, including his own, Merton never seemed, from an early age to early adulthood, to have understood the basic difference between right and wrong, good and evil. This lack haunted him for the rest of his life when important decisions had to be made, and time and time again he would run the other way when responsibility called him to attention. The book of Proverbs speaks to this, pointing out that while one's actions may appear to be innocent in their view, the motives behind them are judged by God. Rationalization may thus occur when no standards exist for deciding between opposite courses of conduct. This was Merton, game, set, match.

Father John Eudes suggested that one of the main reasons Merton was misinterpreted was his inconsistency. Eudes believed Merton was a spontaneous person who quickly formed opinions without considering past experiences. This view is bolstered by Merton's own words: "My ideas are always changing, always moving around one center, and I am always seeing that center from somewhere else. Hence, I will always be accused of inconsistency. But I will no longer be there to hear the accusation."[8] The topic of conversion was a constant in Merton's life. It began when he wrote *SSM* in his early to mid-30s and would continue to be an area of concern until he died. In his autobiography, he concluded that "because of the profound and complete conversion of my intellect, I thought I was entirely converted." This was because, he swore, that due to his belief in God and the teachings of the church, he could debate his resolve all night, which made him believe that he was a zealous Christian. But he knew true conversion of the intellect fell short, because if his will was not with God then this intellectual conversion was indefinite in scope.[9] As late in his life as mid-May 1967, at the age of 52, Merton was still a seeker, writing, "I experience in myself a deep need of conversion. . . ."[10] This was not surprising in light of the Catholic view of conversion being gradual, but it was apparently unknown, or disregarded by those who thus wanted to pin down an actual, convenient moment of conversion for Merton.

Scholars have argued the slippery slope of Thomas Merton's true Christian conversion for 50-plus years. How Merton ultimately dealt with the question of Margie or God in 1966 directly relates to whether he was in a state of being one with God, or disabled in his true beliefs, having slid backward as the years passed at Gethsemani. Certainly even being tempted in a sensual way indicated his unrest with the state of his spiritual being and caused him agony while he pondered his decision.

Specific moments of conversion mentioned by those inspectors of Merton's life include his visits various churches in Rome as an 18-year-old in 1932, a mystical vision of his father in a *pensione* room, his baptism at the Church of Corpus Christi, his decision to enter Gethsemani, his monastic vows, and his ordination. Perhaps it occurred when he confessed past sinful deeds in the forthright letter he wrote to the Baroness de Heuck in 1941. Elements of his conversion run the gamut, according to those assessing what truly causes such a transformation. Some note a change of direction, a true reorientation of one's self, or even a personal revolution. Dr. Anthony Padovano, an ardent Merton observer, suggests there is an "'Ah-ha' eureka experience and nothing looks the same again. I guess the closest most come to it is love. When you are in love with someone, the whole world looks different all of a sudden."[11]

Certainly a crisis may create a path to conversion, whether it is from no religion or spirituality to one, from one to another, or the complete abandonment of any. Conversion expert Dr. Lewis Rambo believes experiencing a crisis causes one to become a "religious seeker," where the "crisis destroys the old so that something new is required."[12] Rambo's commonsense view fits perfectly with Merton's acknowledgment that his path to Gethsemani was highly influenced by disgust for his previous, unfulfilling lifestyle. This spurred Merton to seek a new religion (Catholicism), which led him to a monastic life with lasting consequences.[13] This squares with his words in *The Seven Storey Mountain,* "And then it suddenly became clear to me that my whole life was at a crisis. . . . It was a moment of crisis, yet of interrogation: a moment of searching."[14] Merton's personal correspondence with theologian and friend Rosemary Radford Ruether in 1966–67 is important to understand how Merton truly was in crisis and would deal with Margie. He respected Ruether's opinions because "she is very Barthian—which is why I trust her. There is a fundamental honesty about her theology."[15] Ruether joins Dr. Gregory Zilboorg as the only ones who appeared to see beneath the mask of holiness Merton wore, morning to night, as he suffered within. In late March 1967, after hearing from Merton about various aspects of his life, Ruether told him of her disappointment in him due to his defensiveness and his constant need for "proving, proving how good your life is, etc." She chastised him for not listening to her about balancing his life and for his inclination to distort her words with reactive responses lacking sufficient thought. A follow-up paragraph was even more direct, with Ruether telling Merton he was in crisis, but fighting it with lengthy arguments. She admitted catching only a glimmer of what was bothering him, but believed the depths of his troubled soul were not monastically related, but based on the "rhythm of your personal development." She told him he needed a new point of view and if he didn't find one, if his inner turmoil was not addressed properly, "it will surely mean a regression to a less full existence for you, while if its meaning is properly discerned, it will be a new *kairos* leading to a new level of perception."[16]

Ruether's insights into Merton's state of mind included her observation that his subconscious needed a change of attitude while the "super conscious . . . [was] fighting it off." This was causing, she believed, a defensive posture toward his monastic life whenever the topic turned to his present mental condition. Merton responded by telling his friend, "You are perhaps more right than I think about the 'crisis,' though I have the impression I am not in much more of a crisis than I have been for the last ten years or more."[17]

This frank admission of being in crisis well back into the 1950s was telling, but even earlier, during the late 1940s, he acknowledged his conversion was not complete, that it was continuing and that it was something occurring over a whole lifetime with alternating peaks and valleys.[18] Predictably, Merton saw conversion as an open-ended journey, "an on-going development," and "a dynamic thrust forward and upward." He liked the metaphor of a journey.[19] Merton scholar Anthony Padovano agrees, believing Merton experienced "many transformations" and "many conversions," ultimately "accepting one transformation after another."[20]

Merton explained his own definition of being a Christian on many occasions. He called it a "way of life, rather than a way of thought" and decided one could only "understand the full meaning of the Christian message" by living the Christian life. He further concluded that being a Christian meant being holy, and such was possible only if one was free from "the tyranny and the demands of sin, of lust, of anger, of pride, ambition, injustice, and the spirit of violence." When the person renounced sin and selfish living, peace and seren-ity resulted, because God lives and acts within. Being truly holy was not easy, he suggested, and possible through willpower or good intentions. Only through a difficult struggle could a person recognize the limitations and weaknesses in-festing them. Trusting in God and imitating Jesus, wrote Merton, were the keys to receiving "mysterious strength that has no human source." This permitted more of an identification with Christ, a oneness where God lived within, and was a true strength. At this point, the old external self was renounced, and with it any selfish desires and illusions preventing one from being a true Christian since God literally took possession of everyday experiences. The old self had truly died, permitting the new self to emerge.[21]

Merton's revealing words bring to mind theologian Sally McFague's defi-nition of conversion or transformation and rebirth: "[It] will be a process, usu-ally a painful and lifelong process, fraught with doubt, with ambiguity, with great discomfort, with risk; and certainly it will demand courage to a high de-gree."[22] Based on admissions Merton wrote in a letter to friend Miguel Green-berg in the mid-1960s, "Now I am in my fiftieth [fifty-plus-years] skin and trying to get it [sin] off like a tight bathing suit, too wet, too sticky and irri-tating in the extreme,"[23] he would need all the courage he could muster to once and for all lose the bathing suit of sin and march forward with a pure heart toward deciding whether he should choose Margie or God.

CHAPTER SIXTEEN

SUBSTITUTE MOTHERS *and* FATHERS

Only through suffering, Thomas Merton concluded, could one test his or her true Christian beliefs. Based on his childhood and early adulthood experiences, including the distant relationship with his mother, feelings of abandonment by his father, being orphaned at an early age, the rejected love affairs in his youth, the sinful days at Clare College, the shallow relationships at Columbia, and the "last adulterous affair" shortly before entering Gethsemani *after* being baptized, Merton was certainly tested; he certainly suffered. Discarded women were strewn along the way without a shred of regret until much later in life, when he had time to reflect on his distasteful conduct and experience true guilt for his actions. It is not a stretch to believe, based on brother monk Paul Quenon's assertion that Merton wrote and spoke "from experience,"[1] that Merton alerted those who read his words or heard his lectures to inner struggles but disguised them enough so that no one realized *he* was the one suffering as the days and months passed at Gethsemani. That Merton revealed himself in such a way was not surprising, for the burden of Merton's pre-monastic transgressions was a heavy yoke to bear.

This yoke centered around one aspect of Merton's life more than any other: relationships with girls and women. Merton's interaction with women provides revealing clues not only as to his mental state when he entered the monastery, but how he would ultimately handle the Margie affair. Recalling the words he used to describe these relationships assists the search for the truth.

If one pays close attention, the true answer as to why Margie impacted him so deeply becomes crystal clear.

The parade of women in Merton's life begins with his mother, Ruth. Much has been written about her, the "slight, thin, sober little person" who Merton recalled as "anxious, worried, precise, and quite critical of him."[2] When she scolded Merton for leaving the "h" out of "which,"[3] he was full of fury and "tears of rage" similar to those he experienced when he was chastised by Dr. Gregory Zilboorg years later. Certainly it appears clear that Merton was quite distant from his mother, and objected to her dominance and abusive language, a disturbing experience for a youngster, and one that ignited future unkind emotions about women. Like his later hero, Ernest Hemingway, who hated his mother and often referred to her as an "All-American bitch,"[4] Merton's memories of his mother were less than complimentary.

Little text is devoted to Ruth in Merton's writings, compared with those about his father, but it must be recalled that she died when he was six years old. Certainly, he never admitted to "loving" her or to "being loved" by her, terms he also never employed to describe his father or, for that matter, nearly anyone else in his pre-monastic life. Merton, it may be recalled, later remembered "the pain of his nascent sexual longings in a world seeming to him to have been shaped in its attitudes by the woman-hating Plato."[5]

While consideration of Thomas Merton's relationship with his mother reveals much about his attitude toward women, it is the woman who almost became his step-mother, Evelyn Scott, who provides even a better indication of how Merton viewed women. Close inspection discloses potential trauma that may have adversely affected his relationships with women *more than any other,* except for perhaps his mother. Owen Merton fell in love with Scott, a budding novelist, when he and his son lived in Bermuda in 1922. She was very attractive, with high cheekbones, a slim figure, a pointed nose, soft, large eyes, and wavy brown hair tucked at times under fancy cloth hats.[6] Scott became an important figure in American literature, important enough to have two biographies, *Pretty Good for a Woman: The Enigmas of Evelyn Scott,* and *Fighting the Current: The Life and Work of Evelyn Scott,* written about her. In the former, author D. A. Callard wrote, "[Scott] was instrumental in the introduction of [James] Joyce's work to America and in the elevation of William Faulkner from the rank of minor Southern writer to major novelist. She wrote a dozen adult books, two books of verse and a play, yet she is mysteriously absent from most memoirs of the period and from almost all critical surveys."[7] In the latter, author Mary Wheeling White professed, "Evelyn Scott's shockingly modern first novel, *The Narrow House* (1921), led Sinclair Lewis to exclaim in his review of her effort, "She has done it! 'The Narrow House' is an event; it is one of those recognitions of life by which life itself becomes the greater." Also listed among her works were *The Wave, A Calendar of Sin, Breathe Upon These Slain,* and *The Shadow of the Hawk.* In a 1940 interview, Faulkner, asked if there were any good women novelists, replied, "Evelyn Scott is pretty good . . . for a woman." Praising her further, White wrote, "the life and works of Evelyn Scott supply the twentieth-century scholar with a portrait of one of the most active, creative minds of twentieth-century American literature and criticism . . . Simply put, [she] lived a fascinating life, driven by her adherence to personal and aesthetic ideals."[8] Scott died in 1963, five years before Merton passed away.

Through the years, some biographers have brushed away the potential impact Scott had on the impressionable, seven-year-old Merton. She found Merton to be "oddly *un*childlike," and admitted Merton hated her. Scott's son, Creighton, painted a horrifying portrait of how his mother punished Merton for incidents she let pass when he was the culprit. More to the point, Creighton said she exhibited "a knowing and adept brutality, calibrated to [Tom's] youth, his ignorance and the obscure grief and uncertainty that evidently consumed him."[9] In *Pretty Good for a Woman,* Callard observed, "Tom did not like [Scott], though a strong friendship grew between him and Creighton." He added, "Evelyn may have tried to hope to take the place of Tom's mother. If she did, she failed dismally. Creighton recalled one occasion where she screamed at Owen, 'I'm sick of his damn mother, sick of her. I hate her, I hate her, do you hear?'"[10]

Regarding how Scott treated young Merton, Creighton told Callard, "my mother was ruthlessly and uncouthly indifferent to whatever his private sorrows and obsessions may have been." Creighton then added, "In my late twenties, when she and I were still on speaking terms, her reminiscences about Tom's 'badness' and intractability were all accompanied by little unctuous giggles, like that of a schoolgirl using a dirty word for the first time."[11] This behavior must have made Merton think of his mother because Evelyn's actions were reminiscent of Ruth Merton's domineering and uncaring attitude for her son. Is it any wonder Merton's heart was scalded and untrusting when he began to meet and be interested in loving girls and women early in life?

White barely mentioned Merton in her biography but noted that "Tom never warmed to Evelyn." Regarding the relationship between Scott and

Owen, whom Evelyn called "Mutt," White suggested, "Their relationship had become primarily sexual, for Scott still felt that her physical urges, if not satisfied, resulted in grave depressions. At the time, she described Owen . . . 'as a very lovable romantic who thinks himself in love with me.'"[12]

What Scott did not mention was that Owen may also have been in love with her *husband,* a theory proposed by Merton scholar Robert E. Daggy, albeit with some skepticism from other Merton scholars. Daggy believed that Merton, "like many sons (and daughters, too), [had] problems admitting that his father was a sexual being" since "he may have had little knowledge of his father's sexuality." Continuing this theme, Daggy suggested "that Merton's father had had homosexual experiences and that he was certainly bisexual" due to his "sleeping with Evelyn *and* with her common-law husband, Cyril Kay Scott."[13] Whether Merton actually witnessed such behavior is unclear, but if he even sensed it, negative ramifications were likely for such a young, impressionable boy.

Most important to note is how the young Merton must have felt when Owen was considering abandoning his sons for the love of Scott, who wanted nothing to do with the children. Even if such a possibility was not discussed with Merton, the bright child must have been aware that, already motherless, he might lose his father as well. What severe emotions evolved from this realization cannot be underestimated. Child psychologists could debate all day the effect of Scott's influence on young Merton. But, at the least, he must have had a deep distrust of her, one lingering through the years toward other women who he saw as simply sex objects unworthy of respect or commitment.

Merton's trail of romantic relationships, or relationships he had hoped would be romantic, traveled from young Henrietta to the girl on the English ocean liner to the girl at Bournemouth to girls at Clare College at Cambridge to those he pursued in New York City. Each was a disappointment, but the most devastating was the rejection by the girl on the ocean liner, which, he wrote, was "like being 'flayed alive.' This kind of a love affair can really happen only once in a man's life. After that he is calloused."[14] And Merton was, even more so than anyone realized.

During his days in England Merton had admired his Aunt Maud, whom he called an angel.[15] But she was cast out of his life when Merton was sent away from Europe. His philandering then continued on the streets of New York City, with relationship after relationship squeezed between bouts of drinking, reading dirty books, and drawing disrespectful, soft pornographic pictorials for *Jester* and the Dixie Cup Company.[16] New friendships with party buddies Edward Rice and Robert Lax, among others, permitted more nightlife and the search for women to bed and enjoy without emotional attachment as Merton continued his passion for the flesh. A favorite, according to later writings, was Ginny Burton. Certainly good times must have prevailed in New York, as Merton recalled the Sunday night party, whiskey, swimming in the creek at three in the morning, and "everyone furiously drunk."[17] But Merton could not even be true to a woman he talked of marrying, since he admitted to the "latest" adulterous affair while he was romancing Ginny. He also cheated on her with little hesitation after his baptism, extending a pattern of immoral conduct and deceit that trailed him from childhood and surfaced and nibbled at his soul when he met Margie 25 years later and lied to the abbot about not seeing her. One wonders whether the baptism really impacted Merton, whether he lived up to the beliefs Saint Augustine espoused 15 centuries earlier when he "saw baptism as a step to be taken when and only when the candidate was morally . . . prepared to accept the new responsibilities of Christian life."[18]

Is there any question Merton was not free of the "tyranny and the demands of sin [and] of lust" he described in *Honorable Reader?*[19] Clues abound. Amazingly, *during* his days at the monastery, the human, flawed Merton *still* flirted with the flesh. Visits from Father Anselm's sister, Carolyn, and the "girl from the coast," Margo Dennis, triggered sexual fantasies in Merton. Sensual dreams, if they truly were unconscious dreams and not simply thoughts expressed as dreams on the journal page, also infected his soul as he fantasized about women, including his literary agent, and his relationships with them. One he recalled in specific detail was the meeting the two women dressed in white along with his friend Dan Walsh and his pairing with the one who did not look like a nun, holding her close. He recalled that she was not only fresh but "firm" and "freely intimate," sensual terms of description. He noted her warning that he should not kiss her or try to seduce her—a truly amazing account for a priest supposedly immersed in the monastic life, but not for one who was obsessed with pleasures of the flesh deep into his years at Gethsemani.

I n January 1963, Merton believed he was still "the same self-willed and volatile person who made such a mess at Cambridge." This distasteful person, he admitted in a passage written just a few months after his dream about the two women with Dan Walsh, had "kept some of the old vain, inconstant, self-centered ways of looking at things."[20] Besides his father, the center of Merton's male world during a critical time in his growth while at Clare was Owen's good friend Dr. Bennett, Merton's godfather and guardian and the one who had circumcised Merton as a baby.[21] He was a rather dashing figure, with swept-back oiled hair and protruding ears. A bushy mustache covered half his upper lip, and he dressed immaculately in tweed suits and stylish, colorful ties. Colleagues considered him an expert on disorders of the alimentary tract and on metabolism. One unforgettable characteristic was his voice, which spouted words with care and precision. He spoke fluent French and some Spanish, enjoyed bridge before dinner, and exhibited a bit of "natural irascibility under a calm manner."[22]

Colleagues described Dr. Bennett as quite opinionated, with "strong feelings and prejudices with the outstanding point the "unpredictable nature of his outlook." He was provocative yet could be annoying even though he was an "attractive companion." He died at age 58 shortly after Merton finally informed him of his entry into Gethsemani five years earlier. At his funeral Dr. Bennett was hailed as a "witty speaker," one who appreciated such qualities as individualism, restless energy, and imaginative vision.[23]

Because Merton had little time with his father once Owen became bedridden, it was Dr. Bennett who must be considered a highly influential role model. Recall Father John Eudes's perception of Bennett: It was "the influence of his urbane guardian," whose example taught [Merton] that "perhaps the most effective criticism of all is a light superior mockery, the urbane and gentle murder of pretense and genius alike."[24] Merton must have admired the suave, sophisticated, and polished characteristics in his substitute father.

Monica Furlong, British like Bennett, apparently researched him thoroughly for her biography of Merton, in which she was quite critical of the godfather's influence on him, especially concerning the fathering of an illegitimate child. She wrote that while it was common for a "gentleman" to father a child by a "lower-class" girl and then "disown her," it was "perhaps tragic that Bennett encouraged Merton to do this." The result, Furlong decided, was that "A cloud seemed to spread over [Merton's] life, a cloud that he associated particularly with England."[25]

Merton spent school holidays at the doctor's expensively furnished Harley Street flat near Middlesex Hospital, where Dr. Bennett worked, and listened to Louis Armstrong and Duke Ellington jazz records. Living the life of luxury, Merton was served breakfast by the maids. Merton held Dr. Bennett in such high esteem that it approached hero-worship. The youngster admired his "worldliness" and "hung on his words and his opinions as years before he had had hung on the words of his father." Trips to Paris to view Chagall paintings broadened Merton's world, and it was from Bennett and his wife, Iris, that he learned to appreciate, perhaps even idolize, the writers Ernest Hemingway and D. H. Lawrence, as well as Picasso. From these men, each a lover of ladies with no qualms about womanizing or adultery, Merton was etching into his mind the "new attitude to life" that Bennetts advocated, one that was "a kind of wry detachment from the conventional world that felt excitingly naughty but fun to do." The influence was clear, and Merton later decided he had developed "a habit of wholesale and glib detraction of all the people with whom I did not agree or whose taste and ideas offended me."[26]

Merton's "don't give a damn" attitude stretched to include the Bennetts in his novel *My Argument with the Gestapo,* in which they appear as "Uncle Ralph (Rafe) and Aunt Melissa."[27] For pages on end, the character while writing in the summer of 1941 months before he entered Gethsemani, Merton addressed his uncle in adoring terms. He mentioned Rafe's buying the character Merton the best wallet he ever owned from Finley's, on Bond Street for his eighteenth birthday. It was brand new, smelled great, and was full of travel tickets to Italy. Merton enjoyed time in his uncle's flat, where he could be himself and say what he wanted without a care for what anyone thought. He could talk straight and say that Picasso, Matisse, and Cézanne were "great artists," and not be crazy as everyone believed. A list of all the things he had learned from Uncle Rafe, Merton said, would have included books, painters, cities, wine, languages, races, writing, and "curious facts about all the people of the world." He gave Uncle Rafe credit for introducing him to Evelyn Waugh, James Joyce, and Lawrence, and "the picture galleries in the Rue de la Boetie, in Paris." Summing up, he admitted to being amazed at "Uncle Rafe's knowledge of the world."[28]

Following the pages where he idolized Uncle Rafe, aka Dr. Bennett, Merton acknowledged wedges in his moral psyche. From English drunks and London whores, he decided that "pleasure was what was applauded." He discovered that it was "all right to have a good time so long as you didn't interfere with the good time of anybody else." But he was unable to understand how his pleasures had hurt others "until it was too late." since he didn't know how to say so "because problems of right and wrong didn't exist."[29]

Merton's evident guilt over his behavior at Cambridge oozed into the novel. He recognized after his scholarship had been withdrawn and he had to leave England for good that he wanted to say he was wrong, but "didn't know how, because the word wrong didn't exist in the novels" and he didn't "have any words to say it with." He acknowledged wanting to say he was sorry, but the "word sorry is the one you use when you step on someone's foot in the bus." He thus couldn't confess his wrong; he couldn't admit sin, because confession embarrassed people, and there 'was no such thing as sin: sin was a morbid concept . . . it would poison you entirely and you would go crazy." In the end, he concluded, he "had nothing to say, and sat like a man ready to be shot."[30]

In Merton's novel he was a man who never figured out right from wrong, never understood his conduct to be sinful, never admitted he was wrong. His real-life hero was Dr. Bennett, who truly became a substitute father figure, an intellectual sort who Merton admired for his irreverence and strong opinions. He was one whose taste for swashbuckling heroes like Hemingway and Picasso impacted how Merton felt about morals in general, and sexual conduct in particular. If Bennett thought these dashing men and their adventurous attitude toward women, complete with lack of respect for them and seeing them as no more than sexual conquests, was proper, then Merton believed likewise.

When Merton decided to become a barker at a pornographic sideshow at the World's Fair in Chicago, this was just part of the adventure, as was his visiting vulgar burlesque shows in New York when he was eighteen. This occurred in the company of an artist named Reginald Marsh, a friend of Owen's and another substitute father. Merton's view of life was to live it to the fullest, and from it Merton shed any inhibitions about sex, unusual for an English lad of the time. This permitted him to feel later that he was truly a real man, the "man of the world" his idol Tom Bennett promoted.[31]

Edward Rice's recollection that this "man of the world" frightened women by being too pushy as a way of not getting involved is pertinent to understanding Merton's reluctance to truly love.[32] Rice also noted Merton's reports of roaming with a Viennese whore he picked up in Hyde Park, the Hungarian woman he bedded while she taught him the language, and the endless string of "nubile, compliant girls" who adored him. He was a virtual Don Juan, if Rice—or Merton, for that matter—is to be believed.[33] The naughty mind Merton possessed as late as 1938, just three years before entering Gethsemani, is represented by his use of the word "cunt" in the August 11 letter to

Robert Lax.[34] Such language was glib and sassy, but certainly most disrespectful of women in general.

Merton the romantic troubadour certainly left a wide swath of women in his wake for a man who knew so little about loving and being loved. But the shallowness and sinfulness of the relationships obviously infiltrated his soul. Merton later wrote, it may be recalled, "I am aware of the foolish sin that has always nested in my nature . . . It is from this folly that I probably deserve all the bitterness that is in my life."[35] He was right.

CHAPTER SEVENTEEN

"WE ARE TERRIBLY
in LOVE"

Was it possible that Thomas Merton, the priest, the man dedicated to "God Alone," would scamper away from Gethsemani into the night and marry Margie Smith during the spring of 1966? Certainly the man of many contradictions strongly considered doing so.

As the month of May had appeared with warm temperatures and the sight and smell of colorful flowers at every turn, Merton was perplexed. One can only imagine the crosscurrents blazing through his mind with recurring thoughts of yesteryear and lost opportunities with women caused by mistakes for which he had never forgiven himself. Now he had another chance, a chance to truly love for the first time in his life. What an unexpected blessing. He must have viewed it as divine intervention.

Attempting to be realistic during a time of unparalleled bliss, Merton pondered the future. The day after the May 9 picnic, he decided Margie's idea of living in Louisville in August after graduation, purchasing a car, and driving out to see him once a week, was unworkable. This was due to limitations on his free time and his resistance to ask her to lead that type of life instead of marrying. But she said she refused to marry anyone but him.[1]

Still puzzled by the fresh love affair, Merton considered whether the couple should live together as if they were married. But, he recognized while milling about the hermitage as if in a daze, "the problems are appalling. Excommunication *fuga cum muliere* [flight with a woman] and all the hounds [will be] after me perpetually, from Dom James to the Roman Curia!"[2]

Merton, acting like a smitten teenager, questioned whether he was rational due to being obsessed with Margie and unable to concentrate on anything other than figuring out how to live with her the remainder of his life. This behavior was acceptable, he believed, since it stemmed from the feeling that he was not lacking fidelity to God by loving Margie since love emanated from the Father. Reading her beautiful letters over and over, he called them "cries of love out of the late night."[3]

Alive with the spark of love inside him, Merton turned to writing poetry to express his feelings. One titled "I Always Obey My Nurse," would later be published in *Eighteen Poems*. All the while, Merton was baring his soul, trusting the one he loved with secrets never revealed to anyone else. Although he felt she idealized him, he was pleased to make his true self known to her, and thankful she loved him despite personal characteristics he believed humiliating. As he gazed up at one of the tall pine trees near the hermitage, he was certain that he loved her the same way she loved him and that God approved. As a thunderstorm pounded in the distance, and a scared deer stood right in front of the hermitage porch, staring at him, he thought to himself, "I can only regard this as kind of miracle in my life. . . ."[4]

Merton called the affair beautiful. He wrote that "when we kiss each other our lips say everything—without any effort or any of the smokey wisdom of passion."[5] A visit to a physician in Louisville to receive a shot to treat bursitis in his left elbow provided an excuse to see Margie again. After a cozy lunch at Cunningham's Restaurant, where the couple held hands, exchanged vows of love, and "talked too freely about what we would like to do," Merton realized that he truly was blessed to find Margie. But the bubble of euphoria he had been experiencing finally burst when, nearly three months after Merton met her, he woke up in the middle of the night worried and anxious. While walking in the woods, he "saw clearly that it can't go on like this. I simply have no business being in love and playing around with a girl, however innocently." He admitted "it is simply a game. A fascinating, pleasurable exciting game that she plays perfectly and I have enjoyed it almost to ecstasy (Saturday again)." Wrestling with his conscience, he reminded himself of his vow of chastity and "though I have kept my vow, I wonder if I can keep it indefinitely and still play this gorgeous game." Progressing toward a decision he knew had to be made, he realized telling her the affair must end would be painful, but it would be better for both of them. He intended to inform her of his decision to break up, but planned to suggest they see each other from time to time. As he anguished over his decision and prayed to God for guidance, he called her "sweet" and admitted he would love her as long as he lived.[6]

His emotions flip-flopping by the hour as a rain glistened the countryside, Merton sat on the edge of the porch trying to dodge the uneven drops. He decided calling the romance a game was "in large part a shameful evasion." He blamed his having called it a game on having convinced himself he had to terminate the affair, even though he knew getting out of love was not easy. Upset at himself for playing with her emotions, he rushed to the abbey and called Margie twice, disturbing her on a day when he discovered she was quite lonely and terribly depressed.[7]

Potential exposure of the illicit affair continued to haunt Merton, but as the physical nature of the relationship intensified he was more concerned about his vow of chastity. Noting that "she wants me too," he decided that "a crude botched-up affair in the woods would be worse than nothing." Calling her love "the tenderest, simplest, sincerest thing that has ever come into my life," Merton feared not being able to "see each other" or "kiss each other" while recognizing "we are not the only ones in the world."[8]

On a beautiful day in late May, Margie was driven to Gethsemani in a light blue Ford by a fellow nurse. Passion intensified as the two lovers walked in the woods near the Vineyard Knobs, carrying picnic essentials, ice dripping from a paper bag she was holding. Hidden by the dense brush, they were completely alone. The two lovers ate sparingly of herring and ham, drank wine, read poetry, talked, and "mostly made love and love and love for five hours." When he considered the interlude later, which he swore had not included intercourse, he decided they had been too passionate, but rather than feeling guilt, he felt what they had done was "right." Back at the hermitage, with thoughts of her voluptuous figure still fresh in his mind, Merton concluded, "We now love with our whole bodies anyway and I have the complete feel of her being (except her sex) as completely me."[9]

Such ecstasy permitted Merton to connect with past relationships as he recognized he and Margie were "moving slowly toward a complete physical ripening of love, a leisurely preparation of our whole being, like the maturing of apples in the sun . . ." As he sorted through piles of books and papers searching for a favorite article about love, he suddenly realized he had never experienced this type of bliss before, since in his youth he had always been "too hurried." He decided this was why he had been unhappy, another lesson learned from the gift of Margie. His heart aflutter at every turn, Merton felt his love was slowly, gradually mounting with the vise of a deep, warm, sexual love inside him. He could feel the emotion flooding through his body, "shaking my whole being from the heart (not just genital excitation)—and it was as yet only a little!" Instead of feeling anguished and panicky, as he had with previous interludes, he felt pure, realizing that because of being close to her "my sexuality has been made real and decent again after years of rather frantic suppression . . . I feel less sick. I feel human."[10]

The picnic bliss refused to leave Merton's mind and it bothered him. He decided the affair was a foolish, dangerous game, and must stop. He began reading *The Last Gentleman* by Walker Percy while he waited for his fellow monks to sleep. Then he walked down the hill to the monastery and silently entered the cellarer's office like a thief in the night. He telephoned Margie and the couple agreed that whatever passion had been shared at the picnic had not been regrettable, but certainly contrary to what they had promised to resist and a strict violation of what their love was all about. Just before the call ended with duplicate promises of love, the two agreed that consummating the relationship would wreck the love they shared and they would have to break up. On the way back up the hill to his hermitage, he looked skyward for guidance, realizing that Margie, like him, was frightened by how intense the relationship had become.[11]

As May ended, Merton was frenzied as he attempted to sort out his feelings after a second secret interlude, where "we got ourselves quite aroused sexually" and he suffered "a great deal of confusions, anguish, indecision and nerves." He decided, "I *cannot* let this become a sexual affair, it would be disastrous for both of us." Placing at least part of the blame on Margie and her being "too curious . . . and too passionate for me (for her body to tell the truth was wonderful the other day, ready for the most magnificent love)," Merton, praying he could resist her, recalled more talks about the need for the love to be chaste. He was fearful of another meeting alone on the Gethsemani grounds, and told her it was unwise.[12]

Wary of temptation, Merton was relieved when Margie could not travel to Gethsemani and spend May 28 with him, despite beautiful weather. Expressing trepidation about the closeness they were experiencing in the woods, he noted there might be "too much stirring of sex." Condemning what had already occurred, he knew that any "full sexual consummation" was wrong and harmful, as was "the more or less 'licit' lovemaking we have indulged in."[13]

When he sat in the porch rocker and sorted out his feelings, Merton knew Margie was very lonely, upset, and on the verge of tears. He anguished over her anguish as he begged "God to forgive me and not to take away the gift of love He gave us." Alone in his hermitage with only the sound of crickets to keep him company, Merton relished her acceptance of him, her willingness to accept the worst in him.[14]

In June 1966, Merton looked back and acknowledged that in view of the love affair with Margie, he realized how much he had been loved in the past by girls whose names he could not recall. Bringing those thoughts forward, he did not believe Margie was obsessed with sex, but instead desired to be loved, a love that could include sex. He decided what was important was their union, and sex was only a sign of that love. Criticizing himself for his thought process, he felt he must stop making sex such a big deal and letting it cause him torment, since he wanted it so much but knew having sex was wrong. He hoped that he and Margie would not succumb to sex "in some messy, dishonest way!"[15]

Such fear did not diminish Merton's love for Margie or his acknowledgment that the affair was a learning experience for him. On an evening of deep thought about what had transpired, after he had watched the sun set over the tall trees next to the hermitage, he sat on the porch thinking solely of her. He concluded that while her love on the surface might appear to be some sort of enslavement, it was part of a special liberation that expanded far beyond feelings of affection and expression. But he decided whatever was right or wrong about the love affair, what was most important was for him to be himself, his true self, instead of his ideal self.

Armed with good intentions, self-assurance, and the confidence he was acting in tune with Christlike actions, Merton was thrilled to visit Margie at Cunningham's in Louisville. She looked lovely and full of joy in her light dress as her hair flew in the wind and her face shone with the look of love. He enjoyed the time they spent together, more than four hours. They "talked and loved and scarcely ate anything, but drank Chianti and read poems and loved and loved. . . . It was "simply perfect." The day after the interlude, he was "haunted and comforted by her womanliness, her sweetness, her hair, cheeks, neck, lips, her lovely look of love and surrender."[16]

When he had felt the eyes of others in the restaurant staring at them, Merton suddenly realized an unlikely truism: "[I am] a priest who has a woman." Telling himself the couple had done nothing wrong, even though others might disagree, in view of their "lovemaking . . . [stopping] short of complete sex," he decided to focus on establishing a warm and long lasting friendship where pure love could exist, so that neither he nor Margie would get hurt.[17]

Dedicated to this goal, and hopeful he could resist Margie's charms, Merton met with her on June 12 when they borrowed Dr. Wygal's Louisville office. Champagne brightened the afternoon togetherness. When Merton woke up the next day, it was "without self-hate or guilt but with the realization that something has to be done. We can't go on like this." During a telephone call, the two lovers discussed the idea of living together or marrying. When he carefully considered these alternatives, Merton believed both were ludicrous since social barriers would never permit the two to be together. More important, he finally admitted that he really was not that intent on marriage, and instead wanted to rededicate himself to his monastic vows.[18]

Fear of exposure struck suddenly in mid-June, when Brother Clement informed Merton that another brother had listened to one of Merton's calls to Margie and told Dom James. After praying for divine guidance, Merton decided to meet with the abbot and admit only the telephone calls, nothing else. When the two sat down to discuss Merton's transgression, the abbot was somewhat understanding. But the result was predictable, with Dom James calling for a complete breakup and forbidding Merton to see Margie again. When Dom James suggested writing Margie to end the affair, Merton objected, believing the idea fraught with potential disaster for everyone concerned as he had no idea how Margie might react. Following the meeting, Merton felt alienated from the monastic community, realizing that when he looked at the abbot's secretary, the monk looked away in embarrassment. The gatehouse brother now smiled all too politely, and Merton concluded he was now "known as a monk in love with a woman." Stung by the abbot's reprimand, Merton spent the night wide awake in his rocking chair trying to make sense of whether the abbot truly understood the repercussions caused by his order. He believed that while Dom James could relate to Merton's suffering and perhaps even understand that he was "half dead . . . all covered with blood, that I have been nearly ruined, that I am in terrible shape, etc. etc," the abbot was clueless as to Margie's suffering.[19]

Estranged from Margie, Merton longed for her love on a lovely afternoon when he walked on the grassy hillsides with tears splashing down his face. When he looked at the puffy clouds overhead, he swore the essence of her love was within them. He was upset when the abbot refused to give him a letter from her. Philosophizing later at the hermitage, Merton, seeking some sense of reality about the affair, looked to the teachings of Buddha: "In order to untie a knot you must first find out how the knot was tied." Meandering through the woods, alone with his thoughts, he suddenly sensed a whiff of freedom. Sorting through his emotions, Merton, his face reflecting his soft tone, talked of loving Margie in a different manner, one filled with peace and no disturbance of inner tension. As darkness hovered over his simple dwelling, Merton decided "once again I am *all here*."[20]

I n mid-June, spurred on by memories of the passionate interlude with Margie in Dr. Wygal's Louisville office, upset over the confrontation with Dom James, and angry over the abbot's order banning him from seeing his true love, Merton sat alone in his hermitage amidst the sounds of the birds, the squirrels, and the bees. He set about creating a lengthy diary spanning 32 single-spaced pages—in all nearly 23,000 words, each one typed with love. Merton titled it "A Midsummer Diary for M." Described as "part journal, part love letter," it portrayed Merton as Margie's lover: "passionate, tender, vulnerable, melancholy, full of longing, lonely, confused, and anguished." Before presenting it to her, Merton told her of the abbot's edict: "You will not try to contact her in any way whatsoever, anywhere, either by phone, by letter, etc., etc. You will never go to that hospital again."[21]

Merton delivered a handwritten note to Dom James addressing his concerns about the affair. He told the abbot the whole matter was painful for each of them, and that he was not excusing his conduct since he had been wrong. But he said he hoped "this business" was over and that he could resume living like a hermit. If the abbot had doubts Merton said he could build a fence around the hermitage and promise he would stay inside the fence at night. He closed by writing "please accept my sincere apologies and please don't blame others for my faults I beg you."[22]

Despite the promises of good conduct, "this business" was not over. Merton felt Margie's presence everywhere as he gazed into the starry skies while sweeping the porch or doing dishes. He decided all the feelings of love and sorrow in him were summed up by Joan Baez's song "Silver Dagger." Believing the song symbolized their love, he admitted an obsession with the lyrics. Later, he told Margie they were one voice where your "womanness blends with the man I am, and we are one being." This emotion permitted the two to complete each other even though they could no longer embrace. During a moment of reflection, he decided love was nothing to be understood because it was a combination of joy and then sorrow, but perhaps more joy.[23]

A June 18 visit from his friends Victor and Carolyn Hammer, who had both attempted to dissuade him from continuing the affair, prompted Merton to realize any sustained love with Margie was on one level an impossibility, and on another, pure fact. Deep in the night he reached a conclusion: "We cannot see each other, we cannot meet, we cannot hold each other, we cannot bring our lips together and cling to each other warmly, helplessly, in a long embrace. That is all over." But Merton still believed he could be only half a person without his true love. He told Margie that unless he was with her always, he would never be able to live alone. He felt incomplete without her and told her he could not even be a true hermit without her in his life.[24]

During the third week of June, after having read Albert Camus's *Sisyphus* and being bored with it, Merton backslid toward the days of old when he drank too much. After drinking some wine he had hidden from his superiors, he fell and hurt his back, his arms, and his legs, but was not sorry for himself. Instead he thought he might sleep if he could only quit thinking about Margie's body. After complaining about a lack of sleep (four hours one night), Merton wrote of how intense the relationship was: The two were "fast learning every aspect, every inch of each other. . . ." Wiping a tear from his eye, he decided "that if we had only had a chance, we could have grown magnificently into a beautiful dual organism of love." Merton was certain the abbot would never come between them, because they shared secrets more beautiful than any wedding ring or other symbol of union. Only God, he believed, understood their love.[25]

Attacking himself for his actions, Merton decided he not been a good monk or a good lover. This left Margie, he believed, confused and in pain, because no one could fall in love without experiencing pain. Merton wondered whether he was supposed to live the absurd life of a hermit when he was not truly a hermit. He questioned whether he should live as a writer when he was not certain he wanted to write anymore. Merton prayed to God for strength to live without Margie. On a scorching hot day when walking in the woods was akin to stepping into a furnace, he decided he wanted Margie to move on, to love and marry another.[26]

Perhaps it was this mindset that caused Merton to again write Dom James regarding his feelings. He told the abbot not to worry about him, that a "clean break" was the solution, because he was more clear about what he had to do. He promised Dr. Wygal would help him since he shared the abbot's view of the affair. Merton maintained he was not suffering from loneliness—"certainly not as much as you think I am." He believed solitude and his vocation were the answers as he faced temptation with the view that anything worthwhile must be tested. He closed by thanking Dom James for everything.[27]

The diary dedicated to Margie was now ready for delivery. But with three days left in June, Dr. Wygal warned him about continuing the affair during a trip they took off the grounds of Gethsemani. But Merton ignored him, and when they visited a liquor store Merton called Margie. Wygal told Merton he was on "a collision course."[28] But Merton could not bear to be away from his true love and deliberately violated Dom James's edict, and his words of promise in letters to him, by inviting Margie to meet him at Dr. Wygal's office in Louisville. Merton was angry when he learned Wygal had answered a telephone plea for help from Margie by telling her to leave Merton alone. Margie, who was distraught over learning her fiancé might be missing in action in Vietnam (later she told Merton, "N. is safe in Vietnam—landed in the jungle and got back to his own side."), disregarded Wygal's advice, but when Merton saw her, "she was trembling like a leaf in the elevator." They sat down and he gave her the diary. Wygal's hostility toward Margie not withstanding, at lunch the two lovers fell into each other's arms in desperation, "kissing each other over and over, swept with love and loss. In it, knowing it would probably never be like that again."[29]

Sixteen days later, on July 12, Merton remembered "her body, her naked ness, the day at Wygal's, and it haunts me." He admitted that at the base of his soul that what he had "really secretly planned was to have her as a kind of mistress while I continued to live as a hermit. Could anything be more dishonest?" He was spared a discussion about the possibility when Margie did not visit Gethsemani after all.[30] To him, the decision to end the relationship was final, but was it?

Besieged with doubt as to the right course of action, Merton, at the insistence of Dom James, sought the advice of Father John Eudes in early July. Father Eudes called the visit a consultation, not a confession.[31] Father Eudes cautioned Merton for his susceptibility to "self-defeating programs as a way of life" and suggested Merton be "more self-critical and more self-disciplined and to "take into account [his] need to create and exploit the relationship with the young lady." The straightforward advice caused Merton feelings of loss and deception without understanding exactly what he was experiencing. He wondered if he had been a fool to end the relationship.[32]

On a mid-July morning, one of the hottest days of the summer, Merton drove around drinking beer with Jim Wygal. To Merton's annoyance, the doctor told him of his negative opinion of Margie, and that she was "narcissistic, selfish, is not really capable of loving" Merton. No matter; Merton's love would never be abated. He believed Dr. Wygal was too tough on Margie and that he did not recognize the real love she had for him. When Merton told Wygal he wanted to call Margie, "Jim would not cooperate at all."[33]

Temptation was apparently too strong. Despite the edict from the abbot and discouragement from Dr. Wygal, Merton picnicked at Cherokee Park in Louisville with Margie on a hot, dry July 16. The couple kissed and loved each other passionately, and Margie clung to his body with true love and warmth even though she was tired. Merton admitted that he was too passionate, and in a way he thought unfair since at "one point she was getting worked up and so was I." Margie, Merton believed, was certain he loved God, but to the contrary, Merton wished he did as much as she believed he did. But her observation did not quell the bliss of the moment, with Merton recalling, "As I kissed her she kept saying, 'I am happy, I am at peace now!' And so was I."[34]

Two days before the end of July, Linda Parsons, a friend of Merton's visited. Dom James reprimanded Merton for being intoxicated on the scalding hot afternoon and for taking an unauthorized swim at Dom Frederic's lake, another violation of monastic rules. Worse, to his dismay, Merton was told by Parsons that superiors thought he was "an *enfant terrible* who by some fluke wrote a best-seller."[35] Such a disclosure must have muddled a mind more confused as the days passed, but Merton let the comment slide since breaking up with Margie was once again on his mind. He sent her a letter the day before her graduation from nursing school telling her good-bye. Immediately, he regretted it. He was tormented, and later, unable to sleep. He was mad at everyone in general, the abbot in particular, and the world at large.[36]

Flip-flopping from one day to the next as to whether the torrid affair was truly over, Merton also agonized over the behavior of Dom James when they met on August 5. Merton presented a lecture about spiritual morality and felt the abbot was mocking him when he suggested he should write a book on how hermits get to heaven. To get even, Merton shocked the abbot by shouting, "When the baby is born you can be its godfather!" A "slight shadow crossed Dom James' face and he laughed with less enthusiasm" wondering if Merton was serious. Later, Merton decided, "we are a pair of damn cats."[37]

Nevertheless, Merton could not quit thinking about Margie. He concluded she was "a living and suffering question mark."[38]

Dom James was so concerned over Merton's behavior that he demanded Merton discontinue his medical visits to St. Joseph's Hospital in Louisville and instead receive care in Lexington. In a midsummer 1966 letter to the abbot, Merton informed him that "the person who had created the problem" had moved and would not be returning. He also told him there was no one who knew of the special nature of the relationship, and that Margie would not divulge it to anyone, especially since she was far away. "In any case," Merton wrote, "she is engaged to a boy in Chicago. I just think there is no problem anymore."[39] But there was, with Merton acknowledging that deception had crept into his life and delusion threatened an entry.

With his freedom to see Margie or to communicate with her in any way cut off by Dom James, Merton again targeted his anger at the abbot. Merton questioned his character, his prejudices, and his background, noting he was "the very incarnation of New England middle-class, efficiency-loving, thrifty, crafty, operating, sanctimonious religiosity."[40] Merton decided to express his dissatisfaction to the abbot in another letter that summer. Addressing it to "Dear Rev. Father," Merton criticized the abbot's controlling authority and his struggle with "suspicion, half-baked reports and distorted suggestions." These, Merton believed, slanted the abbot's viewpoint and inflamed his mind because he wanted to be in control. Regarding Margie, he told the abbot he wanted to protect the rights of his friend and asked for respect in doing so. He again promised the affair was over and that no further trouble would ensue. He said there would be no "sinister underground activities" at the hermitage and the abbot could check on this if he wished to do so.[41]

A week later, Merton lamented having not being able to see Margie on her graduation day. When they finally talked, he was choked up with emotions. Though it was a relief to hear her voice, he was troubled and disturbed when he arrived back at the lonely hermitage after a visit to Dr. Wygal's home. He had been uncomfortable while looking at copies of *Playboy* while at Dr. Wygal's and was disgusted with the "whorehouse mentality" of the magazine.[42]

Feeling guilty about the affair, Merton wrote an August 7, 1966, letter to Dom James. He promised to work hard on his "problem" and avoid any temptations to smuggle letters or make illegal telephone calls. Merton assured the abbot that the "source of trouble" was in the past and when in Louisville, he would not frequent friend's homes. These actions, he decided, would cure any difficulties and permit return to a friendly relationship with Margie.[43]

Nearly seven months into the love affair, Merton prayed for guidance as he gazed upward and pleaded to know God's will for him. He wondered whether he should stay at Gethsemani and be devoted to the blessings of solitude or let his personal affections dictate the future. Summing up conflicted feelings, Merton concluded, "I see that I am floundering around in the dark . . . And that it is true that this summer I have done some very foolish and dangerous things."[44]

CHAPTER EIGHTEEN

"MARGIE LOVES YOU *and* WILL ALWAYS LOVE YOU"

Among all of the questions surrounding Thomas Merton's love affair with Margie Smith, it is easy to lose sight of what pulled these two people together: a magical moment in time when they met and shared true love with an intensity that surprised them both. If there is such a thing as love at first sight, it occurred between Merton and Margie. As the love affair blossomed, Merton could not forget the special nature of the moments they shared during the initial stages of the relationship, especially the spark between them after Margie had comforted his body with the sponge bath in the dimly lit Louisville hospital room on March 31, 1966. He learned she was from Cincinnati and that her father was an artist. Margie knew who he was because she had read *The Sign of Jonas*. She said she mostly enjoyed the book, but found some parts troubling. They talked of *Mad Magazine* and the characters, including Snoopy, in the "Peanuts" cartoon strip. Her black hair shone brightly in the light and he noticed her pale skin, "almost almond eyes," and the beauty of her face.[1]

During Margie's subsequent visit, after a weekend had passed, they laughed about more silly things in *Mad Magazine*. She asked him about what it was like to be a hermit, and whether this was what he wanted in life. He lent her his draft of the preface for the Japanese edition of *Thoughts in Solitude*, which included the line, "Love is not a problem, not an answer to a question.

It is the ground of all, and questions arise only insofar as we are divided, absent, estranged, alienated from that ground." Phrases also included were "Love remains the ground of history," and "One disappears in Love in order to 'be Loved.'"[2] Based on an interview with Margie about the preface, Michael Mott concluded, "She had a lot of questions . . . especially what he said on the hermit's life—he couldn't be a hermit."[3] This revelation gave her the impression he was seeking a companion, perhaps even someone to love.

If Margie had read Merton's words in the original version of *Thoughts on Solitude,* she would have been certain of his desire to find someone to love based on a chapter titled, "Love and Need: Is Love a Package or a Message?" In it he conveyed his feeling that the concept of falling in love could be described like water collecting in pools, lakes, rivers, and oceans. One could, he believed, either fall into the water or walk around it. He compared love to falling in the water, where one was forced to swim and even those who failed to do so and did not discover love were still blessed. Merton believed falling in love reflected a special attitude toward love and life, one that was fearsome, awe-inspiring, fascinating, and confusing. When one loved, many emotions surfaced, including suspicion and doubt. In love, he concluded, a person lost himself and fell into the swimming pool. They might get hurt, but only after being foolish and vulnerable. The end result: "Love is, in fact, an intensification of life, a completeness, a fullness, a wholeness of life." Merton spoke of life, and thus love, never stepping on a straight line but one with curves of intensity. He concluded no one was fully human until they surrendered to another in love. He cautioned that surrendering was not just about sex, but about giving to the other "total love." This included, he believed, a capacity for sharing, for mutual care, and for spiritual awareness. Conclusion: "Love is our destiny."[4]

These revealing comments from *Thoughts in Solitude*'s Japanese edition about love were written in mid-March 1966, days before Merton met Margie at the hospital in Louisville. He kept revising the text until mid-April, less than two weeks after he met her.[5] One may only imagine the impact any of these poignant thoughts must have had on a 25-year-old, woman in the company of the famous Thomas Merton. Margie's heart must have been bursting with excitement over the possibility Merton might seek, with her, the very love he wrote about.

Two days later, unable to contain her emotions, Margie stopped by his hospital room before she left work for the day. She had discarded her nurse's uniform and was wearing a dress and raincoat, her hair flowing freely. Merton, smiling as if the sun had visited his room, and calling her "Margie" as she called him "Thomas," requested she inscribe her name in his notebook, along with an address to which he could send some of his writings. Bold and impetuous, Margie asked Merton if she could visit him at Gethsemani, but he quickly said that would be impossible. A bit hurt, perhaps, at the refusal, she announced she had plans to travel to Chicago for the Easter holiday to see her fiancé. How Merton took this news of a love in her life was never noted, but it must have dented his high spirits to think she loved another. Before leaving the hospital, the dazed Merton, lying still to ease the pain in his back, left Margie a letter indicating that she could write to him in confidence by noting "Conscience Matter" on the envelope. He mentioned his need for friendship and encouraged her to write.[6]

When she did, on Tuesday, April 19, 1966, the lighthearted Merton recalled opening the envelope in the quiet of the infirmary and discovering a four-page letter accompanied by a drawing of Snoopy's doghouse, symbolizing Merton's hermitage. Snoopy was stretched out with the balloon commentary, "It's nice to have a friend." Just 20 days after meeting her, Merton replied with a declaration of love. He telephoned Margie to request that she meet him a week later when he traveled to Louisville for a checkup at the Medical Arts Building. Did he envision a chance to put into practice all he had learned about love? His mind must have been stirring with thoughts of doing so. Merton must have also believed that the Holy Spirit was blessing him, for here, right before his eyes, was the perfect partner with whom to test his capacity to truly fall in love for the first time in his life. That he already cared deeply for her was evidenced by his disappointment when he learned she was traveling to Chicago: "I was so terribly lonely, and lay awake half the night, tormented by the gradual realization that we were in love and I did not know how I could live without her."[7]

If Merton was hooked, Margie had questions about the budding love affair he apparently never knew about. Before Margie was to meet with Merton after his checkup, shocked by the suddenness of his affection, she consulted with a priest, who told her she should stop the romance at once. (Alarmingly, the priest apparently made advances toward her before she scurried out of the meeting, amazed at the turn of events.)[8] Margie then entered the Medical Arts Building "like Joan of Arc, ready to do battle with the world, inwardly terrified." Merton had attempted to calm her by showing her a lengthy poem he had written, titled "With the World in My Bloodstream."[9]

When he had time to reflect on their private interlude, he remembered being captivated with Margie's youth and beauty. They hugged and kissed like newlyweds even though they had just begun to love each other. At the Derby Day Louisville Airport meeting in May, just two months into the affair, Merton noted her spunk and fresh zest for life. He took her photograph. Later, New Directions publisher James Laughlin, one of those present along with the lovers, said he "found her very Catholic, very much a lady, very pretty. He had been moved by her obvious love for Merton, while he sensed her distress."[10] Regardless, the love affair zoomed forward toward the fall months with increased intensity.

Memories of the early days of the romance must have been dancing in Merton's head as the calendar turned to September 1966. But one day in particular stood out causing Merton to admit, "The past is what it is and I cannot really regret anything in it except what my conscience sincerely regrets—the day in Wygal's office." Merton never divulged exactly what had occurred in the psychiatrist's Louisville office on September 4, but to calm himself, he had walked deep into the Gethsemani woods near Dom Frederic's lake four days after the office interlude. Guilt crept into his mind and he decided he had been wrong in the first place to ever send the first love letter and set a time to meet.[11]

The stillness of the woods provided a place where Merton could join his feelings for Margie and for God and recall His "gift to me—her love—and the way that love (against all that the books say) seemed to bring me (and still does) closer to them." As he sat quietly on the hillside grass across the road from the hermitage warming himself in the sunlight, he questioned whether the concept that loving God and another human being were necessarily in conflict with what he perceived to be God's perfect love. While Merton walked at a slow, reflective pace, stopping occasionally to pick up a brightly colored leaf, or touch an overhanging branch, an aura of holiness caught his attention. He admitted later that night that any step toward a "fully involved erotic and sexual love for [Margie]—completely fulfilled and frequently so" would affect his life and vocation as never before. This was because he knew the loving affection he had for her—"with the explicit *sacrifice* of sex and of erotic satisfaction"—was more in harmony with God's love than against it.[12] Did Merton's words mean no consummation of the relationship had occurred?

Confused as to what lay ahead, Merton, while lauding the beauty of the countryside near his hermitage, read his journal to discover whether he could make sense of the affair. With mist in his eyes, he recalled how lonely he had been during the first days after he met Margie. He had missed her so. Continuing to reflect, Merton, after passing by a huge wooden cross erected just outside the hermitage, decided he and Margie had been crazy to continue the love affair despite "the evening at the airport and the picnic at Derby Day—I have never experienced such ecstasies of erotic love (except on other days with her)." Without providing any details as to what eroticism had occurred and whether this meant the two had sex, he then questioned his stability and whether he had been dishonest during the relationship. Merton, with a cup of steaming coffee beside him at his work table, decided that he and Margie were really "messed-up people." After glancing over his left shoulder at the bookcase tucked neatly into the cement block and peeking at a wooden cross on the wall, he faced the fact that they could do each other significant harm.[13]

Concluding that he needed to spell out his commitment to being a hermit, he arose early on September 8 as the birds were slowly awakening, and walked down the uneven path to the abbey. There he surprised Dom James with a sacred vow of sorts. It read:

> I Brother M. Louis Merton, solemnly professed monk of the Abbey of Our Lady of Gethsemani, having completed a year of trial in the solitary life hereby make my commitment to spend the rest of my life in solitude in so far as my health may permit.

The vow was signed: "Made in the presence of Rt. Rev. Dom M. James Fox, Abbott of Gethsemani, September 8, 1966."[14] If Merton kept his word, God had won the battle with Margie. But had he?

The drama escalated. September 10 was a day of separation, with Merton enjoying late walks through the woods. When it was time to record his thoughts for the day, he posted a journal entry just after dusk. Believing his declaration to be a hermit the remainder of his life significant, the 51-year-old Merton decided this was the end of his struggle and his selfish hold on Margie. He spoke of still loving her, but no longer craving her.[15] He believed he could end the affair without anyone getting hurt.

Merton's decision to end the romance did not prevent him from admitting he thought of her constantly while enduring X-rays of his sore back, or from calling her after the X-rays were completed. During the conversation, Margie was surprised by Merton's interest in Bob Dylan's song "Just Like a Woman." But more surprising, especially for a man who had earlier decided his break with her was final, was the fact that they talked about their mutual love still running deep. When he returned to Gethsemani and sat on the porch, he recalled the essence of their talk as cheerful and friendly, and quite affectionate. Three days later, he felt guilty about the call.[16]

Merton also considered the symbolism of thoughts he had the day he traveled through Cincinnati's train station in 1941 toward Gethsemani. He recalled passages in Proverbs 8: "And my delights were to be with the children of men." He connected those words with feelings in his heart "between [Margie] and the 'Wisdom' figure—and Mary—and the Feminine in the Bible—Eve, etc.—Paradise—wisdom." He called the connection "mysterious, haunting, deep, lovely, moving, transforming!"[17]

Thoughts of Margie once again mingled in Merton's mind when he received a September 17 letter from "Sister K.," apparently a friend of Margie's in Louisville. The letter described Margie's reaction to one of Merton's previous letters. Sister K.'s letter provides rare insight and understanding concerning Margie's feelings about the love affair.

> Had you seen her expressive little face while reading her letter you would have been amply rewarded for your thoughtful efforts to reach her. She was ecstatic. She is well, looking her usual lovely little self. . . . Sensitive to the tremendous gift that is hers, aware of your powerful love and all it means to her as a woman, grateful to your leading her closer to God; to your every token of communication.
>
> You know her experience overwhelms her. The irony is that she discovers love and is in love with the impossible. . . . Woman is meant to be a 'Yes.' Not to live with that 'yes' in its fullness with the one she loves is something only God can understand. . . . You are saving, in your love and suffering, the one you love. She is charged with your love; you're not denying her its greatest significance nor are you being denied it. She loves you and will always love you. . . .[18]

Four days later, Merton recorded his recollections of a dream he had about Margie. She was swimming in one of the lakes, but he was fearful of jumping in to join her. He saw her wading in the water looking quite inconsolable and very much alone. He wanted to join her, even if he had to take off his habit and be naked. But he swiftly backtracked when one of his fellow monks showed up. He woke up in true distress.[19]

Although he had sworn to leave Margie alone, Merton contacted her in late September when the sky was gray and rainy, and fog cast a shadow over the landscape. She wanted to see him, but it was impossible. Feeling lonely without her, he allowed his strong emotions to spill onto the page that evening after a light supper. He knew he still loved her with his whole being and that she likewise loved him. He called the affair, besieged by conflicting emotions, true love nonetheless. But he knew in his heart there was no hope the two could be together.[20]

In early October, Merton, after learning a gas heater might be installed in the hermitage, received a beautiful letter from Margie, one sweet and warm in tone and filled with love. As he sat in a porch rocker while colored leaves sifted toward the ground and a chipmunk paid him a visit, he read the letter with moist eyes. Margie told him the happiest she had ever been was when she cared for him in the hospital. She explained that not being with him wasn't as difficult as not being able to give him anything except her thoughts and prayers. Sobbing at her words, he read that she felt he kept her, guarded her, and protected her in all ways. She told him her belief that they had been given to each other to love with no holding back, with complete abandon. She said his love sustained her.[21] When Merton finished reading, he tilted his head back and cried and cried. Had he made the right decision to give her up?

Deaths of brother monks around him consumed Merton's thoughts for a time. On a visit to Louisville, he walked into the Brown Hotel bar in mid-afternoon, drank a bottle of beer, and tried to finish a letter to Margie. A visit from peace activist Father Daniel Berrigan brightened Merton's spirits before he traveled to Louisville again for a doctor's appointment and was able to see Margie for a short time. When he returned to his hermitage he felt a sense of peace about him. The moon was full as he sat on the edge of the porch and thought about his love. He realized that for the first time since the month of April, the affair was less intense, providing some sense of freedom. Thinking further, he concluded there was no logic to believing he could ever discover happiness by loving Margie or any other woman. To convince himself he was not meant to love anyone, he decided on the final day of October, two days before a heavy snowstorm blanketed Gethsemani and the surrounding valley, that Margie was really "a mixed-up person with many conflicting trends." Beating her up even more, he concluded she was selfish and conflicted and too spontaneous with whatever interest she had at the moment. But a few days later, Merton had changed course once again and concluded that "[Margie] and I are so much, in so many ways, Eve and Adam."[22]

Merton's confused mind suddenly switched gears again in mid-November, eight months into the forbidden love affair. Having for the most part rid his mind of Margie, he received a letter from her in which she reiterated her love for him. He concluded that the two were, in a "strange way," already married. Dressed in overalls, denim jacket, and a wool cap, Merton walked through the silent snow, trying to make sense of her emotions. When he returned to the warmth of the hermitage and sat at his work table, stunned by the roller-coaster ride of his mind, he realized that neither could withstand the pressure marriage involved. He knew they both knew it, despite their mutual love. Discovering hidden strength that surprised him, he decided he must renew his vow of hermitude and not even think of doing something that would destroy his monastic community, and himself and Margie as well. The same night, as a full moon began to materialize, Merton received a visit from a priest who had left his diocese to get married. Merton thought the man was strained, looking and acting like a tired salesman. Asked his advice, Merton encouraged the man, who would soon be a father—a development that must have triggered thoughts in Merton's mind as to what he would have done if Margie had been pregnant with his child.[23]

On a gray afternoon, when heavy snow was in the forecast, the day was brightened when folk singer Joan Baez[24] and her mentor, Ira Sandperl, arrived to visit the hermitage. She was a pillar of hope for the peace movement Merton advocated, but it had been reminders of her song "Silver Dagger" that glued him and Margie together at 1:30 each morning, when she left work at the hospital and he lay awake thinking of her. Merton never mentioned this to Baez, but he noticed that when she met Dom James, there was an instant dislike on her part. At the hermitage, they played one side of her new record, ate goat-milk cheese and honey, and drank tea. Merton later described her as very forthright, with purity of heart, "a precious, authentic, totally human person," and as a true saint regarding the peace movement.[25]

Baez's recollections of the visit were vivid. She recalled that Merton had craved a hamburger and milkshake, and how, after sneaking him out of the monastery, she laughed when he sat in a field and enjoyed both. Baez said Merton produced a "secret" bottle of whiskey at his hermitage and drank with

Sandperl until the two were "pie-eyed." She said they resembled "two old Russ-
ian convicts." Baez recalled that Merton had "a wonderful sense of longing"
for Margie, to the extent of being ready to take an airplane to see her if necessary. Baez said she wasn't surprised, since he was "in love, or close to that."
She concluded that "watching him drinking and in love showed how the greats
are human, too." Baez said Sandperl egged Merton on as to whether he wanted
to see Margie. When he finally admitted he did, she and Sandperl readied
themselves for a 90-mile drive in the pouring rain to Cincinnati. Merton was
disappointed when Margie was unavailable.[26]

When Baez later discovered Merton and Margie's special love song was
"Silver Dagger," she was surprised. After some thought, she suggested that to
Merton the lyrics, "Don't sing your love song, you'll wake my mother . . . in
her right hand is a silver dagger . . . she says I can't be your bride," may have
referred to the Catholic Church ("Mother") forbidding the love affair. She
also agreed that the lyrics "chains five miles long" may have resonated with
Merton because of his feeling like a prisoner at Gethsemani.[27]

After the Baez visit, Merton admitted he was lonely for Margie. James
Laughlin, Merton's publisher at New Directions, knew the close bond between the two lovers during this time since Margie wrote to Laughlin telling
him Merton never realized "how much he had meant to her." Laughlin sent
her a copy of the published version of *Eighteen Poems* along with a note saying, "You were as close to him as any mortal person can be. He always spoke
to me of you with the deepest affection and gratitude for what you brought
to his life."[28]

Merton's feelings paralleled Margie's; he realized he still loved her deeply
and knew she still loved him. Loneliness was his bedmate as he ruminated
about the "deep, permanent value of our love. And also its complicatedness."[29]

As 1967, Merton's 52nd year, and 26th at Gethsemani, slid into view, he was
determined to change his lifestyle amidst a continuing whirlpool of confusion. On the warm and rain-soaked first day of the new year, when it was not
necessary to break the ice in the rain barrel so his bird friends could drink, he
told himself something he thought he already knew, that a radical change in
the relationship was demanded. Even though he experienced a "dark, depressed
day," one filled with anguish, he was hopeful when he retired to bed late at
night. A few days later, a clearly frustrated Merton, enduring the pain of splin-
ters in his hands incurred while chopping wood, vented not toward Margie or

himself but toward Dom James. He called him and Father John Eudes the "Abbot-Psychiatrist combination," believing they were part of some sort of tyranny, a "deadly business." At night, he noted Dom James's "totally repellent, sickening mentality, emotionalism, . . . and the *ludicrousness* of it." Pressing the thought as he glared down at his desk, Merton decided Dr. Wygal was right about the abbot. He was indeed pathological.[30]

Despite intentions to the contrary, Merton was unable to leave Margie alone, calling her during the third week of January from a gas station near Bardstown. Both were "glad" they spoke, but Merton's anger showed shortly thereafter, when Dom James denied him permission to visit France to attend a Legion of Honor award ceremony for a monk friend. On the 28th, Margie was once again on Merton's mind with his admitting being lonely for her and "troubled and wanting to write to her, wanting to hear from her, wanting to see her."[31]

In early February, Merton visited Louisville on a brisk, windy day and attempted to contact Margie, but was unable to. He knew he was being foolish, and should stop writing letters and making telephone calls. After he returned to the hermitage, he realized he had experienced an illusion with Margie. He wondered whether either of them had been truly happy. He decided the love had been real, but deceptive and an illusion at the same time. He felt as if he were immersed in an unhappy dream. Two days later, Merton, reflective as the days passed without Margie in his life, concluded the affair had shown him he could never be the person who did not know or love "in a deep, mysterious way, because we gave ourselves to each other almost as if we were married."[32]

Although Merton had decided finally and forever that being with Margie was impossible, he still thought about her as he threw stale breadcrumbs on the porch for the cardinals and mockingbirds, or small, white-footed mice who ambled by to say hello. On the second day of March, he called her and they had a warm conversation. She considered visiting him, but in his heart he knew the love affair was over and that there was little reason to keep going. He missed her, he knew, but reality was staring him in the face. Humbled and confused by his human weakness and continued passion, he succumbed to temptation and called Margie five days later while he was in Louisville. But on the ride home, as rain pelted the car, he was sorry he had done so. In the quiet of the late night, he sipped coffee and chewed on an apple as he wrote about his inability to free himself from her loving ways, while admitting Margie needed to be with a man and that although she was destined to be married, he was not.[33]

In late March 1967, as temperatures warmed enough to permit leafy buds to appear on the trees, Merton, following his hour of meditation, walked through the woods at a weak pace, thinking about how he was still in love with Margie but that it was hopeless. Eight days later, as spring weather began in earnest, he sat stoically on a porch rocker, reminiscing about the first anniversary of his having met Margie in the Louisville hospital. He recalled how she had called him her patient.[34]

In early April Merton appeared to spring to life like the grass and plants all around him as he admitted a great deal had gone wrong in his life. He wasn't certain how this had occurred, since no one factor came to mind. But he knew one thing for certain: his falling in love so deeply was not a cause but an effect, one resulting "from roots that had simply lain dormant since I entered the monastery," an indication that distasteful memories from his experiences with women in early adulthood had never been cleansed from his soul. Memories still possessing his mind as rain finally fell and lightning flashed northwest of Gethsemani, Merton visited the picnic table where he and Margie had enjoyed a sensual interlude one year earlier. He relished the memory, but was certain his actions had been against God's wishes. His closeness with Margie had rendered him helpless to resist her warm body, and he was thankful God had saved him from what he believed would have been a real mess. The more Merton considered the extent of the love affair, the more he was convinced that while he cherished her love, he was upset with the mutual untruths he believed prevailed in the relationship even though he could not pinpoint exactly what they were. As the embers in the fireplace dimmed one evening, he thought of how difficult marriage must be.[35]

In late April, Merton telephoned Margie from the Brown Hotel in Louisville as traffic snarled in the streets. They chatted about simple things, but more important, about whether she was going to marry. He believed she did not truly love her fiancé, but could make him happy. She surprised him by saying she was "sort a of masochist, which made it all worse," an ambiguous statement he could not clearly understand. When he returned to the hermitage, he swore he would leave her alone even though he wanted to call her again. Under the light of the crookneck desk lamp, he decided loneliness was his bedfellow and he should accept it as such.

But could he, or was he going to suddenly decide to leave the hermitage and flee with Margie? Intent on doing the right thing in God's eyes, he said a Mass for her and her fiancé, and prayed that they would truly fall in love and marry because he was convinced that any true love between him and Margie was over. Certain that he had crossed a barrier in terminating any future romantic relationship with Margie, Merton wrote on April 22, "So in a way it is liberation day—and I have made up my mind to be what I am supposed to be (Finally!)." In early May, another milestone occurred in Merton's quest to end the relationship. As he burned some brush while a masked raccoon watched from nearby, he recounted the passion of a romantic interlude in the woods with Margie, but suddenly realized his being away from her permitted him to feel "peace, silence, freedom of heart, no care, quiet joy."[36]

Merton decided in mid-May that his journals must not be published until 25 years after his death. But he wanted to be clear about one thing: "I have no intention of keeping the [Margie] business out of sight." Issuing an order he knew would not be read for many years to come, Merton noted that he wanted to be completely open about his life, including his mistakes and his effort to make sense of his life. Drawing his feelings to a close before extinguishing the lights, he added, "The affair with [Margie] is an important part of it—and shows my limitations as well as a side of me that is—well, it needs to be known too, for it is part of me."

As October neared, complete with the metamorphosis of the trees' color change, Merton was continually reflective, alternating thoughts of distaste for Dom James with sprinklings of depression about the world at large. He was denied permission to travel to Chile, extending what he believed to be his imprisonment at Gethsemani. When he sat at his work table after a supper of pinto beans, applesauce, and coffee, he knew he was subject to mood swings as he tried each day to rid himself of the temptation of Margie. Had he finally done so, or would he become weak and rush to her side to prevent her marriage to a man he knew she did not truly love?[37]

CHAPTER NINETEEN

MARGIE *or* GOD

"The other day I called [Margie]. . . . —first time in months . . . It was sad . . . and in the end she was crying."[1] The mid-November 1967 telephone call to Margie, who had decided to move to Miami, rekindled Merton's longing for his true love. He sat by Dom Frederic's lake and tried to make sense of the conversation. He recalled her having suggested he ought to reach for happiness, but he realized he could not be happy living with a woman and causing disaster for everyone involved.[2]

Winding down toward his moment of truth, when he would finally, and for certain, decide between Margie and God, Thomas Merton appeared to have decided on the latter. Letting go of the woman he truly loved was not easy, and Merton struggled with emotions that changed on a daily basis, despite his having pronounced finality over the affair on many different occasions. He was trying hard to think more of her than himself, an attitude absent from any pre-monastic relationships.

At the age of 52, Merton continued to receive thousands of letters from readers of his books, essays, articles, and poems. In early December, as he warmed his feet by the fire and sipped hot cider from his mug, he opened two. Both writers were teachers at Keele University, in England, thanking him for his "Notes on Love" article in *Frontier,* a spiritual publication. Merton was pleased. If his ideas helped two people realize how better to love each other with mutual trust and truth, then his love affair with Margie was worthwhile.

As the new year approached, Merton thought of Margie less and less. She was in Florida and he did not have a telephone number for her, which eased the temptation to track her down. One evening after he had finished shoveling snow off the porch and clearing a path to the woodshed, he wrote her a note but decided there wasn't much to say, since she continued to believe he should leave the monastic life to live with her. When he realized she was calling his actions a sort of betrayal, his feelings looped toward realization that the affair had fallen into the sink of hopelessness.[3]

Having apparently decided on God over Margie, Thomas Merton moved on to other matters in his life as 1967 came to an end. Perhaps he saw the retirement of Abbot Dom James on a cold mid-December day as a bonus from God for his decision to resist temptation. Merton's nemesis was finally headed for a hermitage in the same woods Merton inhabited, with no ability to rule the famous monk's life anymore. In 1977 the abbot would endure a severe beating from intruders at the hermitage but live on to the age of 91 before he died on Good Friday of 1987. Writer Dianne Aprile suggested "somewhere between humble sainthood and absolute dictatorship lies the true character of Dom James Fox."[4]

Two days before Christmas 1967, Margie returned to Merton's mind when he received a card from her. He admitted thinking of his true love, of visiting her, but he reaffirmed his belief that marriage was a terrible idea. Later, alone with his thoughts while sitting on a porch rocker, he concluded that at nearly age 53, it was crazy to think of being married for the first time.[5]

As the calendar turned to 1968, Merton was invited to attend a monastic-ecumenical meeting in Bangkok the following December. A new abbot, Father Flavian, was now in charge. Merton was ecstatic about the change in leadership, observing: "Result: a real sense of liberation."[6] An opportunity for Merton to backslide into the old sinful ways appeared in early April 1968, when girls visited to interview him for the Washington University (Saint Louis) magazine. One of them, Sue, asked leading questions about controversial topics, including premarital sex. Merton had dinner with them away from the monastery where the group shared a bottle of bourbon and Sue got drunk. After the girls left, Merton was upset with his behavior, recalling "her neurosis, her mini-skirt, buxomness, etc. etc."[7] He decided the two of them could stir up trouble and somehow make each other miserable. He warned himself to be careful.

Some days later, Merton was drinking beer at a nearby tavern when he learned of Dr. Martin Luther King Jr.'s assassination. He asked himself, "Is the human race self-destructive? Is the Christian message of love a pitiful delusion? Or must one just 'love' in an impossible situation?"[8] Late April brought more sad news for Merton when a newspaper arrived from New Zealand, reporting a shipwreck of a giant ferry in Wellington Harbor. Among those listed as dead was Aunt Kit: "Agnes Gertrude Merton, 79, Christchurch."[9] Merton held a special Mass for her.

In May, the newly liberated Merton, free of Margie and free of Dom James, traveled to northern California for the first time, for a conference and seminar. He recalled flying over mountains covered with snow, of being 39,000 feet over Idaho, the desolate nature of the desert, and of enjoying two daiquiris in the San Francisco airport, where he believed he had recovered "something of myself that has been long lost."[10] Images of peace grasped Merton's mind when he walked along the beach, where he saw a huge shark swimming south, dorsal fin exposed. He heard the faint cry of a lamb on a nearby mountainside and escaped the rain by ducking under some pine trees while watching sheep in a nearby field. He enjoyed the calm blue ocean and the wild calla lilies as an unrecognizable bird flew over, perhaps an eagle.[11] It appeared Margie was no longer on his mind; he had moved on and could enjoy nature without interruption.

In San Francisco, Merton met renowned poet Lawrence Ferlinghetti and enjoyed chatting with him at a small outdoor café. He stayed in an apartment above City Lights Bookstore. Free from Margie, he decided loving God was now more personal than before. When he visited the Monastery of Christ in the Desert in New Mexico, he was amazed by the emptiness and the silence. When he returned to Gethsemani, he longed for the Pacific and the redwoods, where he had felt at home, in contrast to the monastery, where he still felt he was a stranger.[12]

In early June, Merton mourned the assassination of Robert F. Kennedy. A few days later, Father Flavian approved Merton's travel to Bangkok for a series of conferences and lectures. He looked forward to meeting Buddhists, but would have preferred to spend "a couple of months entirely alone on the shore of the Pacific." In early July, reflecting back on the Margie affair, he decided, in an apparent attempt to convince himself he was right to abandon any contact with her, that he had wasted time and energy during the previous three years on things that had nothing to do with his real purpose and vocation, leaving him frustrated and confused.[13]

The new abbot brightened Merton's spirits. He looked forward to a stop in California on the way to the Far East where he could find "a really quiet, isolated place where no one knows I am (I want to disappear)."[14]

Pain from vaccinations sapped Merton's strength as the long trip approached, but then he became excited over the prospect of visiting Alaska on the way. In mid-August, he was visibly moved about his new life, one free from the grip of Margie and of the clutches of Dom James. The idea of becoming a hermit in Alaska led him to decide that he was on the "edge of something totally new, completely unplanned, and unforeseen, something that simply dropped out of the sky." The result, he concluded, was "very inspiring and does much to lift the burden of depressions, suspicion, doubt that has become almost second nature with me after years of the other kind of policy."[15]

On August 20, 1968, a day marking three years of residence in his hermitage, Merton burned Margie's letters as a symbolic act to end once and for all his romantic relationship with her.[16] It had been 30 months since that first special day in the hospital. With the apparent intent of finality, Margie disappeared from his journal entries and from his life, and while it is fair to assume he thought of her often, Merton had chosen God over his love for her. It had truly been an amazing experience, one he had longed for, being in love for all the right reasons, loving and being loved. Initially, acting like the old Merton, he had been infatuated with her youthful body and exuberance, but lust had turned to love, and he finally loved her enough to let her be free.

Regardless, in Merton's "Evening: Long Distance Call," he wrote,

> We are two half people wandering
>   In two lost worlds.[17]

When finally the two "lost worlds" parted and the kindred souls went their separate ways, no one could prevent Merton and Margie from recalling days of wanderlust and bliss. Their sacred moments of togetherness included clandestine meetings in Dr. Wygal's office, where they first felt the warmth of each other's bodies and enjoyed passion beyond Merton's comprehension; the time spent at the Louisville airport on Derby Day, where the two snuggled and shared inner feelings about love; the picnics at Gethsemani, where emotions erupted into a sexual togetherness; and a multitude of sharing encountered at every turn. They knew the love affair was over, but the love they had known would last forever.

Free of Margie, in September 1968, Merton decided he wanted to be open to everything—including not returning to Gethsemani. The most important thing, he decided as he pondered the trip to Asia while gathering clothes to take, was to do God's will.[18]

Brief stops in New Mexico, Alaska, and California preceded Merton's voyage to the Far East. On October 17, he landed in Bangkok in the wee hours of the morning before traveling to Calcutta. Merton met Vatsala Amin, a young Jain laywoman born in Bombay, whose "great, soft, intelligent, dark eyes" he admired. While traveling to New Delhi, he saw the Himalayas, the tallest mountains he had ever seen, in the far distance. In Tibet, he listened intently to a monk humming a prolonged "om" sound as he walked a mountain path.[19]

Prior to his meeting with the Dalai Lama, Merton had decided no world leader was loved as much as His Holiness. On a bright day in early November, they met and this impression was confirmed. Merton decided the Dalai Lama was quite impressive—stronger and more alert than expected, solid, energetic, warm, and generous. The two men spoke of religion, philosophy, and meditation with mutual respect. The discussion made Merton appreciate Gethsemani more. A second visit concerned various theories of knowledge, and Merton decided he liked his spiritual counterpart's ideas about detachment. A third meeting permitted Merton to answer questions about Western monastic life, vows, the rule of silence, and the ascetic way. When they parted, Merton felt they did so as very good friends and shared a mutual spiritual bond.[20]

Visiting Polonnaruwa, Merton was struck with the magnificence of the huge Buddhist figures, the reclining Buddha, and the seated one. The feelings of beauty and spiritual awareness filled his mind with an inner clarity. The result, he decided, was that: "my Asian pilgrimage has come clear and purified itself . . . [I] have pierced through the surface and have got beyond the shadow and the disguise."[21]

Six days after writing this journal entry and giving a speech to the conference conclave gathered to hear his blessed words on the subject of Marxism and the monastic perspective, Merton, known for being clumsy, apparently stepped out of a Bangkok Red Cross Center room shower and touched a faulty standing electric fan after showering. He was electrocuted and died 36 days short of becoming 54 years old. His final effects: "one Timex watch, one pair dark glasses in Tortoise Frames, one Cistercian Leather Bound Breviary, one Rosary (broken) and one small Icon on Wood of Virgin and Child."[22]

Longtime friend Edward Rice wrote of Merton's life and death: "[Merton] was an Aquarian, born January 31, 1915, and died in the early days of the Aquarian Age, under the sign of the Archer, Sagittarius, who had stuck him down with a bolt from the heavens (disguised as faulty wire) in Bangkok, the gilded city of the kingdom of the Thais."[23]

BOOK VI

the TRUE MERTON

"A [great deal] of my spiritual seeking began with Thomas Merton. He [was] an incredible source of light and comfort and humor."

—*Traveling Mercies* author Anne Lamott

CHAPTER TWENTY

BROKEN VOWS

Assessing Thomas Merton's affair with Margie Smith, historian and author Jonathan Montaldo called it "Romeo and Juliet—he's fifty-one, she's twenty-five—they can't drive, they can't see each other." Regarding Merton's conduct during the romance, Montaldo concluded, "Merton broke every vow he had."[1] Had he, and if so, how does such conduct fit with the overall Merton legacy?

At Gethsemani, Merton had sworn to the vows—obedience, stability, and conversion of manners, which included poverty and chastity—on the feast of Saint Joseph, March 19, 1947.[2] This provided "structure, support, and encouragement to persevere in the journey, the work, in the search" allowing the monks at Gethsemani to "intently and joyfully . . . live the mystery of Christ-among-[them]." The vows were set against the backdrop of the sixth-century Rule of St. Benedict, "interpreted by the Cistercian Usage in the eleventh century and more strictly enforced in the seventeenth century by reforms begun by Armand-Jean de Rance, the Abbot of La Grande Trappe in France."[3]

Determining Merton's obedience requires common-sense definitions and a close examination of Saint Benedict's Rule without becoming too technical. Simply put, being obedient required a commitment to live in the model of Jesus, whose obedience was never shaken, despite His being nailed to the cross facing death. In agreeing to the vow of stability, one committed to remaining at the monastery until death. Conversion of manners demanded a commitment to the lifelong pilgrimage toward a perfect love of God and neighbor within a specific framework of monasticism. Within this third vow was poverty, which included no private ownership of any material worth, and celibate chastity.[4] Merton was certainly aware of the governing Rule of Saint

Benedict, birthed by the disenchanted Roman monk more than 1,500 years ago. It was "called a rule because it regulates the lives of those who obey it."[5]

Aside from determining how Merton's actions with Margie conflicted with the Rule, edicts exist concerning the conduct of abbots (must "avoid all favoritism," must not "love one [monk] more than another," and should not "gloss over the sins of those who err, but cut them out while he can, as they begin to sprout").[6] Did either Dom Dunne or Dom James violated these rules by favoring Merton with special treatment, including permission to write letters and promotion through the release of *SSM* and subsequent books? In Dom James's case, he failed to "cut" Merton the sinner from the monastery pack when he knew Merton was engaged in a love affair he had forbidden.

As to Merton's conduct, Chapter Four of the Rule of St. Benedict, titled "The Tools of Good Works," condemned deceit, ordering that no one "should act in anger or nurse a grudge . . . but speak truth with heart or tongue." Addressing the matter of passion, the Rule stated "Do not gratify the promptings of the flesh, hate the urgings of self-will . . . live by God's commandments every day; treasure chastity." Further rules covered "unhesitating obedience . . . given gladly," and warnings that "evil speech" must be curbed so punishment for sinful conduct could be avoided.[7]

In a chapter titled "Humility," Saint Benedict noted, "Truly, we are forbidden to do our own will for Scripture tells us, 'Turn away from your desires'." Focusing on individual conduct, the text read, "As for desires of the body, we must believe that God is always with us, *for all my desires are known to you,* as the Prophet tells the Lord. We must then be on guard against any basic desire, because death is stationed near the gateway of pleasure. For this reason Scripture warns us, *Pursue not your lusts.*" Saint Benedict also outlined 12 steps of humility designed to permit the monk "perfect love of God which casts out fear."[8]

Evaluating Merton's conduct regarding his vows and the Rule is a subjective matter. Was simply seeing Margie a violation? Of course not. Was enjoying a simple friendship with her one? No. Did he violate his vows and the Rule by initially becoming infatuated with Margie? Perhaps. But if Merton consummated the relationship with Margie through intercourse, he certainly violated the vow of chastity and the Rule prohibiting such behavior. If he did not have intercourse, but instead everything short thereof (based on his admission of naked bodies and erotic conduct), then in the literal sense, he did not break the Rule. But he disregarded the essence of its purpose with the lust in his heart. When this lust and his infatuation with Margie turned to pure love, perhaps one could say his breaking of vows and the Rule was discontinued as the relationship played out and he obeyed the abbot by finally ending the affair.

Certainly, Merton's lies to Dom James and his anger toward him, displayed before and during the affair, violated the spirit of the Rule against such evil emotions. Montaldo believed Merton "literally was not in a consciously obedient, stable, poor, and chaste state when he was swept away by his feelings for Margie . . . his flaws manifested themselves big-time." Of Merton's behavior pattern, Montaldo said, "[He had] acted like an adolescent. Maybe he grew up a little bit with Margie's help."[9]

Regarding the true nature of the physical relationship with Margie, Merton danced around the amorous aspects of their closeness, using language that hinted at everything short of sexual intercourse. Whether Merton consummated the relationship will never be known for certain unless Margie speaks out. Some would say Merton's repeated denials indicate a Shakespearian "doth protest too much" attitude, proving the relationship was consummated, while others point to the continued denials as his way of making certain that readers knew he never broke the vow of chastity. Author Paul Elie believed otherwise, based on interviews with Merton publisher and friend Robert Giroux. Referring to the romantic interludes Merton and Margie spent at Dr. Wygal's Louisville office, Elie concluded, "There, one afternoon in early summer, Merton and Margie met once more; there, they drank champagne and made love."[10] When asked the context of Giroux' revelation, Elie said it occurred while he was speaking to the publisher about "excised material" from the original text of Merton's private journal entries. Elie did not follow up on the striking comment and could not provide additional context for Giroux' statement.[11] But this author attempted to corroborate the fact that editors had cut some of Merton's original journal entries. A reliable source confirmed[12] that the ugly stamp of censorship had once again been inflicted on Merton's true words, albeit long after his death since what was subjectively termed "irrelevant material" was clipped by certain journal editors. This author attempted to substantiate the accusation with those close to the Merton Legacy Trust, but was turned away.[13]

The author's source said that the specific words, "A botched job" had been deleted from journal text following Merton's disclosure of one romantic afternoon with Margie at Dr. Wygal's office.[14] This language is similar to words Merton used earlier in the journals, when he wrote "that a crude botched-up affair in the woods would be worse than nothing."[15] Whether use of the similar phrase after Merton and Margie's afternoon at Dr. Wygal's office proves the two had sex is subject to interpretation, but the crude language Merton used must be considered in the context of his tendency to write without considering the true consequences of his words. Certainly Merton meant no disrespect to Margie; this is quite clear based on his loving feelings for her.

The best way to uncover whether the two had sex begins with pinpointing *which* romantic interlude "A botched affair" followed. Elie suggests June 12, the day when they drank champagne. But his curious lack of following up by questioning Giroux complicates his resolution, since Merton's strongest words about any meeting with Margie follow a June 26 interlude at Dr. Wygal's office. During this time together, Margie mentioned she was distraught over the possibility that her fiancé was missing in Vietnam, an emotion causing her to be quite vulnerable. Merton recalled her "body, her nakedness, the day at [Dr.] Wygal's, and it haunts me. . . ." Later, he added, "The past is what it is and I cannot really regret anything in it except what my conscience sincerely regrets—the day in Wygal's office."[16]

No such language exists regarding any of several other romantic interludes—for instance, their togetherness on the grass outside the Luau Room at the Louisville Airport, or during the Gethsemani picnic, when he admitted the two "made love" for five hours, became "rather sexy" and loved with their "whole bodies" despite denial of sex.[17] No, it was only the day of June 26 at Dr. Wygal's office that haunted him and caused a regretful conscience. Recall his exact words about their time spent together: "We fell on each other in desperation and love, kissing each other over and over, swept with love and loss." And then, most important, "In it, knowing it would probably never be like that again."[18] If Merton was telling the truth, it is not a stretch to believe he and Margie had sex that day. Certainly the fact that he had noted her "nakedness" made this possible.

Whether Merton and Margie consummated the relationship may be irrelevant to many and should not overshadow the depths of the true love they knew. If they did make love, it was because they truly loved each other; a true love Merton had never known before. Perhaps more surprising is Merton's admission that he considered having a secret love relationship with Margie as his mistress. This thinking reverted back to the days at Clare/Cambridge, when he tended to think of himself as a Hemingway or a D. H. Lawrence, a dashing and adventurous figure, a ladykiller par excellence. Comparisons with

Hemingway abound, because the great novelist was also shunned by the first love of his life—a nurse at that, named Agnes—when she rejected his advances following World War I. She had called him, "just a boy" (she was eight years older than Hemingway), a phrase reminiscent of the scalding words Merton heard from the older woman on the ocean liner.

Like Merton's idol Hemingway, who never met a woman he didn't covet, Merton was obsessed with women from late childhood to Margie. W. H. "Ping" Ferry witnessed the love-stricken monk when he asked for a few coins to use to call Margie during a visit Ferry made to Gethsemani. Ferry recalled Merton telling him, "What I want to do is go away with this woman for a month. What do you think of that?" Ferry answered, "Are you out of your mind?" triggering a discussion about the potential for publicity if Merton ran away with the woman. Ferry said Merton was dumbfounded to hear that there might be a fuss, and asked for his assistance in dealing with any scandal.[19]

Such transgressions raise the question as to why Merton was not booted out of Gethsemani. Montaldo believes "he was never in danger of being removed from the Cistercians at any time in his monastic career." Was this because of his celebrity status, of a church not wanting to risk embarrassment by punishing its poster boy? If he was banished, people would ask why, questions the church wished to avoid to protect its image. Merton was thus never confronted with the consequences of failing to heed Dom James's warnings to stay away from Margie, a warning from a superior he ignored in violation of the Rule of St. Benedict. Such behavior caused Merton's fellow monk, Dr. Rudy Bernard to believe "Merton was violating all sorts of rules, those of the abbot and the monastery and its rule, not to mention the Commandments and his own solemn vow of chastity as well as obedience." But, Bernard concluded, Merton eventually made the choice to honor his vows and return to being a faithful monk. "He was severely tempted . . . but in the end he converted and remained faithful, not exactly an unusual occurrence in the spiritual life, going all the way back to the desert fathers, who report all sorts of temptations, especially sexual ones."[20]

Granting Merton understanding for his irreverent conduct is possible since there is no doubt he was weak and vulnerable during a time of midlife crisis when ill health caused him to face mortality. Denied the right to leave Gethsemani, he felt like a prisoner. He was thus susceptible to temptation, but even more ready to act boldly when a woman appeared to test his mettle. Throwing caution out the window, Merton consciously decided to take the risk, break his vows, and break the Rule, possessed as he was with his one chance to love and be loved. Are not compassion and forgiveness necessary for one so confused, one still seeking a true identity in view of the rocky road he experienced since fame had unexpectedly entered his life? Didn't Merton, denied the alternative to be Frater Louis instead of Thomas Merton, have the right to love after instructing so many, through his writings, as to how they should love? Absolutely, especially when the source of his love was a beautiful, sensual woman half his age, whose passionate affinities matched his. What man in his position, so starved as he was for love, could have resisted her web of intrigue, her willingness to bare her naked body to him and excite his as they lay together holding each other like lovers do? After all, as Joan Baez mentioned, "Watching Merton . . . in love showed how the greats are human too," and Merton was certainly human and as susceptible to Margie's considerable charms as any red-blooded man would be. Such a stereotypical identity may seem unfair to those offended by Merton being interested in sex, but, at least in the beginning stages of the relationship, Merton acted the part. How is Merton's situation different from that of many modern-day priests who desire to marry but are forbidden to do so in accordance with archaic Catholic Church precedent? Certainly Alberto Cutié, the well-known Roman Catholic Miami priest caught in tabloid photographs kissing a woman was torn between his vows and a woman he loved. In the end, he chose to leave the church and join the Episcopalians so he could marry her. Merton chose to stay with the church and forsake the woman he loved, the woman he had waited his whole life for. Both men exhibited courage, albeit it in different ways.

Understanding how strongly Merton felt about experiencing love and even marriage is evident through a slow and careful reading of his words in *Conjectures of a Guilty Bystander.* The book features a series of "conjectures"— "more than guesses but less than definite positions" presented by Merton, who classified himself as a "guilty bystander." It is written more from the point of view of "where he had come from than where he was when he wrote the book."[21] But Merton made it clear in the preface that his words, taken from various private journal entries, "add up to a personal version of the world in the 1960s" and that "elaborating in such a version one unavoidably tells something of himself." As a caveat, he pointed out that his writings should not be viewed as answers to questions, but only as thoughts for dialogue, since "man is better known by his questions than by his answers,"[22] a clue to understanding Merton's intention with the multitude of vignettes, which some scholars have equated to Jesus' parables.[23]

Merton began with a bold statement: "Man is most human, and most proves his humanity (I did not say his virility) by the quality of relationship with woman." He then decided, "obsession with virility and conquest makes a true and deep relationship impossible." The reason: "Men think today that there is no difference between the capacity to make conquests and the capacity to love." Merton then considered the female role: "Women respond accordingly, with elaborate deceit and thinly veiled harlotry—the role assigned to women by fashion—and there is a permanent battle between the sexes, sometimes covered over with the most atrocious and phony playacting." Having tendered strong opinions that must have been based on his pre-monastic romantic dalliances, Merton chastised both sexes: "In all this everyone completely forgets the need for love. A desperate need: not the need to receive it only, but the need to *give love*." How far this man had come from the days when he admitted knowing nothing about the subject.

Turning to thoughts about his own plight as of 1965, Merton explained, "In the monastery, with our vows of chastity, we are ideally supposed to go beyond married love into something more pure, more perfect, more totally oblative. This should then make us the most *human* of all people." This is terrific, Merton believed, "but that is the trouble: how can one go 'further' than something to which one has not yet attained?" Elaborating, he noted, "this does not mean that one cannot validly embrace a life of virginity until he has first been married, a nice contradiction to put a person in!" But, he decided, "it does mean that we cannot love *perfectly* if we have not in some way loved maturely and truly."[24]

Wow! In tandem with his apparent state of mind at the time, and all he had learned during 24 years at Gethsemani about the subject of love, Merton had in two paragraphs, 222 words in all, summed up his view of why it was essential for a monk to experience love and being loved, so as to have the potential to discover the ultimate goal: perfect love, of being with "God alone." Whether he was still sorting out his exact feelings about the subject is unknown, but he appeared to possess clear insight as to his state of mind at the time. Did this mean that all along he had intended to discard Margie so as to move toward the perfect love with God? Perhaps at the beginning of the relationship such feelings existed, but as the relationship grew and blossomed, there was no doubt he loved her more than himself.

Based on these revelations, when a chance to love "maturely and truly" occurred out of the blue with the gift of Margie, Merton grabbed it. Can anyone blame him? This was the mark of a man who had lived in a dark tunnel for so many years, but was emerging into the light through God's grace, a woman to love, and be loved by. This connected to his belief about what he called the "Law of Love . . . the deepest law of our nature." He believed a deep and most fundamental part of any divine law within one's heart was fulfillment reached by loving.[25]

Merton's mindset regarding the need to risk, to let oneself go and realize such love, was evident in a story brother monk Paul Quenon said Merton told twice during the time of the Margie affair. According to Brother Quenon, Merton said, "one of the Desert Fathers patronized by a wealthy woman was permitted to live at the hermitage. To test his spirit, the wealthy woman sent a prostitute to him. The man's response to the girl was, 'I am a dried-up stick; you are wasting your time.' When the wealthy woman was told of his response, she said, 'That man is a phony; throw him out.'" Quenon believed the woman "understood the monk had lost his ability to feel." According to his interpretation, the moral of the story was that "spiritual maturity does not mean a deadening of the sensibilities" and "[Merton] was glad he could still have such feelings" since "a phony gets cut off from his sexuality because he is in too much denial. Instead of integration, there is isolation."[26] Since Merton had the capacity to love, as demonstrated by his journals, he was ready to let loose with feelings of love if the chance occurred. When Margie appeared, he took that chance.

Certainly timing played a part in Merton's willingness to risk all with the love affair. While he knew he had the capacity to love, there was no one to love, which made him frustrated, anguished, and depressed. He had used the terms "depressed" or "depression" many times throughout his writings, with the first occurring after he read his mother's note telling him she was going to die.[27] Later, in 1931, Merton, age 16, described a depressed state in *The Labyrinth*, where he fell into "into the middle of a great depression." Within a short time, he felt himself souring as his insides turned to ashes.[28] In *The Sign of Jonas*, written in 1953, Merton referenced another nervous breakdown, a reminder, he lamented, of the time in 1936 when he thought he was cracking up on the train and, more recently, since ordination. Edward Rice noted Merton's state of depression even after he became a priest.[29]

In early 1963, Merton's mind was full of confusion, and he decided that his life had been "kind of a lie, a charade," and he had been through a "kind of dazed desperation in my half-conscious attempt to preserve my identity." In June 1963, Merton decided his chief weakness was a lack of courage to handle the monastic way of life. He admitted he was worn down and "easily discouraged. The depressions are deeper, more frequent. I am near fifty. People think I am happy."[30]

Though he loved nature and the solitude of the hermitage, he knew his pose as a writer and a monk was a false identity. He compared it to a cocoon that "masks the transition stage between what crawls and what flies."[31] Merton concluded anyone who called himself a "Mertonist" did not realize how much misery he had in his life. He said anyone who tried to imitate him did so at his own risk. To them, he promised times of naked despair. This admission, and others of similar ilk, had triggered comments from Merton biographers, including Monica Furlong, who observed, "[Merton] regretted the way he had tried to live up to an illusion of the person he ought to be, instead of simply trying to be himself."[32]

Merton addressed this attitude in May 1967 when he wrote to Rosemary Radford Ruether, "People still have me categorized in terms of *The Seven Storey Mountain*," a bold comment of vast importance indicative of Merton's knowledge that he was not, in fact, the contemplative monk who had been promoted through the years. This was the man who acknowledged he could be the protagonist in a Graham Greene novel, the "man who tried to be virtuous, and is in a certain sense holy," but was nevertheless overwhelmed by sin.[33] This was the troubled Merton, the one no one knew existed.

Proof that Merton's mind was tormented is further documented by psychiatrists in Louisville and Chicago. Dr. Gregory Zilboorg, the noted analyst, ridiculed him as no one had done before, causing Merton to confront his neuroticism. Even Abbot Dom James questioned Merton's mindset, accusing him of being a baby who by fluke had written a successful book.[34] Such instances of psychological warfare reveal that Merton's soul must have been much more tormented then anyone realized. The hurtful experiences of childhood and early adulthood—feeling unloved, abandoned, rejected, and later, imprisoned and persecuted at Gethsemani—cut much deeper than any of Merton's closest friends or fellow monks understood.

Yes, timing was everything for a man who had been suffering for so many years, the man who experienced anguish, loneliness, and depression. As 1966 approached, Merton's writings about love in *Conjectures of a Guilty Bystander* proved that thoughts were stirring in his mind regarding the necessity for a monk to love a woman "maturely and truly" so as to discover perfect love with God. And then he had written fresh words on the subject for the Japanese translation of *Thoughts on Solitude*. With this in hand when he visited the hospital for his back operation in late March, he could let Margie read those words and show her that although he was a hermit and devoted to God, he truly sought love in his life as well. It is no wonder Merton must have seen it as a sign of divine intervention when she walked into his life. God had blessed him with the gift of love; his prayers had been answered.

CHAPTER TWENTY-ONE

the NEW MERTON

During the first century B.C.E., the Roman poet Virgil exclaimed, "Love conquers all things; let us too surrender to Love."[1] Thomas Merton put it this way: "[Love] transforms our entire life. Genuine love is a personal revolution. Love takes your ideas, your desires, and your actions and welds them together in one experience and one living reality which is the new *you*."[2]

From the ashes of the Margie affair a new Thomas Merton had emerged. Dante needed Beatrice; Yuri Zhivago, Lara; Romeo, Juliet; and Ernest Hemingway, a bevy of young beauties, including the half-his-age Adrianna Ivancinch, whom he once missed so much he said it felt as if a leg had been amputated. Like them, Merton needed Margie, and by having the courage to risk loving and being loved, he had conquered many of his fears. He had learned how to truly accept the gift of love, to love back, and then survived the test God presented by choosing to love Him more than any human being. When Merton left for Asia, he was free, free of the demons haunting him since childhood, free to finally realize he was the true Christian, the peaceful, free man he had pretended to be for so many years. Like any human being, his dedication to God would waffle, but the solid foundation was there as never before—thanks to Margie.

Merton's close friend and brother monk Father Basil Pennington agreed. He said Merton told him that asking "Am I happy?" was the wrong question, with the real one being, "Am I free?" Pennington concluded Merton meant the freedom from need, whether it was happiness, pleasure, things, or people, combined with the ability to choose and enjoy special things with joy and thanksgiving.[3]

Pennington believed that in tandem with the image of the title of Merton's autobiography, there were seven stages in his quest for freedom. These were his "quest for basic human freedom, which he exploited and abused," a quest of faith, and a more complete freedom through the monastic life. During his time at Gethsemani, Pennington decided Merton wanted to be free to experience all reality, and then "freedom of the eremitical [hermit] life." Within this process, he sought "freedom of final integration, which prepared him to enter into the ultimate freedom of the Kingdom of Heaven." Pennington concluded Merton understood Dante's concept of false self. He viewed the world as tantamount to hell, where one strayed away from God. This caused Merton to encounter "the seven mountains of purgatory" in progressing toward the goal of becoming free.[4]

What was the lesson Merton learned, according to Pennington? He believed Merton was certain that total freedom was never possible by following one's own passions, thoughts, and ideas. But hope lingered if one aligned his mind and heart with reality, with the truth, and with God.[5] The result: "Thomas Merton's vocational struggle was an open one, a struggle for freedom, to be free enough to do what he really wanted to do and do it as his true self."[6] When this occurred, Merton could give up the gift of Margie since he no longer wore the mask of false self. This led to enlightenment, peace, and salvation instead of the unhappiness and torment he experienced while trying to be something he was not.

Brother Paul Quenon believed the end result of the Margie affair was relevant to understanding how "the choice had to be made for solitude, and the result was a larger freedom and maturity" for Merton. Even before the affair, said Quenon, Merton "sensed something was still unresolved in his attitude to women and was due to be addressed."[7] Apparently it had been to his satisfaction, since Merton's brother monk and longtime secretary Patrick Hart noted his lively step just before he left for Asia, describing him as being "like a young boy off to the circus, full of life, full of joy."[8] Certainly this was the indication of one truly free.

The new Merton's mindset was even more apparent when considering a handwritten letter he had sent to Dom Frederic Dunne just after entering Gethsemani in 1941. Merton wrote of being disgusted with everything in his life, disappointed as he was with his lifestyle. But he concluded the answer was to be dedicated to nothing but Christ's will. He did not want to enjoy any specific pleasure or satisfaction, or "shine in any way." He wanted to be a "non-entity."[9]

Desiring not to "shine," to be anything special, indicated Merton's dedication to the contemplative life. The goal would sour a decade later, when publication of *SSM* changed the course of his existence and cast him in the glow of worldwide fame, depriving him of the very freedom he had sought from such things. Bolstering this view requires recalling how he entered the monastery as Thomas Merton, but lost this identity when his head was shaved and his name changed to Frater Louis. He lived under this identity until the birth of *SSM,* when he became Thomas Merton again. Hopefully, when he died, he felt as if the symbolism of Frater Louis had been restored by experiencing Margie's love and casting off the pre-monastic, sinful Merton once and for all. But this had been a slow process, years in the making.

In 1962, Merton spoke of interior freedom and how he had blocked it through a false sense of independence. Three years later, he was concerned with the illusion in his life and yearning to lose it, although he knew it would be a struggle.[10] In a lecture to his beloved novice students in December 1965, Merton suggested that the purpose of the ascetic existence at Gethsemani was freedom: freedom from sin, freedom to love, freedom to do what one wanted. He asked what was really important, what they wanted? His answer: to live without any impediments so as to become free, to really love God. Doing so meant disconnecting from all illusion so one was "fully awake, fully aware, fully alert, and fully in contact."[11]

Regarding false self, Merton noted freedom was only possible if one was truthful, so one could be who he or she truly was. He admitted struggling to rid himself of the imaginary person he had to be, and the need to get rid of this double, of the person who was always hanging around. This coincided with early proclamations that he could only be a monk when he quit trying to be one, when he stopped trying to live up to an image consciously created in the minds of other people.[12]

The clearest window into Merton's mind, revealing an absolute resolution about the subject of freedom, occurred just months before he died. With emphasis ringing from the words he spoke about the essential purpose of asceticism, he wrote that a person was in a true state of freedom when he was ready to do anything, including die; to go ahead and "meet the bridegroom at any moment." A person, he decided, was "free to take the last step that will take him into God." This meant the person was always "living at the point where with one step he [could] walk over the line and there [was] no unfinished business to fool around with." This resulted in being prepared to respond to any grace permitted, anything God requested with an attitude of readiness at the call.[13]

When Merton was asked in 1966 to contribute to noted religious composer Alexander Pelloqin's "Four Freedom Songs," first performed by members of the Ebenezer Baptist Church of Atlanta, he wrote verse symbolic of his enlightened attitude concerning how one must conquer demons so as to find the true self leading to freedom. He spoke of being "down in a cavern, to the bottom," even lower than Jonas and his whale. He was so far down nobody could find him; so far most believed he was gone forever. But then, to the surprise of everyone, he emerged and rang a bell to alert his return.[14] From the Margie affair, and what he learned about true love from it, Merton had emerged from being gone forever and had rung his bell. This was in true accordance with what he called the "ingredients" of freedom: "In order to become myself I must cease to be what I thought I always thought I wanted to be, and in order to find myself I must go out of myself, and in order to live I have to die."[15] Died, he had, but through Margie, lived again.

The Thomas Merton who emerged from the Margie Smith affair was a man who had met the woman of his dreams and therein experienced a part of himself that had been denied. He had learned about love, struggled with the challenge of whether to choose her over his God, chose God, and thus emerged with a pure heart and a reformed soul and inner peace. Because of his struggles, Merton's spiritual self was stronger and surer than it would have been without the gift God presented. As Merton stated in *New Seeds of Contemplation,* "the highest freedom is found in obedience to God."[16]

Within this context, Merton's thoughts and writings about true and false self prior to and just after meeting Margie make perfect sense, because it is easy to realize that when he wrote about how others should lead their lives, he was speaking, as Brother Paul Quenon agreed, about *his own personal experiences.* But he could not take his own advice at the time, because he was besieged by the expectation of being the contemplative, peaceful monk enablers wanted him to be instead of the humanistic Merton who hurt and suffered like others who hide behind a mask. Whether it is the contest for the highest office in the land, a worker's quest to be promoted, or a youngster trying to impress a teacher, when people lose their true identity, they experience turmoil and suffering, and ultimately fail. Merton realized this early on while pondering whether to leave the monastery when he decided, "perhaps it is I who am the liar."[17]

Merton's writings in his many books pre-Margie take on a fresh meaning when one understands the man beneath the mask of holiness, the one who, as Quenon noted, sensed something unresolved with his attitude toward women. Nowhere is this more clear than in *New Seeds,* published four years before he met Margie. Examples abound in which he cried out to the world in anguish, and while some realized this, many never understood how personal the tone was. He wrote of being unable to receive any seeds of freedom since he was a prisoner and had hardened his heart against any sense of true love. He realized he had to change his habits and become a new man by leaving himself and then finding himself so as to yield to God's love. He knew people were "at liberty to be real or unreal . . . be true or false, the choice is ours." Merton believed we may wear "one mask and now another and never if we so desire to appear with our own true face."[18] Later, he added, "We have a choice of two identities: the external mask which seems to be real and which lives by a shadowy autonomy for the brief moment of earthy existence." This conflicted, he believed, with the hidden, inner person who appeared to be nothing but could give "himself eternally to the truth in whom he subsists."[19]

To discover the new man Merton aspired to be, it was important for him not to lie to himself or others, since no one could expect to discover truth and reality on a whim. During the first year of the Margie affair, Merton noted the danger of taking one's "vulnerable shell" as his true identity, taking the mask as one's own true face, and protecting "it with fabrication even at the cost of violating ones own truths," an indication he knew he was wearing a mask, knew he was not the Merton others thought him to be. Instead, he had been a man who had loved out of lustful desire, causing that love to be dominated by lust and desire. The antidote, he knew, was to love for love's sake. When this occurred, one could be completely free.[20]

Attempting to understand who he really was, Merton, as always using the gender-exclusive language of the day, believed the origin of man's alienation could be attributed to how a culture divided a person against himself, threw a mask on him, and presented him with a role he may not have wanted to play. Alienation was complete when he identified with the role and thus the mask, and finally determined that any other role or identity was impossible. Merton realized the man who sweated under the mask, "whose role makes him itch with discomfort," the one who hated the conflict within himself, was already tasting freedom. But he warned that God would not help him if he simply wanted to wear the mask another man wore, since the other man was not sweating or itching, since the other man might not be human enough to itch or "[pay] a psychiatrist to scratch him."[21] These words of wisdom project issues so relevant to today's world, in which confusion and despair run rampant.

In *New Seeds,* Merton wrote that the key was for this new man, obviously himself, to detach himself from material things so that he might attach himself to God. He knew the challenge was quieting the selfish "external, egotistic will." If this was not successful, he believed he would be alienated from both reality *and* God. The false self then became a god of sorts, and the false self received the love. The result was a relationship full of corruption and sin.[22]

Merton believed everyone was "shadowed by an illusory person: a false self." This was "the man that I want myself to be but who cannot exist, because God does not know anything about him."[23] Focusing on love of the divine, he was certain that if man were not one with God, the world could be harmful. This was especially true when one was dead to the pain inflicted by the world, and therefore worshiped the false self. This was tantamount to worshiping nothing, and "the worship of nothing is hell."[24] These are the people in today's world whose financial empires have collapsed through deception, fraud, and corruption and who sit in a prison cell shaking their heads in disbelief over the harm they have caused others, including family and close friends who trusted them (think Enron executives; Ponzi scheme financier Bernard Madoff, impeached Illinois governor Rod Blagojevich).

Sin, Merton asserted, was the result when the false self existed because of ego-perpetuated desires and false motives. He believed this was a fundamental reality of life around which the world orbited. In an amazing admission, one that would have already been apparent to those aware of his checkered past, Merton admitted to having led his life desiring pleasure and the experience of power and knowledge to favor the false self, while attempting to turn it into something real. This mindset, however, did not produce a true spiritual foundation, but instead "my own nakedness and emptiness and hollowness, to tell me that I am my own mistake."[25] How many people today may relate to this state of affairs, having thrown their lives away seeking the almighty dollar, material objects that theological-ethicist H. Richard Niebuhr agreed were "little-g gods," or pleasures of the flesh (think former New York governor Eliot Spitzer), as poisonous as any rattlesnake that ever roamed the desert? Merton the prophet knew of what he spoke, with words as relevant to today's decaying morals as they were 50 years ago.

Above all, Merton realized his secret identity, his true identity, was hidden in God's love and mercy, where only the true self could be discovered, an indication of how he might have decided he had to give up the woman he loved to be hidden in God's love. What was important, he decided, was the admission that being made in the image of God meant that love was the true reason for any existence, since God *was* love. This led to the bottom line: "Love is my true identity. Selflessness is my true self. Love is my true character. Love is my name."[26] When love prevailed, hatred, the sign and "the expression of loneliness,"[27] disappeared—another lesson to be learned from the gifted healer. This is a truism whether one believes in God, in another spiritual power, or in no power at all. When hate disappears and love rules, the world is, plain and simple, a better place. The source of this love, Merton knew, could only be found in a sanctuary where the mystery of God existed. In this sanctuary, too, was his true self; it was the place where he could be transformed by possessing his true identity and losing himself in Him. Merton realized the "root of Christian love is not the will to love, but *the faith that one is loved. The faith that one is loved by God.*"[28] This was more important, he realized, that love of any human being.

One obstacle that Merton recognized could keep someone (in this case, himself) from being one with God was sex. Connecting this with solitude, he noted how an important aspect of solitude was its intimate dependence on chastity. Once again speaking about his own experiences, he decided that the virtue of chastity was *not* denial of sex, but denial of the *wrong kind* of sex. Since sex was the most difficult of man's appetites to control, undisciplined gratification blinded man to any interior light. This prohibited man from being whole, since he could not be in one spirit with God. Instead, the Christian way to lead his life was to find a balance where the body, "with its passions and instincts, the mind with its reasoning and its obedience to principle and the spirit with its passive illumination by the Light and Love of God form one complete man who is in God and with God and from God and for God."[29]

No doubt exists that Merton's mind was alive with thoughts about how shedding his mask would lead to living in Christ, being one with God, or being with "God alone." But the intermediary step was learning about loving and being loved, and Margie was the instrument God used for this purpose.

The world would never know his heartfelt feelings until decades after he died. But Merton had been able to shout out his love for a woman on nearly every page of his journal during the days when the romance was flourishing. This love would transcend his initial feelings of infatuation and wonder to a ripe, real, complete love of her for all the right, Christlike reasons. Whatever form of "sex" they enjoyed was the right kind of sex, he believed, since they were so deeply in love. This was a true departure from the sex of old, when he craved passion/satisfaction instead of truly loving. He hadn't married Margie, but he had learned what it was like to enjoy love as if he were married. Now he could reach "beyond married love into something more pure, more perfect . . ." and that doing so would make him the most human of all people.[30] Perfect love with God was now possible.

It was no wonder Merton called the love affair with Margie a miracle. Even after he chose God over her, the new man he had become was still in place. He had been truly transformed, and he knew he would never again be the man he was before, never again be the man who "did not know or love in a deep, mysterious way, because we gave ourselves to each other almost as if we were married."[31] One may only imagine how Merton must have felt when he wrote these words, truly liberated as he was after so many years of anguish and despair.

Those who studied Merton inside and out concur that the transformation had taken place through his experience with Margie. Michael Mott concluded Merton "loved greatly and was greatly loved. He was overwhelmed by the experience and it changed him forever . . . Thomas Merton never again talked of his inability to love, or to be loved."[32] William Shannon concluded: "What that experience showed was that he could love and be loved . . . At last he had discovered a relationship in which he was loved as a person and requited that love. . . ."[33] Nazareth College professor Dr. Christine Bochen wrote, "at the age of fifty-one, in midlife, with a new clarity born of solitude and mature prayer, [Merton] saw what had hitherto been obscured: *that he had not allowed himself to be loved.* The episode with [Margie] revealed for the first time what intimacy actually means. He allowed himself to love and be loved, to know and be known."[34]

Alternative perspectives on Thomas Merton's love affair with Margie abound. Author Paul Elie's opinion: "[Merton] had written exhaustively about love: the love of one's enemy, the love of one's neighbor, the love of God alone. Now it was time to know love firsthand—to place himself in love—even if, in worldly terms, it would come to nothing." Dr. Rudy Bernard, the novice at Gethsemani with Merton from 1949 to 1951, viewed Merton's love affair with more simplicity: "I was not totally surprised although I remain disturbed and puzzled by Merton's conduct with Margie because he was thumbing his nose at the monastic life and the monastery." But, as Bernard observed, "Merton really wasn't living the life of a monk. Monks don't go on picnics with girl-friends; monks don't drink bourbon. He just didn't fit the mold and he broke every rule of the monastery. He was in full rebellion, a midlife crisis, for fool-ish." This was due, Bernard believed, to "severe psychological difficulties. I have sympathy for him, but he was immature—he really wasn't grown up until he had this experience with love."[35]

Father John Eudes viewed the relationship through an alternative lens: "I think Merton was caught off-guard by being alone in the hospital, where he suffered physical pain as well as from a period outside his customary environ-ment. He was exposed to an attractive, sympathetic young woman's attentions in a manner he had never experienced earlier, and at a time when he was more vulnerable without usual defenses at hand." Commenting on Merton's mo-tives, Eudes observed, "[They involved] human weakness, to which all more or less normal men are subject. I believe he was going through a period of spiritual drought that contributed to his vulnerability, so that he did not suf-ficiently resist the early stages of the mutual attraction. Such attraction is com-monly accompanied by delusional anticipation of a happiness that proves elusive." Eudes added, "I certainly did not expect it, but in retrospect, I had no trouble in understanding how it could happen. We are all vulnerable crea-tures. Even Saint Augustine acknowledged that he was not sure what he might do on the morrow."[36]

Paul Quenon learned of the affair from a fellow monk, Father Columban, who had talked with Abbot Dom James. But Quenon "didn't want to hear about it," since he "had idealized Merton's image." When he saw Merton and Margie walking toward Frederic's Lake across the road from the abbey, he thought, "How nice. He's got a friend." But the seriousness of the affair was apparent when Quenon overheard Merton talking to "a woman, obviously someone spe-cial," in the cellarer's office and saying, "This is a holy thing. I love you."[37]

While these observations clarify Merton's transformation, questions remain. Why did he fall so madly in love with Margie just days after meeting her?

What was it about her that captivated him so entirely that he would violate his vows and the Rule of Saint Benedict, risking scandal of a proportion he could not have even imagined? The answers, based on the totality of Merton's writings, appear to rest with an unlikely source, a young girl Merton had met during his early childhood. When one recalls all of the important girls/women in Merton's life, it is truly amazing that the one he could never forget, but recalled with feelings of love, was Ann Winser, Andrew's younger sister. Recall that in a journal entry dated June 1965, just nine months or so before meeting Margie, Merton wrote of her with the utmost affection, admitting that after Mass, he suddenly remembered Ann. She had been 12 or 13 when he visited the Winsers at the rectory on the Isle of Wight. Merton remembered Ann fondly, as the "quietest thing on it, a dark and secret child."[38]

Merton revealed meeting Ann after a hoped-for love affair with the girl at Bournemouth failed miserably. He recalled being enamored with her when she applauded a painting he had created of the fall of Lucifer. Later, she appeared as a character in his novel, *My Argument with the Gestapo:* "I respected [her] a lot, although she was nothing but a little girl and never said anything much or was of any account at all." In the novel, Merton wrote of having a wonderful time with Ann at a fancy-dress party at "Admiral Mayhew's house." He noted wearing a pair of riding breeches and a South American sombrero. He thought he looked like a horse thief. But Ann, to him, was the star attraction, wearing a big hoop skirt to emphasize her disguise as a shepherdess. Merton wrote that she had no wig, but was pleased she didn't so as to be a shepherdess with "her bobbed, dark, child's head of hair."[39]

Most important, Merton decided later that while a person did not fall in love per se, with a child so young, he realized he had not forgotten her, and if things had been different, if he had "taken another turn in the road [he] might have ended up married to Ann."[40] He further admitted she was the "symbol of the true (quiet) woman I never really came to terms [with] in the world, and of this there *remains an incompleteness that cannot be remedied*" (emphasis added).[41] This "incompleteness," this emptiness from childhood that remained in spite of all the women who entered his life, Merton thus believed, could have been avoided if he had discovered a woman like Ann Winser. Somehow her memory, her quietness, her gentle way had truly impacted him like few realized.

But was Margie Smith Ann? Was Margie the "dark and secret child," the little girl, the childhood friend, who might "complete" Merton? Was he obsessed his entire life with finding another Ann with the hope that this would permit the true love he sought? If this was his quest, he appeared to have discovered his Ann in Margie, for he wrote in April 1966, "All I know is that I love [Margie] so much I can hardly think of anything but her. Also I know that in itself this love is a thing of enormous value (never has anyone given herself to me so completely, so openly, so frankly, and never have I responded so completely)." Speaking more directly, he admitted, "I see how badly I need her love to complete me." Later, he would decide that Margie's "womanness blends with the man I am, and we are one being,"[42] indicating her having completed him as he believed Ann would have done.

Significant images of Margie as the one meant for him were certainly on Merton's mind in late June 1966, three months into the love affair. He was puzzled by them, admitting, "I almost never dream of [Margie] as she is, but of someone who, I instinctively know, represents her. Yet this girl is 'different' from [Margie]. How does one explain this? Still, just as I wake up, the archetypal [Margie] and the reality merge together." Searching for answers, he decided in this reality he found that "the [Margie] I love in the depths of my heart is not symbolic and not just the everyday [Margie] either, but the deep, mysterious, personal, unique potential that is in her."

Does this mean Merton was dreaming of Ann Winser and thinking of Margie, but that when he woke up, Margie was foremost in his mind? If so, this lends credence to the consideration that Margie represented the Ann he had always coveted, as evidenced by his admitting, "I now realize I had found something, someone, that I had been looking for all my life."[43] If so, this was truly Merton's miracle and he had discovered the woman who could fill the "incompleteness that cannot be remedied" mentioned when he spoke of Ann. Having finally discovered a woman to complete him must have meant that the decision to choose God over Margie was even more difficult than anyone imagined. What courage it took to give up the woman he loved, the woman he had searched for his entire life. This was truly selfless love.

Learning what true love was all about permitted Merton to share his thoughts, ideas, experiences, hopes, plans, strengths, and weaknesses with his true love. By being in love, he accepted the treasures possible when two people truly love each other. He could now sit in the hermitage and recall the special times he and Margie had known, the times when their hearts beat as one.

This freedom, and the absence of the abbot who had imprisoned him for so many years, permitted Merton to visit the Far East so as to continue his curiosity with Eastern religions and shed what he described as the burdens of depression, suspicion, and doubt haunting his soul for years. He could even admire Gethsemani. This despite contrary feelings Edward Rice said Merton had expressed to him prior to the Asia trip, leading Rice to believe Merton never would have returned to Gethsemani. Rice also suggested Merton somehow knew he was going to die in Asia; he had established a trust to handle his papers and written farewell letters to three friends, one of which included his suggested plans for burial. Rice surmised Merton's life at Gethsemani was over, and if he did not die, he would spend the rest of life away from his monastery. If Rice was right, Merton had indeed gained a true sense of freedom.

On the final day of 1966, Merton had written a revealing letter to Don James, laying out his true feelings about the Margie romance. He admitted an "emotional problem" was difficult to shed but necessary in order to discover solitude so as to give himself to God. Merton admitted "this problem" had provided him with a great learning experience, allowing him to think and pray, and more important, to "grow in a way that was not possible before." Most revealing was Merton's admission: "I have been more truly myself than ever before. . . ."[44] Such emotions connected to his belief that "perfect freedom equaled perfect love, and that love and solitude were the true sign of maturity and freedom."[45]

Certainly Merton deserved this newfound freedom and solitude. One hopes that if he had lived longer, he would have continued on the "right road" where he would "just . . . go for walks, live in peace, [and] let change come quietly and invisibly on the inside."[46] The best evidence that Merton appeared to be in this state of grace was a letter from the abbots attending the Bangkok conference where Merton died. Sent to Gethsemani, it read, in part, "In death Father Louis's face was set in a great and deep peace, and it was obvious that he had found Him Whom he had searched for so diligently."[47] Scholar Paul Wilkes, for one, agreed that Merton had found his peace, his God before he died, writing that after Merton witnessed the gleaming Buddhist statutes at Polunnaruwa, his "hand-wringing days were over, the myriad questions now rendered irrelevant, the once precisely delineated steps to enlightenment—or union with the almighty—were now but a feeble ladder that would soon be kicked away."[48]

Exposing the paradoxical Merton had required unmasking the man who abhorred masks, the actor who kept inner anguish to himself yet hated actors, those artificial in nature. Some may feel that dissecting Merton's private life, a dark side of sorts, is akin to blasphemy, but his preserving so much of his life story indicates that he wanted others to learn from, and be inspired by, his humanistic struggles. Anthony Padovano believed Merton wrote in his journals "about his pettiness, his envy, his sexual temptations, his doubts" so everyone would know that "the mystical journey was profoundly human, that it wasn't exotic, that it wasn't artificial." Father John Eudes, after noting Merton's "tortuous way he was to travel to God," said, "[Merton] knew that ambiguity and contradictory tendencies mark every monk's life and, in fact, are a feature of every human character." Regarding the importance of Merton's journals and their exposure of "intimate material," Eudes suggested, "They provide a window into his lifelong search for authenticity of life, especially of his life of prayer. His honesty leads him repeatedly to confess his failures with a clear-sighted frankness that surprises at times." In mid-May 1967, Merton himself mentioned how he wanted to be completely open about mistakes made and his quest to make sense of life with the "affair with Margie," as he called it, an important part of him indicating his limitations. Biographer John Howard Griffin concluded: "No matter how it [the love affair] turned out, no matter how it made him look, he wanted the truth of its essentials to exist in an unembellished state."[49]

Griffin's words depict a true, loving, converted Christian, the new Thomas Merton, the compelling spiritualist who had become liberated as never before, since he had not only conquered sinful inner demons, but broken free of the chains the Catholic Church imposed upon him, the ones connected with preserving "the good image of the Order."[50] They are the words of a man, a monk, flawed as he may have been, human beneath the mask of holiness, one who had become "empty" so as to discard his false self, and one who truly died so he might live. This transformation, triggered by his finally understanding the true meaning of love, permitted Thomas Merton to conquer, not once, but twice, the obstacle first mentioned in *The Seven Storey Mountain,* a "mountain of purgatory, steeper and more arduous that I was able to imagine."[51] Now he could look in the mirror and see the true image of himself since he had regained self-respect and dignity so as to love not only his God, but himself. He was Frater Louis again, one who, by finally adhering to his vows by resisting the temptation of Margie, had done God's will so as to be with "God alone."

That Merton was able to climb these mountains and many more during a life inspiring millions of people recalls the words of Father Basil Pennington. Intent on presenting a unique, positive bent to Merton's life, he wrote, "Thomas Merton was a man. Much of his attractiveness lies in the fact that he was, indeed, a person of flesh and blood, body and feeling, time and place."[52] Amen.

CHAPTER TWENTY-TWO

THOMAS MERTON:
the MAN, *the* LEGACY

In Herbert R. Lottman's superb biography of Albert Camus, the author notes, "Sometimes the biography of an author can seem like a banquet from which the guest of honor is absent. So what the biographer must do is to draw attention to the work without pretending to substitute his book for the collected works of the subject."[1] Such has been the intention of this Thomas Merton portrayal; since no one can write like Merton, no one can create the magical language he wove together in his books. Hopefully this contribution to his story will inspire many to search out his writings and benefit from his wisdom, regardless of one's faith or lack thereof. Merton was certain, as he noted in Louisville in 1958, that "my vocation does not really make me different from the rest of men or put me in a special category. . . ."[2] He spoke to all of us when he wrote, "My Lord God, I have no idea where I am going. I do not see the road ahead of me. I cannot know for certain how/where it will end. . . ."[3] This is the bond Merton has with everyone; this is the certain link connecting him to modern-day society. The road Margie Smith shared with Merton ended for certain when he died. We will never know whether he would have resumed the relationship when he returned to the United States from Asia or whether he would have stayed at Gethsemani.

Some scholars, including Michael Mott, suspect that Merton died accidentally, but he also noted that "some grounds" existed that Merton might have been murdered, but they did not appear "plausible."[4] If Merton was killed, the logical suspects would be directives hired by the Catholic Church hierarchy, who were afraid of a scandal if Merton were to return to his lover or leave Gethsemani. This possibility appears remote, but Merton's words in Bangkok implying that "conditions had changed, and that celibacy, even for a monk, was a thing of the past," must have been cause for concern for Catholic officials watching his every move.[5]

Without the famous monk in her life, Margie carved out her own existence. In 1998, she spoke to Paul Hendrickson of the *Washington Post*. He reported that "Margie Smith went back to Ohio and married a doctor[6] and raised sons. In all these years she has never once spoken publicly of Merton. Even Michael Mott, the authorized biographer, never met her. (They spoke on the phone.)" Hendrickson added, "She has painted, she has taken advanced studies in nursing, she has kept up with the Louisville friends who were close to Merton. She has declined to become part of a culture in America that would reward somebody with millions for writing a book titled 'I was Thomas Merton's Secret Love.'"[7] Apparently disappointed with Hendrickson's report, Margie cut off further communication with those interested in her relationship with Merton.

Merton died in 1968, at age 53, 27 years to the day after he entered the Gethsemani gates, and it is possible to view his life and times through multiple lenses. Robert E. Daggy believed the spiritual guru was a "Poet and essayist, biographer and critic, translator and diarist, novelist, autobiographer, sometime satirist . . . a letter writer of extraordinary ability,"[8] Dr. Rudy Bernard, Merton's brother monk in the late 1940s, said Merton had a "twinkle in his eye . . . he was jovial, almost a jokester . . . He had a winsome personality, very democratic, self-effacing and earthy" despite his fame.[9] R. A. DeSutter, a brother monk with Merton from 1957 until 1963, said he was "a superb teacher, extremely intelligent, and one who could see below the surface of questions." DeSutter's wife, Lynn, recalled a social occasion with Merton and Dan Walsh in 1968, where Merton was "very present in the moment, genuine," and had "a hearty laugh that went to his toes." When she asked for a reading list, he suggested *Black Like Me,* a biography of Malcolm X, and books on the Vietnam War."[10] Brother Paul Quenon remembered Merton's "vivid imagination; [he] expressed himself poetically."[11] Father Matthew Kelty recalled Merton as "saucy, bouncy, young, boyish, English, cool, laid back, subtle, whimsical, [and] merry . . . [He was] a man of great hope." "[Merton] was convinced that God spoke through him," Kelty said, "and that his way of writing allowed people to hear things that seemed to be written *for* them."[12]

Father Flavian Burns concluded, "Many people would read such and such Merton, and then say, 'That's not Merton, that's me; that's my own life.'"[13]

His Holiness the Dalai Lama viewed Merton as one who took "a deep interest in Eastern philosophy, mainly Buddhism, and especially meditation . . . he was very open-minded."[14] Author Lawrence Cunningham's opinion of Merton: "I think that [he] could easily be called the greatest spiritual writer, . . . of the twentieth century in English-speaking America."[15] Poet and longtime friend Ron Seitz liked the human side of Merton: "He was a guy with big, baggy pants, needed a shave, laughed too much, drank too much beer, just an ordinary guy."[16] Sister Elena Malits said Merton "by temperament, I think, was basically a risk taker. He knew that to learn anything is to leave a safe ground." Colman McCarthy perceived a different face of the famous monk: "[Merton] was a rebel . . . You're not supposed to be a rebel in the Trappists . . . I think he realized after the popularity of his autobiography that he was now a product."[17]

Joan Baez said Merton was "this red-cheeked lovely man, who was "cheerful, joking," and "always giggling like the Dalai Lama with a smile on his face, ready for joy." She recalled him as a mentor "known and loved. He had a true sensibility." Merton, she decided, was "a true man, with a lightness like the Dalai Lama, with all the depth anyone could have."[18] Baez' recollection of Merton becoming "pie-faced," an apparent reference to his being drunk during her visit with him in 1966, connects with several instances where he drank alcohol, whether it was borrowed from Brother Camillus; from a hidden stash of wine; with Dr. Wygal or friend Linda Parsons; or with Margie on picnics, at restaurants, or in Dr. Wygal's office. Does this mean any true portrayal of Merton must include his being an alcoholic, one who never shed pre-monastic tendencies based on bouts of drunkenness both at Clare College and Columbia? Did this mean his drinking contributed to his sometimes confused, depressed mental state, and perhaps even to his initial infatuations and continued passionate relationship with Margie Smith?

As with all reflections about Merton, the truth is embedded in the words he wrote and from those who knew and observed him. While he chose to drink on many occasions, labeling him an alcoholic would be unfair. But a valid interpretation based on his journal entries leaves little doubt alcohol was, at the least, a contributing factor in the romance with Margie. Certainly his words indicate alcohol was a constant companion as the relationship intensified, perhaps a fortifier of the courage he needed to keep the love flame alive despite a reality check now and then. His passion for Margie was intense, and the alcohol may have bolstered his feelings of manhood. Few Merton scholars have approached this subject, perhaps out of respect for him, or because no one has heretofore connected the dots between his pre-monastic conduct and Merton's intermittent drinking during the Margie affair. It does appear that after he had finally decided to choose God over Margie, the drinking was curtailed, evidence that alcohol was less of a crutch than before. This would mesh with the view that he was truly free—free of all of the demons haunting him for so many years.

To be certain, Merton shared his transgressions with other famous spiritual leaders from the past. Saint Francis, known for his sexual appetite as a youngster at 15, later achieved strict celibacy, as did Saint Bernard, the Cistercian abbot of Clairvaux, "who had passed through a dissolute phase in his early life," where, as "middle-class, rich, vain (he vaunted a velvet cloak), and attractive; he used these assets to give good parties and seduce girls of a lower class for whom he had feelings no deeper than sexual pleasure."[19] But it is Saint Augustine, who took two mistresses and fathered a son, with whom Merton should be most readily identified. In his *Confessions,* which some scholars have compared to *SSM,* he recorded his famous prayer "Give me chastity, but not yet." Like Merton's, Augustine's father died when he was young. Like Merton, Augustine was consumed with love of the flesh, with "adolescence and sexual temptation." He was described as "too much a man of the flesh," and "a man awash in sexual temptations." But Augustine saw the light and moved from "sexual love to divine love."[20] Merton moved from sexual love to true love to a new sense of divine love with "God alone" through the Margie experience, freeing him from the shackles of lust as forbidden by the Rule of St. Benedict.

Merton is still, 40-plus years after his death, a beacon of light for those who admire his writings. Addressing Merton's continuing popularity, Robert Toth, director of the Merton Foundation, stated, "Maybe the notion of popular spirituality fits in . . . [People] are looking for something to grab in these weird times. When they land on Merton, they discover something really substantial. It clicks. We can see our way out of it—the whole mess—when we read Merton."[21]

Knowing about Merton's secret world should not cause followers, or those interested in him for the first time, any reluctance to pursue his writings. To the contrary, understanding Merton's human, flawed side permits a true connection with everyone who realizes his own failings. This is why he wanted the Margie affair to be known, why he wanted his life, warts and all, to be understood—so those struggling with the same problems he encountered would know hope is their best friend during tough times. Merton's words stand strong in defense of the idea that happiness, joy, and, most important, freedom, are only possible through a spiritual oneness with God and the Holy Spirit, or whatever higher power one may choose. As Pastor Rick Warren wrote in his best-seller *The Purpose Driven Life,* "It's not about you." This is a simple phrase, but one that rings true, especially for Merton, who had to learn that a selfish, "me, me, me" attitude was never the answer, and that he could only find the joy he sought through the love of a woman first, and finally, through being obedient to, and loving "God alone." Then one does not "drive" as Merton once put it; he or she lets the Holy Spirit be in charge.

What is the true legacy of Thomas Merton, and why are his life and his writings still as relevant in today's world as those of Eckhart Tolle, Ram Dass, Anne Lamott, Rick Warren, Deepak Chopra, Houston Smith, Joel Osteen, and others of spiritual prominence? Merton, despite his contradictions, inspires in so many ways through his promotion of contemplative living as a way of life so as to provide love and compassion for others. A true echo of God's voice, Merton encourages people to value the divine moments in life, to savor the deeper meaning of every experience, and to count their blessings while enjoying the simple things: love, family, and good health. This life path extends to any and all religions and spiritualities; Merton was truly a man of inclusion, not division.

Merton knew from his own experiences that God is a loving God, one who will forgive, one who will guide the way for troubled souls when there appears to be no way out. This is especially true for a new generation of young people, many of whom have not heard about Merton, but need to, so as to make sense of a 21st-century world confronting them with challenges too difficult to overcome without some spiritual direction. If more of them knew of Merton's teachings, perhaps his spiritual messages would resonate just as they did among youth in 1949, when *SSM* was published, leading editor Robert Giroux to believe "the book appealed to young people upset with the world" and those "who were depressed and disillusioned, looking for assurance."[22] This assurance, Merton would suggest, is only possible through love, since "man is saved by love."[23]

While Merton contributed his wisdom in so many ways, it is his compelling search for love that arguably provides the strongest impact, since each of us can relate to this struggle. To this end, the greatest lesson to be learned from the spiritual monk's life may be described as follows: If a lonely orphan like Merton, infected as he was with debilitating morals, lustful sin, and guilt, may find love and truly be "in love," then such is possible, he would urge, for anyone, no matter his or her sinful past, willing to open up their heart and soul, and thus witness the magic, the majesty, of the true gift of love.

More than anything, Thomas Merton's life was a love story, a mystical adventure. In essence, Merton had become the man he described when he wrote, "The true Christian rebirth is a renewed transformation, a 'passover' in which we are progressively liberated from selfishness and not only grow in love but in some sense we 'become love.'" Through his experience with Margie Smith, he had reached the perfection of this new rebirth where there was "no more selfishness, there is only love." Having attained this state of enlightenment, he was free to take the last step toward God and walk over the line passing from this earth to his next state of being with no "unfinished business" to worry about.[24] He may have been Thomas Merton in real life, but now his true name was indeed, as he had hoped, Love.

ACKNOWLEDGMENTS

The idea for a fresh biography of Thomas Merton was birthed during a conversion class taught by Dr. Lewis Rambo and Steven C. Baumann during my completion of a Master's degree in Theological studies at San Francisco Theological Seminary. Dr. Rambo continued mentoring me throughout the writing process and I am most thankful for his guidance and friendship. His colleagues Dr. Elizabeth Liebert, Dr. Christopher Ocker, Dr. Herman Weitjen, Drs. Bob and Polly Coote, Dr. Charles Marks, and the late Dr. Doug Adams are also thanked for their contributions to my spiritual journey. Novelist Ron Carlson certainly assisted with the storytelling method used in the book and I thank him as well. I also appreciate the guidance I received from Jonathan Montaldo, associate director of the Merton Institute for Contemplative Living. Jonathan continues to inspire all who will listen to his words of wisdom providing guideposts for daily living. Special thanks are extended to Dr. Paul Pearson and Mark Meade of the Thomas Merton Center at Bellarmine University in Louisville. They were invaluable in assisting me with research. I also thank Anne McCormick and the Merton Legacy Trust for their permission to use excerpts from Merton's private letters.

I am most thankful for interviews with Dr. John Eudes, Brother Paul Quenon, Dr. Rudy Bernard and gifted singer/songwriter Joan Baez. Each provided fresh insight into the Merton mindset both before and during the Margie Smith love affair.

Space concerns permit me only to simply thank many people who contributed their wisdom to the book. They include: Doug Olds, Joe Lauer, Alice Peck, Debbie Dewey, Dave Danforth, Jenn Granat, Jane Arnold, Nancy and Dave Foley, Mike Stipher, Hugh and Pearl Campion, Ronald Malaluan and Fabio Natolli of the Hotel Barocco in Rome, Jerry Bales, Lynn Farabaugh, Margie Rodriguez Le Sage, Pat Riley Anna and Gerd Kortemeyer, Don and Corrine Larsen, Janice and Scott Montross, Jack Lupton, Pete and Alice Dye, Richard and Wendy Boly, Bob Baldori, Bill Castinair, Jackie Munoz, Linda Orzechowski, Peggy Roske, Jocelyn K. Wilk, Susan Hamson, and Sandra and Jim Seaton. Several books certainly impacted my spiritual growth during the creative process. They include a *Study Bible* provided by one of my stepsons, *The Purpose Driven Life, Jesus Life Coach, The Skilled Pastor,* the *Tao Te Ching, Listening for the Soul,* and *The Death of Ivan Illych.* Merton's *New Seeds of Contemplation* has also become a special friend, one guiding me toward the contemplative life.

This book would not have been possible without the assistance of my treasured literary agent, James Fitzgerald, who believed in this book from the moment he read the proposal. He, in turn, discovered one of like mind at Palgrave Macmillan: editor Alessandra Bastagli. Her colleague, Jake Klisivitch considerably enhanced the quality of the book by prodding me to deeper thought about Merton's story. This book is a thousand times better due to his assistance. Thank you Alessandra, Jake, and your Palgrave colleagues Colleen Lawrie, Christine Caterino, Sarah Thomas, Yasmin Mathew, and also David Baldeosingh Rotstein, Letra Libre, Sarah Hanson, and Nancy Hirsch, among others.

For her love, patience, encouragement, understanding, and much-needed advice with both writing and editing, I thank my wife, Wen-ying Lu. She is the bright star in my life, the illuminator, the light, the most caring individual on the face of the earth, one who has showed me what true love is all about. Our beloved Labrador, Black Sox, is also thanked for his loyalty and patience during the writing process. What a wonderful friend he has been through the years.

To Margie Smith, whose privacy I have honored by not attempting to locate her, I am thankful for her loving ways with Merton. When she reads this book, I hope she will realize how much she meant to him and his discovering freedom for the first time in his life. My fondest wish would be for her to permit me to tell her side of the story.

To Thomas Merton, I say thank you for your inspirational words and teachings, ones that have greatly changed my life for the better. There are many more experienced writers and scholars who could probably tell your story better than I have, but I trust my presentation of your struggle to discover true love and freedom is positive and compelling. Your body of work is second to none and I am hopeful people who have not heard about your writings will discover for themselves the wisdom of the words. More each day make their way to my website at www.markshawbooks.net and the Merton weblog at http://merton.markshawbooks.net/ to learn more about you.

From the very moment I began writing this book, it is has been truly guided along by the Holy Spirit. Time and time again, I was led to new information about Merton whether through books, interviews, or ideas permitting a better understanding of the complicated, gifted monk. Many days I could actually feel the spirit infiltrating the writing, causing me to witness firsthand the power of divine intervention. It has truly been an honor to write this book, and I trust it will inspire those reading it to never give up in the quest to learn what true love, and freedom, are all about.

—Mark Shaw

NOTES

PROLOGUE

1. *O, The Oprah Magazine,* May 2005; www.oprah.com/article/omagazine/readingroom/ obc_omag_200505_5books.
2. Author e mail interview with Dr. Paul Pearson, January 12, 2009.
3. Dr. Rowan Williams (Archbishop of Canterbury), *The Tablet,* Dec. 20–27, 2008, 14–15.

CHAPTER 1

1. Merton's audience is designated here as "students" according to various recorded audio tape introductions. During Merton's earlier years, the lectures were exclusively for novices. Later Merton spoke for the whole community on Sundays. For the "student" lectures, lay brothers were excluded, with "only the choir monks in novitiate and before vows being allowed. Lay brothers might listen to the recorded version while completing tasks such as peeling potatoes the next day." E-mail interview with Mark Meade, January 5, 2009.
2. During this period, novices were not permitted to speak to each other, in accordance with The Rule of Saint Benedict. Asking questions or commenting during instruction was permitted in order to allow brother monks to learn some facts and personality traits about each other by the substance and tone of the questions asked or comments made. Interview with Dr. Rudy Bernard, June 18, 2008.
3. Merton's lecture mentioned in this and the following five paragraphs is in Thomas Merton, *Pure Love,* lecture, April 20, 1963 (Credence Communications, 1995), #AA2136, audiocassette.

CHAPTER 2

1. Thomas Merton, *Dancing in the Water of Life: Seeking Peace in the Hermitage,* The Journals of Thomas Merton, vol. V (San Francisco: HarperSanFrancisco, 1997), 32.
2. Merton's description of Meister Eckhart: "[He] may have limitations, but I am entranced with him nevertheless. I like the brevity, the incisiveness of his sermons, his way of piercing straight to the heart of the inner, the awakened spark, the creative and redeeming Word, God born in us. He was a great man. . . ." in *Conjectures of a Guilty Bystander* (New York: Doubleday, 1966), 42; Merton's reference to sermon in Thomas Merton, *Learning to Love: Exploring Solitude and Freedom,* The Journals of Thomas Merton, vol. VI (San Francisco: HarperSanFrancisco, 1997), 38.
3. Merton, *Learning to Love,* 45.
4. Michael Mott, *The Seven Mountains of Thomas Merton* (Boston: Houghton Mifflin, 1984), 435.
5. The monastery near Bardstown, Kentucky, was founded in 1848 by Cistercian (Trappist) monks who came from France under the leadership of Fr. Eutropius Proust. William H. Shannon, Christine M. Bochen, and Patrick F. O'Connell, eds., *The Thomas Merton Encyclopedia* (Maryknoll, NY: Orbis Books, 2002), 175.
6. Merton, *Learning to Love,* 37–38.
7. Ibid., 9, for information on Sheen; for Merton's snow description, 13.
8. Ibid., 15, 16.

9. Ibid., 18, 19, 21.

10. Ibid., 24, 25.

11. Ibid., 26.

12. Ibid., 27.

13. John Howard Griffin, *Follow the Ecstasy: The Hermitage Years of Thomas Merton* (Maryknoll, NY: Orbis Books, 1993) 51.

14. Merton, *Learning to Love,* 40.

15. Thomas Merton, *The Sign of Jonas* (San Diego: Harcourt, 1979), 171.

16. Griffin, *Follow the Ecstasy,* 22.

17. Merton, *Learning to Love,* 41, 42.

18. Ibid., 42.

19. Ibid., 43.

20. Ibid., 43.

21. Ibid., 43, 44.

22. Ibid., 44.

23. Ibid., 44.

24. Little is known about the "fiancé." His full name is never provided, but he will be called "N." later. It appears Margie told Merton about her attachment when they first met.

25. Merton, *Learning to Love,* 44, 45. Merton designates Margie with the letter M. in his journals.

26. Ibid., 45.

27. Ibid.

28. Merton initially visited Dr. Wygal for psychotherapy, but became a good friend. Ibid., 45; Merton's emotions, Ibid., 46.

29. Ibid., 46.

30. Ibid.

31. Ibid.

32. Ibid., 46, 47.

33. Ibid., 47.

34. Ibid.

35. Ibid.

36. Ibid.

37. Ibid.

38. Ibid., 48.

39. Ibid.

40. Ibid., 49.

41. Ibid., 49, 50, 51.

42. Ibid., 51.

43. Merton's description is from Griffin, *Follow the Ecstasy,* 65; Merton's description of where he met Margie, how she looked, and what he did is from Merton, *Learning to Love,* 51, 52.

44. Merton, *Learning to Love,* 52.

45. Information as to Merton's writing the poem is from Griffin, *Follow the Ecstasy,* 66; poem is published in Merton, *Learning to Love,* 53.

46. Merton's description of his emotions are from Merton, *Learning to Love,* 54. Biographer Michael Mott envisions what another monk seeing Merton with Margie might have thought: "There goes Father Louis a hermit, all alone with a pretty girl. Well, perhaps that is a new slant on the hermit's life." Mott, *Seven Mountains of Thomas Merton,* 443.

47. Ibid., 54.

CHAPTER 3

1. Father John Dear, in Morgan C. Atkinson, *Soul Searching: The Journey of Thomas Merton,* DVD, (Duckworks, 2007).

2. Thomas Merton, *Honorable Reader* (New York: Crossroad, 1989), 3.

3. Paul Wilkes, ed., *Merton, by Those Who Knew Him Best* (San Francisco: Harper & Row, 1984), 43–44.

4. Jonathan Montaldo, ed., *A Year with Thomas Merton: Daily Meditations from His Journals* (San Francisco: HarperSanFrancisco, 2004), book jacket text.

5. Elizabeth Renzetti, "Mapping the Mountain that is Merton," *Toronto Globe and Mail,* December 5, 1998, p. C9.

6. Joan Chittister, e-newsletter, www.benetvision.org, December 8, 2008.

7. Wilkes, ed., *Merton,* 147.

8. Thomas Merton, *Introduction to Contemplative Prayer* (New York: Herder and Herder, 1969).

9. Thomas Merton, *The Road to Joy* (New York: Farrar, Straus, Giroux, 1989), 41.

10. Russell Shaw, *Nothing to Hide: Secrecy, Communication, and Communion in the Catholic Church* (San Francisco: Ignatius Press, 2008), 15, 13, 17.

11. Thomas Merton, *The Seven Storey Mountain* (New York: Harcourt Brace, 1948).

12. Giroux opinion from Merton, *Seven Storey Mountain,* introductory page; Mott opinion from Michael Mott, *The Seven Mountains of Thomas Merton* (Boston, Houghton Mifflin, 1984), xvii; Pennington conclusion from M. Basil Pennington, *Thomas Merton, Brother Monk, The Quest for True Freedom* (San Francisco: Harper & Row, 1987), xi. It is also important to remember that the book was first published in 1948, during a very strict age of Catholicism before Vatican II. Rice opinion from Edward Rice, *The Man in the Sycamore Tree* (New York: Doubleday, 1970), 64–65.

13. Mott, *Seven Mountains of Thomas Merton,* 77.

14. Ibid.

15. Ibid., 77, 78.

16. Rice, *Man in the Sycamore Tree,* 65.

17. Merton, *Seven Storey Mountain,* 3.

18. Ibid., 3, 4.

19. Ibid., 5–6.

20. Ibid., 7–9.

21. Monica Furlong, *Merton: A Biography* (San Francisco: Harper & Row, 1980), 5.

22. Merton, *Seven Storey Mountain,* 10.

23. Ibid., 14–15, 16.

24. Ibid., 20–21.

25. Ibid., 22.

26. Ibid., 23, 25.

27. Ibid., 25–26.

28. Ibid., 29.

29. Ibid., 31–32.

30. Ibid., 33, 54.

31. Ibid., 54.

32. Ibid., 54, 57, 61–62.

33. Ibid., 69.

34. Ibid., 71, 76.

35. Ibid., 78–79, 81.

36. Ibid., 84–85, 89–90.

37. Owen Merton obituary: "Mr. Merton was a water-colour painter of distinction who, had he lived long, would have earned a wide reputation . . . His pictures displayed a sense of design and a delicacy of colour which reflected his love of the Chinese masters, together with a strength and individuality which bore witness to the originality and power of the artist's mind," London *Times,* January 21, 1931; Merton's recollections of father from Merton, *Seven Storey Mountain,* 93.

38. Merton, *Seven Storey Mountain,* 94.

CHAPTER 4

1. Thomas Merton, *The Seven Storey Mountain* (New York: Harcourt Brace, 1998), 94.

2. Merton, *Seven Storey Mountain,* 95.

3. Ibid., 97.

4. Ibid., 98.
5. Ibid., 100.
6. Ibid., 98.
7. Ibid., 110–112.
8. Ibid., 116–117, 119.
9. Ibid., 120.
10. Ibid., 122. Merton does not specify the name of the Rome *pensione* he stayed at in 1933, but author research based on the coordinates necessary for him to have "looked down" on the Triton Fountain, the Barberini Piazza, the Bristol Hotel, the Barberini Palace, and the Barberini Cinema from his room is consistent with the location of the Santa Centrale Pensione, located a few meters to the west of the fountain where the Hotel Barroco now exists. Author interview with Hotel Barocco manager Fabio Natolli, March 2008.
11. Merton, *Seven Storey Mountain,* 118, 123.
12. Ibid., 123–124.
13. Ibid., 129.
14. Ibid., 131.
15. Ibid., 133–134.
16. Ibid., 134, 137.
17. Ibid., 137–139.
18. Ibid., 141.
19. Ibid., 145–147.
20. Ibid., 152–153.
21. Ibid., 153–154, 156, 163.
22. Ibid., 165.
23. Ibid., 166, 173.
24. Ibid., 174–175.
25. Ibid., 178–179.
26. Ibid., 180.
27. Ibid., 181, 182.
28. Ibid., 185.
29. Ibid., 186.
30. Ibid., 187–188, 189, 191.
31. James Harford, *Merton & Friends* (New York: Continuum, 2006), book jacket text.
32. Merton, *Seven Storey Mountain,* 206–209.
33. Robert Lax was an Olean native, and the cottage where he and Merton stayed was owned by Lax's brother-in-law, Benjamin Marcus. Merton wrote of Lax: "He was a combination of Hamlet and Elias. A potential prophet, but without rage . . . A king, but a Jew too. A mind full of tremendous and subtle intuitions . . . [he has always had] a kind of natural, instinctive spirituality, a kind of inborn direction to the living God." Ibid., 198, 211, 219.
34. Ibid., 223–224.
35. Ibid., 225–226, 230.
36. Ibid., 231, 233.
37. Ibid., 234, 236.
38. Ibid., 236–237.
39. Ibid., 237–239.
40. Ibid., 238, 242.
41. Ibid., 6, 245, 248. Apparently Merton's baptism as a child in France was not recognized as an "official" baptism, according the edicts of the Catholic Church.
42. Ibid., 250–251.
43. Ibid., 251–252, 253.
44. Ibid., 256–257.
45. Ibid., 261.
46. Ibid., 277–279.
47. Ibid., 280.

CHAPTER 5

1. Thomas Merton, *The Seven Storey Mountain* (New York: Harcourt Brace, 1998), 284–285.

2. Ibid., 287–289.

3. Ibid., 289–291.

4. Ibid., 294, 298, 301.

5. Ibid., 302–303.

6. Ibid., 313.

7. Ibid., 314, 315, 317.

8. Ibid., 319, 320, 323, 324.

9. Ibid., 324.

10. Ibid., 325.

11. Ibid., 325.

12. Ibid., 326.

13. Ibid., 328. Breviaries are books of prayers, hymns, psalms, and readings for the canonical hours.

14. Franciscans promote a "third order" consisting of laypersons who minister to others.

15. Merton, *Seven Storey Mountain,* 328.

16. Ibid., 328–329.

17. Ibid., 332.

18. Ibid., 333–334.

19. Edward Rice, *The Man in the Sycamore Tree* (New York: Image Books Edition by special arrangement with Doubleday, 1972), 45.

20. Merton, *The Seven Storey Mountain,* 339, 340, 343, 345.

21. Ibid., 346, 349, 351.

22. Ibid., 351, 352.

23. Ibid., 354, 355.

24. Merton once described fellow monks as being "hothouse plants, nursed along in a carefully overheated life of prayer." See Thomas Merton, *Conjectures of a Guilty Bystander* (New York: Doubleday, 1966), vii. Merton's emotions and thoughts in Merton, *Seven Storey Mountain,* 359, 362.

25. Merton, *Seven Storey Mountain,* 365, 372, 375, 377.

26. Ibid., 394, 399.

27. Ibid., 401–403.

28. Ibid., 405–406.

29. Ibid., 406, 408.

30. Ibid., 410, 413–414.

31. Ibid., 422, 426, 438.

32. "John Paul became interested in Catholicism while at Cornell, where he had taken up flying together with Fr. Donald Cleary, the Catholic chaplain. In late August, 1942, John Paul arrived in Liverpool at the bomber command in Buckinghamshire. From there he went off to Bournemouth for training." See William H. Shannon, Christine M. Bochen, and Patrick F. O'Connell, *The Thomas Merton Encyclopedia,* (Maryknoll, NY: Orbis Books, 2002), 294, 295; Merton recollections from Merton, *Seven Storey Mountain,* 438–440.

33. "On [John Paul's] disembarkment he took the train to London, where he visited the American Eagle Club, set up for Americans in the RAF. While in London he met Margaret May Evans, a typist, who had enlisted in the British armed forces. They fell in love and were married, February 1943." See Shannon, et al., *Thomas Merton Encyclopedia,* 295. Merton's thoughts about his brother from Merton, *Seven Storey Mountain,* 442.

34. "On April 16 'Mert' (as John Paul was called) took off in a crew of five in a Wellington bomber. For a reason that has never been discovered, the plane began to lose altitude and finally crashed into the English Channel. Two members of the crew were able to get to an inflated dinghy. They managed to pull Merton on board. His back was broken in the fall. He was conscious for a while and spent much of his time praying. Finally he died in the early hours of Saturday, April 17, the Saturday of Passion Week. They watched over his

body for two days, hoping for rescue. Eventually it came, but too late for Merton. His comrades had buried him at sea, in as Christian a manner as possible." See Shannon, et al., *Thomas Merton Encyclopedia*, 295; burial information from Merton, *Seven Storey Mountain*, 442–443.

35. Merton, *Seven Storey Mountain*, 444, 447, 448.
36. Copy of *New Directions* contract in the Thomas Merton Center, Bellarmine University, Louisville, Kentucky.
37. Merton, *Seven Storey Mountain*, 448–449.

CHAPTER 6

1. Thomas Merton, *Run to the Mountain: The Story of a Vocation*, The Journals of Thomas Merton, vol. I (San Francisco: HarperSanFrancisco, 1995), page opposite of verso of title page.
2. Robert M. Durling, trans., *The Divine Comedy of Dante Alighieri*, vol. II (London: Oxford University Press, 2004), 7.
3. Merton, *Run to the Mountain*, 6.
4. Ibid., 18.
5. Ibid., 24–25, 31.
6. Ibid., 32.
7. Ibid., 34.
8. Ibid., 48.
9. Ibid., 59, 62.
10. Ibid., 62–63.
11. Ibid., 72.
12. Introduction to Saint Theresa of Avila, E. Allison Peer, ed., trans., *The Interior Castle*, (Garden City, NY: Image Books, 1961).
13. Ibid., 97–98.
14. Ibid., 137.
15. Ibid., 162.
16. Ibid., 229–237.
17. Ibid., 252.
18. Ibid., 398, 444.
19. A 1954 letter from Jean Leclercq to Merton expresses the Benedictine monk's view of Merton the writer-for-profit: "But it would be a good thing if at least once you could write just for the glory of God with no money involved. And that would have the advantage of reacting to a fairly widespread idea in Europe: T. Merton brings in money, so his Superiors exploit him as much as possible, because of the income." See Brother Patrick Hart, ed., *Survival of Prophecy: The Letters of Thomas Merton and Jean Leclercq* (New York: Farrar, Straus, Giroux, 2002), 49.
20. Morgan C. Atkinson, *Soul Searching: The Journey of Thomas Merton*. DVD. (Duckworks, Inc., 2007).
21. Thomas Merton, *The Road to Joy* (New York: Farrar, Straus, and Giroux, 1989), 10.
22. Ibid., 15.
23. Thomas Merton, *The Collected Poems of Thomas Merton* (New York: New Directions, 1977), 25–59.
24. Thomas Merton, *Entering the Silence: Becoming a Monk & Writer*, The Journals of Thomas Merton, vol. II (San Francisco: HarperSanFrancisco, 1996), 31.
25. Ibid., 33, 35.
26. Ibid., 35, 36, 40.
27. Ibid., 42, 46–47.
28. Ibid., 49.
29. Ibid., 70, 72.
30. Ibid., 77.
31. Ibid., 79–80.
32. Ibid., 89, 100, 101.

33. Ibid., 121, 135, 161. Merton's view of *SSM* included his comment: "Proofs [on the book] came, and there is a lot of it, and still 8,000 words to cut, but that won't be hard. I'll cut more . . . St. Paul, help me out, sharpen my scissors!" .

34. Ibid., 161, 172–173.

35. "I will never argue with a censor. I don't have to. I can say all God wants me to say in the right area where no controversy enters at all." Ibid., 201, 211.

36. Ibid., 218.

37. Merton, *Entering the Silence,* 228.

38. Ibid., 234.

39. Ibid., 237.

40. Ibid., 253.

41. Ibid., 287.

42. Thomas Merton, *The Waters of Siloe* (New York: Harcourt, Brace, 1949), xix, xxxiii.

43. Merton, *Entering the Silence,* 314, 317, 327.

44. Ibid., 328.

45. Ibid., 332, 349.

46. Ibid., 363, 367.

47. Ibid., 371.

48. Ibid., 376, 379, 387.

49. Ibid., 393, 398, 420.

50. Ibid., 420–421.

51. Ibid., 450–451.

52. Ibid., 458.

CHAPTER 7

1. Author interview with Dr. Rudy Bernard, April 12, 2008.

2. Thomas Merton, *A Search for Solitude: Pursuing the Monk's Life,* The Journals of Thomas Merton, vol. III, (San Francisco: HarperSanFrancisco, 1996), xiv.

3. Ibid., 17, 20, 22.

4. Jim Forest, *Living with Wisdom: A Life of Thomas Merton* (Maryknoll, NY: Orbis Books, 1991), 120.

5. Merton, *A Search for Solitude,* 32.

6. Zilboorg meeting information from Michael Mott, *The Seven Mountains of Thomas Merton* (Boston; Houghton Mifflin, 1984), 291: Zilboorg impressions from Merton, *A Search for Solitude,* 59, 60.

7. Merton, *A Search for Solitude,* 60.

8. Ibid., 147, 149.

9. Ibid., 150, 151.

10. Ibid., 181, 182.

11. Ibid., 187, 214.

12. Dr. Rudy Bernard believes that "a foundation—the starting up of a new monastery—was more in line with what Merton believed the modern monastic life should be like—perhaps in an urban setting, rather than in a rural setting." Author interview with Dr. Rudy Bernard, April 13, 2008.

13. Merton, *A Search for Solitude,* 225, 240.

14. Ibid., 268.

15. Ibid., 277, 284. The remedy proposed was for Merton to get "an exclaustration, with the help of the bishop of Cuernavaca, move to Cuernavaca, [and] live for a while as a hermit under the auspices of the Monastero de la Resurreción until I got oriented."

16. Ibid., 284, 285.

17. Ibid., 289, 291.

18. Ibid., 291, 293.

19. Ibid., 309, 319.

20. Ibid., 322, 323.

21. Ibid., 326–327.

22. Ibid., 331.
23. Ibid., 335, 347.
24. Ibid., 350.
25. Ibid., 358.
26. Ibid., 358, 367.

CHAPTER 8

1. Thomas Merton, *Turning Toward the World: The Pivotal Years, The Journals of Thomas Merton,* vol. IV (San Francisco: Harper San Francisco, 1996), 7.
2. Ibid., 8, 13, 17, 21.
3. Ibid., 33.
4. Ibid., 34, 35.
5. Ibid., 73.
6. Ibid., 86, 87, 89.
7. Merton's reflection from Ibid., 97, 108. Rice's statements from Edward Rice, *The Man in the Sycamore Tree* (New York: Image Books Edition by special arrangement with Doubleday, 1972.), 80, 81.
8. Merton, *Turning Toward the World,* 108, 158.
9. Ibid., 158, 159.
10. Ibid., 172, 177.
11. Ibid., 183.
12. Ibid., 197.
13. Ibid., 212, 215, 217.
14. Ibid., 221, 245, 246.
15. Ibid., 246. Merton description included "Let us call her that, the question of knowing her name never really arises at all. It is totally irrelevant."
16. Ibid., 246–247.
17. Ibid., 272, 278, 279.
18. Ibid., 294, 303.
19. Ibid., 323–324.
20. Ibid., 328.
21. Ibid., 336, 340.
22. Ibid., 350.

CHAPTER 9

1. Thomas Merton, *Dancing in the Water of Life: Seeking Peace in the Hermitage,* The Journals of Thomas Merton, vol. V (San Francisco: HarperSanFrancisco, 1997), 3, 15, 16.
2. Ibid., 36, 37.
3. William H. Shannon, Christine M. Bochen, and Patrick F. O'Connell, eds., *The Thomas Merton Encyclopedia* (Maryknoll, NY: Orbis Books, 2002), 358, 359.
4. President Kennedy was revered by the powers that be at Gethsemani. Merton wrote, "Every time Kennedy sneezes or blows his nose an article is read about it in the refectory." See Thomas Merton, *Conjectures of a Guilty Bystander* (New York: Doubleday, 1966), 46. Merton emotions from Merton, *Dancing in the Water of Life,* 37.
5. Ibid., 68, 107, 116.
6. Ibid., 156. Dom James opinion from Dianne Aprile, *The Abbey of Gethsemani: Place of Peace and Paradox,* (Louisville, KY: Trout Lily Press, 1998), 153.
7. Merton, *Dancing in the Water of Life,* 197, 198.
8. Ibid., 198.
9. Ibid., 198, 199.
10. Ibid., 249.
11. Ibid., 256.
12. Ibid., 258–259.
13. Thomas Merton, *The Contemplative Call,* audio tape AA2915 (Credence Communications, 1995).

14. Ibid.
15. Ibid.
16. Merton, *Dancing in the Waters of Life,* 322, 326, 327.
17. Ibid., 327, 328.

CHAPTER 10

1. Robert Inchausti, *Echoing Silence: Thomas Merton and the Vocation of Writing* (Boston: New Seeds Books, 2007), vii, ix.
2. Author interviews with Brother Paul Quenon and Dr. Paul Pearson, November 3, 2008.
3. James Harford, *Merton & Friends* (New York: Continuum, 2006), book jacket text.
4. Ibid., 164 (photo insert caption).
5. Monica Furlong, *Merton: A Biography* (San Francisco: Harper & Row, 1980), book jacket text.
6. Michael Mott, *The Seven Mountains of Thomas Merton* (Boston: Houghton Mifflin, 1984), xxi, xxii.
7. Jim Forest, *Living with Wisdom: A Life of Thomas Merton* (Maryknoll, NY: Orbis Books, 1991), xi.
8. David Cooper, *Thomas Merton and the Art of Denial* (Athens: University of Georgia Press, 1989), 10.
9. William Shannon's comments in "A Note to the Reader," Thomas Merton, *The Seven Storey Mountain* (New York: Harcourt Brace, 1998), 5.
10. Harford, *Merton & Friends,* ix.
11. Michael Higgins, *Heretic Blood: The Spiritual Geography of Thomas Merton* (Toronto: Stoddart Publishing, 1998), 9.
12. Paul Elie, *The Life You Save May Be Your Own* (New York: Farrar, Straus, and Giroux, 2008).
13. Joan McDonald, *Thomas Merton, A Personal Biography* (Milwaukee, WI: Marquette University Press, 2007), Introduction, 2.
14. Furlong, *Merton,* 3.
15. Merton birthplace information from Mott, *Seven Mountains of Thomas Merton,* 391 (photograph text); Merton naming information from Furlong, *Merton,* 3.
16. Furlong, *Merton,* 3, 5. Merton self-description from Merton, *Seven Storey Mountain,* 5.
17. Furlong, *Merton,* 7, 26.
18. Ibid., 8, 15.
19. Ibid., 8, 9, 16, 32.
20. Ibid., 9. Merton childhood memories from Elie, *The Life You Save,* 8.
21. Merton emotions from Mott, *Seven Mountains of Thomas Merton,* 22, 25.
22. William Shannon, *Silent Lamp: The Thomas Merton Story* (New York: Crossroad, 1993), 26.
23. Ibid., 29.
24. Ibid., 33.
25. Higgins, *Heretic Blood,* 15, 16.
26. Mott, *Seven Mountains of Thomas Merton,* 32, 45.
27. Furlong, *Merton,* 41.
28. Ibid., 41, 49.
29. Mott, *Seven Mountains of Thomas Merton,* 62.
30. Ibid., 59.
31. Merton journey information from Ibid.; Merton arrival information from Shannon, *Silent Lamp,* 55.
32. Winser information from Furlong, *Merton,* 52–53. Burning of letters and Winser information from Mott, *Seven Mountains of Thomas Merton,* 63. Thomas Merton, *My Argument with the Gestapo* (Garden City, NY: Doubleday, 1968), 81.

CHAPTER 11

1. Paul Elie, *The Life You Save May Be Your Own* (New York: Farrar, Straus, and Giroux, 2003), 34.

2. Monica Furlong, *Merton: A Biography* (San Francisco: Harper & Row, 1980), 57.
3. Michael Mott, *The Seven Mountains of Thomas Merton* (Boston: Houghton Mifflin, 1984), 80, 81.
4. Furlong, *Merton,* 58.
5. "Friend suicide" from Elena Malits, *The Solitary Explorer: Thomas Merton's Transforming Journey* (San Francisco: Harper & Row, 1980), 25; Merton activities from Furlong, *Merton,* 58.
6. Furlong, *Merton,* 58.
7. Ibid., 58–59.
8. Ibid., 59.
9. Merton noted, "Scar on palm right hand" under the heading "Visible Distinctive Marks" on a certificate of naturalization form required by the U.S. Government in Louisville in 1951. Merton also mentioned it in his "Declaration of Intention" during instruction at Corpus Christi Church in 1938. See Mott, *Seven Mountains of Thomas Merton,* 78–79, 585.
10. Mott, *Seven Mountains of Thomas Merton,* 78, 126, 147, 148,
11. In the manuscript, Mott reports that Merton added, "And that is the lie I want to avoid . . . For there is nothing so dull and tedious and uninteresting and unworthy of historical record, in itself, as sin: but above all is this true of the sins of adolescents who have just entered a university and have got the idea that lust is life, and mean to prove that they are alive." Ibid.,78–79.
12. Ibid., 74.
13. Furlong, *Merton,* 59.
14. William Shannon, *Silent Lamp: The Thomas Merton Story* (New York: Crossroad, 1993), 73.
15. Elie, *The Life You Save,* 40, 483.
16. Mott, *Seven Mountains of Thomas Merton,* 84.
17. Ibid., 91.
18. Shannon, *Silent Lamp,* 75.
19. Furlong, *Merton,*61.
20. Ibid., 60.
21. Ibid., 108.
22. Mott, *Seven Mountains of Thomas Merton,* 85.

CHAPTER 12

1. Edward Rice, *The Man in the Sycamore Tree* (New York: Image Books Edition by special arrangement with Doubleday, 1972), 21–22, 25.
2. Ibid., 13, 25.
3. Thomas Merton, *My Argument with the Gestapo: A Macaronic Journal* (Garden City, NY: Doubleday, 1968), 181.
4. Rice, *Man in the Sycamore Tree,* 20, 32.
5. Ibid., 34, 37–38.
6. Ibid., 40–43.
7. M. Basil Pennington, *Thomas Merton, Brother Monk: The Quest for True Freedom* (San Francisco: Harper & Row, 1987), 49.
8. William Shannon, *Silent Lamp: The Thomas Merton Story* (New York: Crossroad, 1993), 49, 84.
9. Ibid., 86, 87.
10. Rice, *Man in the Sycamore Tree,* 46.
11. James Harford, *Merton & Friends* (New York: Continuum, 2006), 22, 23.
12. Pavadono is interviewed in Morgan C. Atkinson, *Soul Searching: The Journey of Thomas Merton.* DVD. (Louisville, KY: Duckworks, 2007). Assumptions about Merton's conversion appear in such books as Michael Mott, *The Seven Mountains of Thomas Merton* (Boston; Houghton Mifflin, 1984), 123.
13. Mott, *Seven Mountains of Thomas Merton,* 391 (photograph text).

14. Merton's activities at the cottage are detailed in Harford, *Merton & Friends*, 24. Comparisons between Merton and Ginsberg are based on information in Paul Maher, Jr., *Kerouac, His Life and Work* (New York: Taylor Trade Publishing, 2004), 157.

15. Merton's activities are detailed in Harford, *Merton & Friends*, 27. Rice's opinions appear in Rice, *Man in the Sycamore Tree*, 29.

16. Ibid., 29.

17. Ibid.

18. Mott, *Seven Mountains of Thomas Merton*, 125.

19. Merton's affections are described in Monica Furlong, *Merton: A Biography* (San Francisco: Harper & Row, 1980), 87. Merton's nightlife is mentioned in Mott, *Seven Mountains of Thomas Merton*, 133.

20. Mott, *Seven Mountains of Thomas Merton*, 143.

21. Furlong, *Merton*, 101.

22. Ibid., 133, 134–135.

23. Ibid., 135, 139.

24. Ibid., 142–143.

25. Pennington, *Thomas Merton, Brother Monk*, 85.

26. Furlong, *Merton*, 92–93.

27. Ibid., 162, 167.

28. Ibid., 100.

29. Merton, *My Argument with the Gestapo*, 112–113.

30. Furlong, *Merton*, 101.

31. Merton, *The Secular Journal of Thomas Merton* (New York: Farrar, Straus, and Giroux, 1959), 264.

32. Rice, *Man in the Sycamore Tree*, 17, 47–48.

33. Mott, *Seven Mountains of Thomas Merton*, 167.

34. Furlong, *Merton*, 111–112.

35. Merton, *Secular Journal of Thomas Merton*, 76–77.

36. Ibid., 199.

37. Thomas Merton, *The Seven Storey Mountain* (New York: Harcourt Brace, 1998), 400.

38. Merton, *Secular Journal of Thomas Merton*, 199–198.

39. Thomas Merton, *Run to the Mountain: The Story of a Vocation*, The Journals of Thomas Merton, vol. I (San Francisco: HarperSanFrancisco, 1995), 462.

40. Harford, *Merton & Friends*, 53.

41. Mott, *Seven Mountains of Thomas Merton*, 201.

42. Merton, *Secular Journal of Thomas Merton*, 81.

43. Rice, *Man in the Sycamore Tree*, 54.

44. Ibid., 54, 55, 62.

45. Ibid., 65.

46. Pennington, *Thomas Merton, Brother Monk*, xi, xxi.

47. Ibid., xv, xxi.

48. David D. Cooper, *Thomas Merton's Art of Denial: The Evolution of a Radical Humanist* (Athens: University of Georgia Press, 1989), 186.

49. Merton, *Seven Storey Mountain*, book jacket text.

50. Rice, *Man in the Sycamore Tree*, 65.

51. *New York Times Book Review*, October 3, 1948, section 7.

52. Other reviews: *Chicago Tribune*: "*The Seven Storey Mountain* is a contribution to man's knowledge of man," January 10, 1950, 6. *Newsweek*: "The most popular book of the year, a phenomenon in the publishing history" February 5, 1950, 5.

53. Rice, *Man in the Sycamore Tree*, 65.

54. Jim Forest, *Living with Wisdom: A Life of Thomas Merton* (Maryknoll, NY: Orbis Books, 1991), 90.

55. Rice, *Man in the Sycamore Tree*, 65.

56. Father John Eudes' comments during question-and-answer session following Andrea Neuhoff's presentation, "Counterpoint: Merton's Early Years in the Monastery and the

World," Eleventh General Meeting of the International Thomas Merton Society, Nazareth College, Rochester, NY, June 10–14, 2009.

CHAPTER 13

1. Joan C. McDonald, *Tom Merton: A Personal Biography,* (Milwaukee, WI: Marquette University Press, 2006), 97.
2. Edward Rice, *The Man in the Sycamore Tree* (New York: Doubleday, 1978), 92.
3. Ibid., 122.
4. Ibid., 97, 117.
5. McDonald, *Tom Merton,* 170.
6. Ibid., 170, 176, 183.
7. Ibid., 183.
8. Jim Forest, *Living with Wisdom: A Life of Thomas Merton* (Maryknoll, NY: Orbis Books, 1991), 111, 112.
9. Ibid., 184.
10. Monica Furlong, *Merton: A Biography* (San Francisco: Harper & Row, 1980), 198, 207–209.
11. Ibid., 212.
12. Michael Mott, *The Seven Mountains of Thomas Merton* (Boston: Houghton Mifflin, 1984), 297.
13. Ibid., 293, 295, 296.
14. Ibid., 297.
15. Ibid., 297, 298.
16. Furlong, *Merton,* 233.
17. Paul Elie, *The Life You Save May Be Your Own* (New York: Farrar, Straus, and Giroux, 2007), 186.
18. Thomas Merton, *The Sign of Jonas* (San Diego: Harcourt Brace Jovanovich, 1979), 253.
19. Forest, *Living with Wisdom,* 135.
20. Elie, *The Life You Save,* 186.
21. Ibid., 208–209.
22. Mott, *Seven Mountains of Thomas Merton,* 339.
23. McDonald, *Tom Merton,* 237.
24. Thomas Merton, *Turning Toward the World: The Pivotal Years,* The Journals of Thomas Merton, vol. IV (San Francisco: HarperSanFrancisco, 1996), 393.

CHAPTER 14

1. Thomas Merton, *Eighteen Poems* (New York: New Directions, 1986), 57.
2. Thomas Merton, *New Seeds of Contemplation* (New York: New Directions, 1972), 64.
3. Thomas Merton, *No Man Is an Island* (Boston: Shambhala Publications, 2005), xxi.
4. Michael Mott, *The Seven Mountains of Thomas Merton* (Boston: Houghton Mifflin, 1984), 198. M. Basil Pennington, *Thomas Merton, Brother Monk: The Quest for True Freedom* (San Francisco: Harper & Row, 1987), x. *A Taste of Gethsemani: Trappist Monks Remember Merton* (Louisville, KY: Thomas Merton Foundation 1997), DVD.
5. Thomas Merton, *The Seven Storey Mountain* (New York: Harcourt Brace, 1998), 409.
6. Thomas Merton, *The Wisdom of the Desert* (Boston: Shambhala Publications, 2004), 16, 17, 19, 20.
7. Merton, *No Man Is an Island,* xviii.
8. Ibid., xxiii. Merton decided that people could not love others unless they loved themselves, and "a selfish love of ourselves makes us incapable of loving others." Concluding his remarks as he gazed at the paper in front of him, he decided that nothing made sense, unless people admitted, as John Donne proposed, "No man is an island, entire of itself; every man / is a piece of the continent, a part of the main."
9. Mott, *Seven Mountains of Thomas Merton,* 423.
10. Thomas Merton, *Day of a Stranger* (Salt Lake City: Gibbs M. Smith, 1981), 49.
11. Thomas Merton, *Learning to Love: Exploring Solitude and Freedom, The Journals of Thomas Merton,* vol. VII (San Francisco: HarperSanFranciso, 1997), 40.

12. Thomas P. McDonnell, "Interview with Thomas Merton," *U.S. Catholic,* 1968, 118.
13. Gerald G. May, *The Dark Night of the Soul: A Psychiatrist Explores the Connection Between Darkness and Spiritual Growth* (San Francisco: HarperSanFrancisco, 2004), 12, 46.
14. Ibid., 50.
15. Merton, *Learning to Love,* 39–40.
16. Ibid., 38.
17. Author interview with Father John Eudes, May 28, 2008.

CHAPTER 15

1. Thomas Merton, *Learning to Love: Exploring Solitude and Freedom,* The Journals of Thomas Merton, vol. VI (San Francisco: HarperSanFrancisco, 1997), 108.
2. Michael Higgins, *Heretic Blood: The Spiritual Geography of Thomas Merton* (Toronto: Stoddart Publishing, 1998), 4.
3. Thomas Merton, *The Other Side of the Mountain: The End of the Journey,* The Journals of Thomas Merton, vol. VII (San Francisco: HarperSanFrancisco, 1998), xvii.
4. John Eudes Bamberger and Jonathan Montaldo, *Thomas Merton: Prophet of Renewal* (Collegeville, MN: Liturgical Press, 2005), 23.
5. Ibid., 25.
6. Thomas Merton, *A Search for Solitude: Pursuing the Monk's Life,* The Journals of Thomas Merton Journals, vol. III, (San Francisco: HarperSanFrancisco, 1996), 268, 277.
7. Thomas Merton, "The Contemplative Call," Audio Tape AA2915 (Louisville, KY: The Merton Center, 1965).
8. Eudes's thoughts in Bamberger, *Thomas Merton: Prophet of Renewal* (Kalamazoo, Michigan: Cistercian Publications, 2005), 26. Thomas Merton, *A Vow of Conversation: Journals 1964–65,* ed. by Naomi Burton Stone (New York: Farrar, Straus and Giroux, 1988), 19.
9. Thomas Merton, *The Seven Storey Mountain* (New York: Harcourt Brace, 1998), 253.
10. Merton, *Learning to Love,* 234.
11. Walter Conn, *Christian Conversion* (New York: Paulist Press, 1986), 17. Morgan C. Atkinson, *Soul Searching: The Journey of Thomas Merton,* DVD. (Louisville, KY: Duckworks, 2007).
12. Ann Hunsaker Hawkins, *Archetypes of Conversion: The Autobiographies of Augustine, Bunyan, and Merton* (Lewisburg, PA: Bucknell University Press, 1985), 140. Lewis Rambo in Henri Gooren, "The Religious Model and Conversion Toward a Whole New Approach," *Exchange* 35, 1 (2006): 53, 54.
13. Walter Conn, "Christian Conversion: Development and Theological Reflections on Young Thomas Merton," *Perkins Journal* 37, 1, (Fall 1983), 23.
14. Merton, *Seven Storey Mountain,* 279.
15. Merton, *Learning to Love,* 195.
16. Thomas Merton and Rosemary Radford Ruether, *At Home in the World: The Letters of Thomas Merton & Rosemary Radford Ruether,* ed. by Mary Tardiff (Maryknoll, NY: Orbis Books, 1995), 47–48.
17. Ibid., 49, 51
18. Thomas Merton, "The White Pebble," in *Where I Found Christ,* ed. by John A. O'Brien (New York: Doubleday, 1950), 243.
19. Elena Malits, *The Solitary Explorer: Thomas Merton's Transforming Journey* (San Francisco, Harper & Row, 1980), x.
20. Robert Reilly, "Gathering Observes Merton's Baptism and Continual Conversions," *National Catholic Reporter,* December 18, 1998; http://www.natcath.org/NCR_Online/archives2/1998d/1218198/121898i.htm (accessed July 6, 2008).
21. Thomas Merton, *Honorable Reader* (New York: Crossroad, 1981), 98, 131, 133.
22. Sallie McFague, "Conversion on the Edge of the Raft," *Interpretation* 32, 3 (July 1978), 259.
23. Merton, letter to Miguel Greenberg, August 16, 1964 (Louisville: Thomas Merton Center).

CHAPTER 16

1. Author interview with Brother Paul Quenon, November 3, 2008.
2. Merton, *The Seven Storey Mountain* (New York: Harcourt Brace, 1998), 5.

3. Michael Mott, *The Seven Mountains of Thomas Merton* (Boston: Houghton Mifflin, 1984), 17.
4. Michael Reynolds, *Hemingway: The Final Years* (New York: W. W. Norton, 1999), 86.
5. Monica Furlong, *Merton: A Biography* (San Francisco: Harper & Row, 1980), 98.
6. D. A. Callard, *Pretty Good for a Woman: The Enigmas of Evelyn Scott* (London: Jonathon Cape, 1985), 66.
7. Ibid., xi.
8. Mary Wheeling White, *Fighting the Current: The Life and Work of Evelyn Scott* (Baton Rouge: Louisiana State University Press, 1998), 1, 4, 6.
9. Ibid., 26; William Shannon, *Silent Lamp: The Thomas Merton Story* (New York: Crossroad, 1993), 29.
10. Callard, *Pretty Good for a Woman,* 72.
11. Ibid., 73–74.
12. White, *Fighting the Current,* 68.
13. Robert E. Daggy, "Questions and Revelations: Thomas Merton's Recovery of the Ground of Birthwas," Speech delivered at the First General Meeting of The International Thomas Merton Society of Great Britain and Ireland, May 1996.
14. Merton, *Seven Storey Mountain,* 98.
15. Ibid., 69.
16. Edward Rice, *The Man in the Sycamore Tree* (New York: Doubleday, 1978), 38.
17. Merton, *Seven Storey Mountain,* 18.
18. James J. O'Donnell, *Augustine: A Biography* (New York: Harper Perennial, 2005), 39.
19. Merton, *Honorable Reader,* 98.
20. Ibid., 294.
21. Furlong, *Merton,* 4.
22. Obituary, Correspondence Section, *British Medical Journal* 104 (July 20, 1946): 46.
23. "Obituary, Ed. T. F. Fox," *The Lancet* Vol. No. CCLI, Volume Two (July-December 1946): 106, 107.
24. John Eudes Bamberger, *Thomas Merton: Prophet of Renewal* (Kalamazoo, MI: Cistercian Publications, 2005), 23.
25. Furlong, *Merton,* 61.
26. Ibid., 45.
27. Thomas Merton, *My Argument with the Gestapo: A Macaronic Journal* (New York: Doubleday, 1969), 132, 148.
28. Ibid., 142, 144, 148.
29. Ibid., 148.
30. Ibid., 148, 149.
31. Furlong, *Merton,* 45, 57, 60.
32. Rice's comments in Michael Mott, *The Seven Mountains of Thomas Merton* (Boston: Houghton Mifflin, 1984), 142.
33. Rice, *Man in the Sycamore Tree,* 46.
34. James Harford, *Merton & Friends* (New York: Continuum, 2006), 23.
35. Thomas Merton, *Turning Toward the World: The Pivotal Years,* The Journals of Thomas Merton, vol. IV (San Francisco: HarperSanFrancisco, 1996), 212.

CHAPTER 17

1. Thomas Merton, *Learning to Love: Exploring Solitude and Freedom,* The Journals of Thomas Merton, vol. VI (San Francisco: HarperSanFrancisco: 1997), 54.
2. Ibid., 54, 55.
3. Ibid., 55.
4. Ibid., 56–58.
5. Ibid., 58.
6. Ibid., 61, 62.
7. Ibid., 62.

8. Ibid., 63
9. Ibid., 66.
10. Ibid., 66–67.
11. Ibid., 67–68.
12. Ibid., 70.
13. Ibid., 71.
14. Ibid., 73.
15. Ibid., 75, 77.
16. Ibid., 78.
17. Ibid., 79, 80.
18. Ibid., 81.
19. Ibid., 82, 84.
20. Ibid., 83, 84.
21. Ibid., xxi, 304.
22. Correspondence with Dom James, 1966. Series 1, #55, The Thomas Merton Center Archives, Louisville, KY.
23. Music in Joan Baez, "Silver Dagger," *Very Early Joan* (Vanguard Recording Society, 1961); Merton quote in Merton, *Learning to Love,* 305.
24. Ibid., 313, 315.
25. Ibid., 326–327.
26. Ibid., 334, 346, 338.
27. Correspondence with Dom James, Series 5, #60 (The Thomas Merton Center Archives, Louisville, KY).
28. Merton, *Learning to Love,* 86.
29. Ibid., 89, 94.
30. Ibid., 94.
31. Author e-mail interview with Father John Eudes, May 2, 2008.
32. Merton, *Learning to Love,* 107.
33. Ibid., 94–95.
34. Ibid., 96–97.
35. Ibid., 103.
36. Ibid., 104.
37. Ibid., 108.
38. Ibid., 109.
39. Merton Correspondence with Dom James, Series 1, #50 (The Thomas Merton Center Archives, Louisville, KY).
40. Merton felt Dom James was "calculating and sentimental, comfort loving and disciplined," and "a mystically inclined businessman, secretive, solitary . . ." Merton believed the abbot thought he was "irritating and embarrassing." Exposing his own inner emotions, Merton admitted to feeling "like a Negro in the presence of a Southern white man." Merton, *Learning to Love,* 111.
41. Merton Correspondence with Dom James, Series 5, #69 (The Thomas Merton Center Archives, Louisville, KY).
42. Merton, *Learning to Love,* 114, 116–117.
43. Merton Correspondence with Dom James, Series 1, #51 (The Thomas Merton Center Archives, Louisville, KY).
44. Merton, *Learning to Love,* 119–120.

CHAPTER 18

1. Merton's recollections in Thomas Merton, *Learning to Love: Exploring Solitude and Freedom,* The Journals of Thomas Merton, vol. VI (San Francisco: HarperSanFrancisco, 1997), 38. Descriptions in Michael Mott, *The Seven Mountains of Thomas Merton* (Boston: Houghton Mifflin Company, 1984), 435.
2. Merton, *Honorable Reader, Reflections on My Life* (New York: Crossroad, 1989), 111, 112.

3. Mott, *Seven Mountains of Thomas Merton,* 435.

4. Ibid., Thomas Merton, *Love and Living* (New York, Farrar, Straus and Giroux, 1979), 17, 25, 26, 27.

5. Ibid., 40.

6. Mott, *Seven Mountains of Thomas Merton,* 436.

7. Ibid., 437.

8. Ibid., 439.

9. Included were such lines as "I wonder who the hell I am," "I bleed myself awake and well," and "I am Christ's lost cell." Thomas Merton, *The Collected Poems of Thomas Merton* (New York: New Directions, 1977), 615–618.

10. Mott, *Seven Mountains of Thomas Merton,* 439, 441.

11. Merton, *Learning to Love: Exploring Solitude and Freedom, The Journals of Thomas Merton,* vol. VI, 121.

12. Ibid., 122.

13. Ibid., 122, 123.

14. John Howard Griffin, *Follow the Ecstasy: The Hermitage Years of Thomas Merton,* (Maryknoll, NY: Orbis Books, 1993), 86.

15. Merton, *Learning to Love,* 129.

16. Ibid., 130–131, 133.

17. Ibid., 130, 131.

18. Ibid., 134.

19. Ibid., 140.

20. Ibid., 143, 144.

21. Ibid., 145.

22. Ibid., 149, 151, 154, 157.

23. Ibid., 162, 162.

24. Baez was at the height of her popularity during this time. Later, she and Merton collaborated on "The Bells of Gethsemani." Merton wrote the words, Baez the music.

25. Merton, *Learning to Love,* 167.

26. Ibid., 168.

27. Author telephone interview with Joan Baez, February 13, 2009.

28. Lawrence S. Cunningham, *Thomas Merton & the Monastic Vision* (Grand Rapids, MI: Eerdmans, 1999), 141.

29. Merton, *Learning to Love,* 175.

30. Ibid., 182, 183–184.

31. Ibid., 186, 188, 190.

32. Ibid., 191–192, 193.

33. Ibid., 201, 202, 204.

34. Ibid., 211.

35. Ibid., 215, 217.

36. Ibid., 222, 223, 227.

37. Ibid., 234, 297.

CHAPTER 19

1. Thomas Merton, *The Other Side of the Mountain: The End of the Journey,* The Journals of Thomas Merton, vol. VII (San Francisco: HarperSanFrancisco, 1998), 11.

2. Ibid.

3. Ibid., 19.

4. Dianne Aprile, *The Abbey of Gethsemani: Place of Peace and Paradox* (Louisville, KY: Trout Lily Press, 1998), 155.

5. Merton, *Other Side of the Mountain,* 29.

6. Ibid., 41. Merton also observed, "Almost a shock to realize that the secrecy, the suppression and the manipulation exercised by Dom James no longer dominates us. That we have a man we can talk to, work with frankly, exchange ideas with, propose real experiments . . . is a real sense of liberation."

7. Ibid., 75–76.
8. Ibid., 78.
9. Ibid., 84.
10. Ibid., 94–97.
11. Ibid., 98–99.
12. Ibid., 102, 104, 122.
13. Ibid., 132, 137.
14. Ibid., 142.
15. Ibid., 153.
16. Merton scholar Jonathan Montaldo questions whether this occurred: "I think he is deliberately confusing any future reader of his journals in order to protect [Margie]." Author e-mail interview with Montaldo, December 27, 2008.
17. Michael Mott, *The Seven Mountains of Thomas Merton* (Boston: Houghton Mifflin, 1984), 454.
18. Merton, *Other Side of the Mountain,* 166.
19. Ibid., 215–216, 221, 226, 237.
20. Ibid., 245, 251, 252, 258, 259, 266.
21. Ibid., 323.
22. Speech details, cause of death ("Father de Grunne . . . saw Merton lying on the terrazzo floor . . . There was the smell of burning flesh. Merton, clearly dead, was lying on his back with the five-foot fan diagonally across his body . . . A long, raw third-degree burn about a hand's width ran along the right side of Merton's body almost to the groin. There were no marks on his hands. His face was bluish-red, eyes and mouth half-open. There was bleeding in the back of his head," and final effects list from Jim Forest, *Living With Wisdom: A Life of Thomas Merton* (Maryknoll, NY: Orbis, 1991), 212, 215, 216.
23. Edward Rice, *The Man in the Sycamore Tree* (New York: Doubleday, 1970), 11.

CHAPTER 20

1. Author e-mail interview with Jonathan Montaldo, January 5, 2009.
2. http://www.monks.org/whoweare.html, accessed December 31, 2008.
3. Joan C. McDonald, *Tom Merton: A Personal Biography* (Milwaukee, WI: Marquette University Press, 2006), 128.
4 hrrp//www.walburga.org/com_vows.html, accessed December 31, 2008.
5. Timothy Foy, O.S.B., The Rule of St. Benedict. 5,
6. Ibid., 7–9. The abbot must, St. Benedict orders, "avoid all favoritism in the monastery. He is not to love one more than another unless he finds someone better in actions and obedience . . . He should not gloss over the sins of those who err, but cut them out while he can, as soon as they begin to sprout. . . ." Ibid., 9.
7. Ibid., 13, 14, 15. Chapter Four then explains "The Tools for Good Works," relating to conduct. Speaking to the subject of deceit, the Rule orders that no one "should act in anger or nurse a grudge . . . but speak truth with heart or tongue." Addressing matters of passion, the Rule states, "Do not gratify the promptings of the flesh, hate the urgings of self-will . . . live by God's commandments every day; treasure chastity. . . ." Regarding obedience, the Rule states, "The first step of humility is unhesitating obedience, which comes naturally to those who cherish Christ above all . . . they carry out the superior's orders as promptly as if the command came from God himself . . . the disciple's obedience must be given gladly." Concerning criticism, Saint Benedict orders, "evil speech should be curbed so that punishment for sin may be avoided."
8. Ibid., 17, 18, 19, 20.
9. Author e-mail interview with Jonathan Montaldo, January 5, 2009.
10. Paul Elie, *The Life You Save May Be Your Own* (New York: Farrar, Straus, and Giroux, 2003), 389.
11. Author e-mail correspondence with Paul Elie, June 16, 2009.
12. Information from reliable source received by this author during the Eleventh General Meeting of the International Thomas Merton Society, Nazareth College, Rochester, NY, June 10–14, 2009.

13. Author e-mail correspondence with the Merton Center's Mark Meade, June 17, 2009.

14. Information from unnamed reliable received by this author during International Thomas Merton Society Conference, June 10–14, 2009.

15. Thomas Merton, *Learning to Love: Exploring Solitude and Freedom,* The Thomas Merton Journals, vol. VI (San Francisco: HarperSanFrancisco), 63.

16. Ibid., 94, 121.

17. Ibid., 66.

18. Ibid., 89.

19. Paul Wilkes, ed., *Merton: By Those Who Knew Him Best* (San Francisco: Harper & Row, 1984), 91.

20. Author e-mail interview with Jonathan Montaldo, December 27, 2008; Author email interview with Dr. Rudy Bernard, January 15, 2009.

21. William H. Shannon, Christine M. Bochen, and Patrick F. O'Connell, *The Thomas Merton Encyclopedia* (Maryknoll, NY: Orbis Books, 2002), 75.

22. Thomas Merton, *Conjectures of a Guilty Bystander* (New York: Doubleday, 1966), v.

23. Shannon, et al., *Thomas Merton Encyclopedia,* 75.

24. Merton, *Conjectures of a Guilty Bystander,* 172.

25. Ibid., 107.

26. Author interviews with Brother Paul Quenon, November 3, 2008, and November 12, 2008.

27. Thomas Merton, *The Seven Storey Mountain* (New York: Harcourt Brace, 1998), 16.

28. Mott, *Seven Mountains of Thomas Merton,* 69.

29. Merton's depressed mindset in Merton, *Learning to Love,* 22 and Thomas Merton, *A Search for Solitude: Pursuing the Monk's Life,* The Journals of Thomas Merton, vol. III, (San Francisco: HarperSanFrancisco, 1996), 22; Rice recollection in Edward Rice, *The Man in the Sycamore Tree: The Good Times and Hard Life of Thomas Merton* (Garden City, NY: Doubleday, 1970), 79.

30. Thomas Merton, *Turning Toward the World: The Pivotal Years,* The Journals of Thomas Merton, vol. IV, (San Francisco: HarperSanFrancisco, 1996), 323, 324.

31. Ibid., 328.

32. Ibid., 393; Monica Furlong, *Merton: A Biography* (San Francisco: Harper & Row, 1980), 59.

33. Thomas Merton and Rosemary Radford Ruether, *At Home in the World: The Letters of Thomas Merton & Rosemary Radford Ruether,* ed. by Mary Tardiff (Maryknoll, NY: Orbis Books, 1995), 64; Thomas Merton, *Entering the Silence: Becoming a Monk & Writer,* The Journals of Thomas Merton, vol. II (San Francisco: HarperSanFrancisco, 1996), 367.

34. Zilboorg incident in Merton, *Entering the Silence,* 295; Abbot Dom James words in Merton, *Learning to Love,* 104.

CHAPTER 21

1. "Omnia vincit Amor: et nos cedeamus Amori." Virgil, *Eclogues* no. 10, I, 69.

2. Thomas Merton, *Love and Living* (New York: Farrar, Straus and Giroux, 1979), 29.

3. M. Basil Pennington, *Thomas Merton, Brother Monk: The Quest for True Freedom* (San Francisco: Harper & Row, 1987), 15.

4. Ibid., 38–39.

5. Ibid., 64.

6. Ibid., 85.

7. Author e-mail interview with Brother Paul Quenon, November 12, 2008.

8. Michael Higgins, *Heretic Blood: The Spiritual Geography of Thomas Merton* (Toronto: Stoddart, 1998), 268.

9. Correspondence with Dom Frederick Dunne, Section A, Correspondence #2, January, 1942 (Louisville, KY: The Thomas Merton Center).

10. Merton's emotions in Thomas Merton, *Turning Toward the World: The Pivotal Years*, The Journals of Thomas Merton, vol. IV (San Francisco: HarperSanFrancisco, 1996), 197; Merton's thoughts on illusion in Thomas Merton, *Dancing in the Waters of Life: Seeking*

Peace in the Hermitage, The Journals of Thomas Merton, vol. V (San Francisco: Harper-SanFrancisco, 1997), 198.

11. Thomas Merton, "True Freedom" lecture, December 12 and 19, 1965, (Kansas City, MO: Credence Communications, 1995), audiocassette AA2803.

12. Thomas Merton, *A Search for Solitude: Pursuing the Monk's Life,* The Journals of Thomas Merton, vol. III, (San Francisco: HarperSanFrancisco, 1996), 214.

13. Merton, "True Freedom" lecture.

14. Thomas Merton, *Collected Poems* (New York: New Directions, 1977), 669–670.

15. Thomas Merton, *New Seeds of Contemplation* (New York: New Directions, 1972), 47.

16. Ibid., 196.

17. Merton, *A Search for Solitude,* 285.

18. Merton, *New Seeds of Contemplation,* 32.

19. Ibid., 297.

20. Merton on truth in *Merton: A Film Biography,* Paul Wilkes and Audrey L. Glynn producers (First Run Features, 1984); Merton on the mask in Thomas Merton, *Raids on the Unspeakable* (New York: New Directions 1966), 15; importance of love in Thomas Merton, "Pure Love" lecture, April 20, 1963, Credence Communications, 1995, audiocassette AA2136.

21. Merton, "Why Alienation is for Everybody," *The Literary Essays of Thomas Merton,* ed. by Patrick Hart (New York: New Directions, 1981), 381.

22. Merton, *New Seeds of Contemplation,* 21.

23. Ibid., 34.

24. Ibid., 25–26.

25. Ibid., 35.

26. Ibid., 35, 60.

27. Ibid., 72.

28. Ibid., 61, 63, 75.

29. Ibid., 87–88, 140.

30. Thomas Merton, *Conjectures of a Guilty Bystander* (New York: Doubleday, 1966), 172.

31. Merton, *New Seeds of Contemplation,* 193.

32. Michael Mott, *The Seven Mountains of Thomas Merton* (Boston; Houghton Mifflin Company, 1984), 438.

33. William Shannon, *Silent Lamp: The Thomas Merton Story* (New York: Crossroad, 1993), 201.

34. Higgins, *Heretic Blood,* 56.

35. Paul Elie, *The Life You Save May Be Your Own: An American Pilgrimage* (New York: Farrar, Straus and Giroux, 2003), 390, 391. Author interview with Dr. Rudy Bernard, April 12, 2008.

36. Author e-mail interview with Father John Eudes, May 2, 2008.

37. Author interview with Brother Paul Quenon, November 3, 2008.

38. Thomas Merton, *Learning to Love: Exploring Solitude and Freedom,* The Journals of Thomas Merton, vol. VI (San Francisco: HarperSanFrancisco: 1997), 259.

39. Thomas Merton, *My Argument with the Gestapo* (Garden City, NY: Doubleday, 1968), 53, 81, 84.

40. Merton, *Learning to Love,* 259.

41. Ibid., 258.

42. Ibid., 47, 306.

43. Ibid., 328.

44. Correspondence with Dom James, series 5, undated 1966, #03 (Louisville, KY: The Thomas Merton Center).

45. Merton, *Learning to Love,* 39–40.

46. Thomas Merton, *The Other Side of the Mountain: The End of the Journey,* The Journals of Thomas Merton, vol. VII, 113.

47. Jim Forest, *Living With Wisdom: A Life of Thomas Merton* (Maryknoll, NY: Orbis Books, 1991), 214.

48. Paul Wilkes, "Merton's Enlightenment: What He Found in Asia," *Commonwealth* 133,11 (June 2, 2006): 12–14.

49. Padovano's comments in Morgan C. Atkinson, *Soul Searching: The Journey of Thomas Merton,* DVD (Louisville, KY: Duckworks, 2007); John Eudes Bamberger, *Thomas Merton: Prophet of Renewal* (Kalamazoo, MI: Cistercian Publications, 2005), 30, 40; Merton, *Learning to Love,* 234; John Howard Griffin, *Follow the Ecstasy: The Hermitage Years of Thomas Merton* (Maryknoll, NY: Orbis Books, 1993), 61.

50. Pennington, *Thomas Merton, Brother Monk,* xi.

51. Thomas Merton, *The Seven Storey Mountain* (New York: Harcourt Brace, 1998), 242.

52. Pennington, *Thomas Merton, Brother Monk,* xv.

CHAPTER 22

1. Herbert R. Lottman, *Albert Camus: A Biography* (Corte Madera, CA: Gingko Press, 1997), xx.

2. Thomas Merton, *A Search for Solitude,* The Journals of Thomas Merton. vol. III (San Francisco: HarperSanFrancisco, 1996), 182.

3. Thomas Merton, *Thoughts on Solitude* (Tunbridge Wells, England: Burns and Oates, 1975), 81.

4. Mott discusses all aspects of Merton's death including discrepancies based on physical evidence gathered in Bangkok. Michael Mott, *The Seven Mountains of Thomas Merton* (Boston: Houghton Mifflin, 1984), 568.

5. Edward Rice, *The Man in the Sycamore Tree* (New York: Doubleday, 1970), 135.

6. Asked whether the doctor Margie married was the same fiancé "N" she had mentioned during her affair with Merton, Dr. Paul Pearson, director of the Merton Center, stated, "I'm under the impression that it wasn't the fiancé she eventually married, but I'm not aware of any evidence that is definitely the case." Author e-mail interview with Dr. Pearson, February 18, 2009.

7. Paul Hendrickson, "One of Us: Thomas Merton's Writings Gave Spiritual Insights to Millions. But at His Old Monastery, They Know He Was Only Human." *Washington Post,* December 27, 1998, Style Section, F01.

8. Thomas Merton, *Honorable Reader* (New York: Crossroad, 1989), 3.

9. Author interview with Dr. Rudy Bernard, April 2 and December 9, 2008.

10. Author telephone interview with R. A. and Lynn DeSutter on June 29, 2009.

11. *A Taste of Gethsemani: Trappist Monks Remember Merton* (Louisville, KY: Thomas Merton Foundation, 1997), DVD.

12. Ibid.

13. Paul Wilkes, ed., *Merton, by Those Who Knew Him Best* (San Francisco: Harper & Row, 1984), 110.

14. Ibid., 147.

15. Morgan C. Atkinson, *Soul Searching: The Journey of Thomas Merton* (Louisville, KY: Duckworks, Inc., 2007), DVD.

16. Ibid.

17. Ibid.

18. Author telephone interviews with Joan Baez, February 13, 2009.

19. Adrian House, *Francis of Assisi: A Revolutionary Life* (London: Hidden Spring, 2000), 26, 61.

20. James J. O'Donnell, *Augustine: A Biography* (New York: Harper Perennial, 2005), 38, 49, 67, 70, 74.

21. Robert Toth quoted in "One of Us: Thomas Merton's Writings Gave Spiritual Insights to Millions. But at His Old Monastery, They Know He Was Only Human," by Paul Hendrickson, *Washington Post,* December 27, 1998, F01.

22. Thomas Merton, *The Seven Storey Mountain* (New York: Harcourt Brace, 1998), xii.

23. Wilkes, ed., *Merton,* 213.

24. Merton, *Honorable Reader,* 113–114.

INDEX

12-2-10